PRAISE FOR THE SPARTACUS WAR

"[*The Spartacus War*] has all the excitement of a thriller. . . . The account of what it meant to be a gladiator, of the tactics required to be victorious and of the agony of defeat is particularly adrenaline-fueled. Spartacus's death—not on a cross, as in Stanley Kubrick's 1960 movie, but charging the Roman general who led the campaign against him—comes as a worthy climax to an epic that never once relaxes its tension."

—Tom Holland, *The Washington Post*

"The great slave revolt of the gladiator Spartacus shook the Roman world of the first-century B.C. as much as it fascinates us still two millennia later. The classicist and stylist Barry Strauss explains why all that is so in a narrative that is as engaging to read as it is thoroughly researched."

—Victor Davis Hanson, Martin and Illie Anderson Senior Fellow, Classics/Military History, the Hoover Institution

"With his trademarks of extensive knowledge, insights, and great story-telling ability, Barry Strauss brings us as close as we can get to the enigmatic Spartacus, the slave who defied the Roman Republic."

—Adrian Goldsworthy, author of *Caesar: Life of a Colossus*

"The long track of history—especially ancient history—is marred by potholes and chasms of the unknown and unknowable. No contemporary historian bridges these gaps better than Barry Strauss. He does not leap across them so much as build elegant spans of logic, of the likely and the possible. His raw materials are an immense knowledge base, wit and humor, and a welcome sense for brevity. Spartacus comes alive."

—David L. Robbins, author of *War of the Rats* and *The Assassins Gallery*

"A swift-moving, accessible chronicle of the insurgency against ancient Rome led by the charismatic slave leader Spartacus. . . . Strauss colorfully illustrates the making of the durable Spartacus myth."

—*Kirkus Reviews*

"[Strauss] unites a novelist's storytelling skills with the expert's command of ancient sources to retell for classically challenged moderns some of the most important and exciting stories from ancient history. *The Spartacus War* is a worthy successor to those earlier achievements, weaving together evidence from ancient literary sources, archaeology, epigraphy, and personal autopsy of the Italian regions where Spartacus marched and fought to give us a fast-paced, gripping story that tells us everything we can reliably know about Spartacus the man and the revolt he inspired. . . . *The Spartacus War* exemplifies popular history at its finest."

—Bruce S. Thornton, *The New Criterion*

"Barry Strauss, whose previous work is saturated with ancient lore and gore from the Battle of Salamis to the Peloponnesian War, knows his stuff so well that he can spin a great epic tale about the Spartacus rebellion from 73 to April 71 B.C., even though the facts are slim. . . . Riveting."

—Sam Coale, *The Providence Journal-Bulletin*

"Strauss neither condescends to his readers nor panders to them with the desperation of many pop historians. He writes history for adults."

—John Wilson, *Books & Culture*

"The Spartacus revolt is a fascinating and engrossing story, which Strauss relates with great style and energy. . . . Highly recommended."

—Richard H. Berg, *The Post and Courier* (Charleston)

"No one presents the military history of the ancient world with greater insight and panache than Strauss."

—Publishers Weekly

"This is a colourful and thrilling account that deserves the widest possible readership."

—Christopher Silvester, *Daily Express* (UK)

"[A] racy retelling of the real story behind the myth of the rebel slave."

—The Sunday Times (UK)

"This absorbing story is told in the most enthralling way and the reader, either specialist or amateur, will be unable to put the book down without reaching the end—and they'll reach the end fast."

—BBC History Magazine (UK)

"Masterful story-telling. . . . deeply satisfying. . . . Strauss' Spartacus will remain the standard popular history. . . . a well-told reconstruction of a gripping tale."

—Tony Williams, *The Internet Review of Books*

"Strauss delivers a rousing good tale of Spartacus."

—The Library Journal

"The weight of a gladiator's shield, the look of the landscape, the fury of battle—Strauss weaves all this and much more into his account, which reads with the ease of a novel, while constructing historical interpretations that deserve serious consideration. . . . [A] lively and imaginative book."

—Thomas R. Martin, *History Book Club*

ALSO BY BARRY STRAUSS

SPAR

SIMON & SCHUSTER PAPERBAC

THE
TACUS
WAR

BARRY STRAUSS

New York   London   Toronto   Sydney

Simon & Schuster Paperbacks
A Division of Simon & Schuster, Inc.
1230 Avenue of the Americas
New York, NY 10020

First Simon & Schuster trade paperback edition February 2010

SIMON & SCHUSTER PAPERBACKS and colophon are registered
trademarks of Simon & Schuster, Inc.

For information about special discounts for bulk purchases,
please contact Simon & Schuster Special Sales at
1-866-506-1949 or business@simonandschuster.com.

The Simon & Schuster Speakers Bureau can bring authors
to your live event. For more information or to book an event,
contact the Simon & Schuster Speakers Bureau at
1-866-248-3049 or visit our website at www.simonspeakers.com.

Designed by Dana Sloan

Manufactured in the United States of America

10 9 8 7 6 5 4 3 2

The Library of Congress has cataloged the hardcover edition as follows:

Strauss, Barry S.
The Spartacus war / Barry Strauss.
    p. cm.
Includes bibligraphical references and index.
1. Spartacus, d. 71 B.C. 2. Gladiators—Rome—Biography. 3. Slaves—
Rome—Biography. 4. Slave insurrections—Rome. 5. Rome—History—
Servile wars, 135–71 B.C. 6. Spartacus, d. 71 B.C.—Influence. I. Title.
    DG258.5.S83 2009
    937'.05—dc22
                                                    2008054138

ISBN 978-1-4165-3205-7
ISBN 978-1-4165-3206-4 (pbk)
ISBN 978-1-4391-5839-5 (ebook)

To Josiah Ober and Adrienne Mayor

CONTENTS

CHRONOLOGY

Autumn 73   Spartacus raids Campania and Lucania, defeats Varinius

Winter 73–72   Rebels occupy Thurii

Winter–Spring 72   Pompey captures Perperna and ends revolt in Spain

Spring 72   Rebels march to Mutina, defeat consuls; Romans defeat Crixus

Summer 72   Rebels return to southern Italy

Autumn 72   Crassus takes command, decimates cohort, drives Spartacus southward

ca. January 71   Spartacus negotiates with pirates, tries to cross Strait of Messina

ca. February 71   Spartacus breaks out of Crassus's trap

ca. April 71   Spartacus's last battle

ca. May 71   Crassus crucifies six thousand surviving rebels

70   Rebel bands raid Tempsa; December 29, Crassus celebrates *ovatio*

63   Death of Mithridates

60   Octavius wipes out last remnants of Spartacus's followers

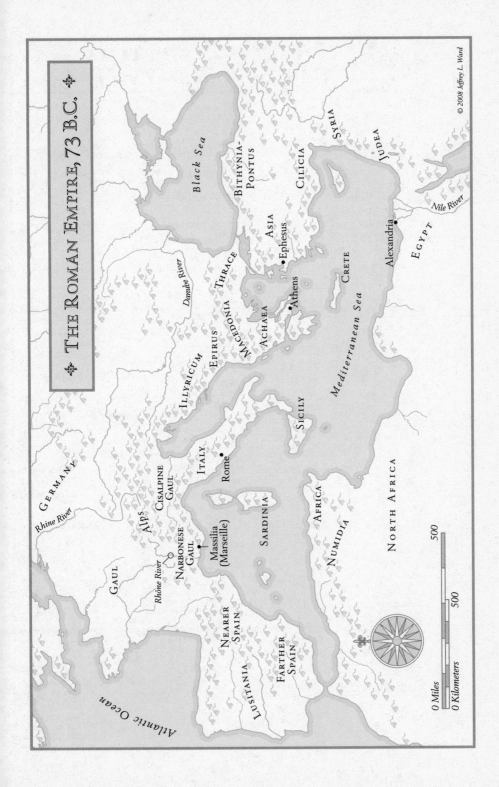

THE ROMAN EMPIRE, 73 B.C.

GERMANY

Rhine River

GAUL

Rhône River

Alps

CISALPINE
GAUL

NARBONESE
GAUL

Massilia
(Marseille)

ITALY

Rome

SARDINIA

CORSICA

NEARER
SPAIN

LUSITANIA

FARTHER
SPAIN

Atlantic Ocean

ILLYRICUM

EPIRUS

Danube River

MACEDONIA

THRACE

ACHAEA

Athens

Black Sea

BITHYNIA-
PONTUS

ASIA

Ephesus

CILICIA

SYRIA

JUDEA

Nile River

Alexandria

EGYPT

CRETE

Mediterranean Sea

SICILY

AFRICA

NUMIDIA

NORTH AFRICA

0 Miles   500

0 Kilometers   500

© 2008 Jeffrey L. Ward

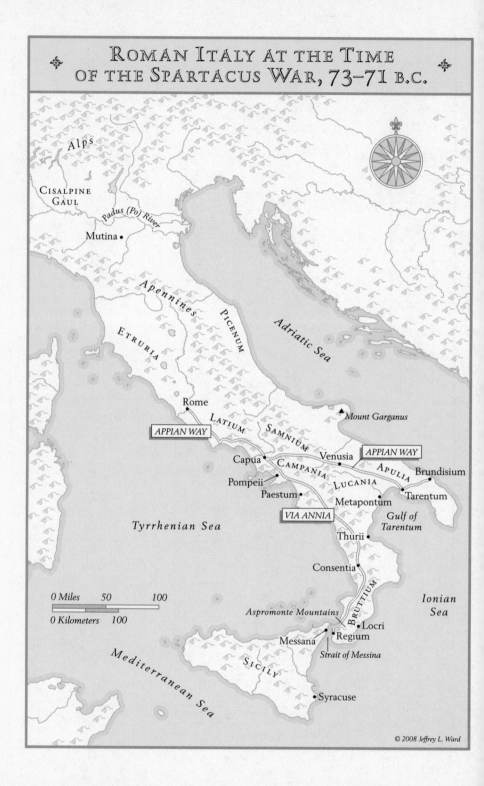

ROMAN ITALY AT THE TIME OF THE SPARTACUS WAR, 73–71 B.C.

Alps

CISALPINE GAUL

Padus (Po) River

Mutina

Apennines

PICENUM

ETRURIA

Adriatic Sea

Rome

LATIUM

SAMNIUM

Mount Garganus

APPIAN WAY

Capua

CAMPANIA

Venusia

APPIAN WAY

APULIA

Brundisium

Pompeii

LUCANIA

Paestum

Metapontum

Tarentum

VIA ANNIA

Gulf of Tarentum

Tyrrhenian Sea

Thurii

Consentia

0 Miles 50 100

0 Kilometers 100

Aspromonte Mountains

BRUTTIUM

Ionian Sea

Messana

Locri

Regium

Strait of Messina

SICILY

Mediterranean Sea

Syracuse

© 2008 Jeffrey L. Ward

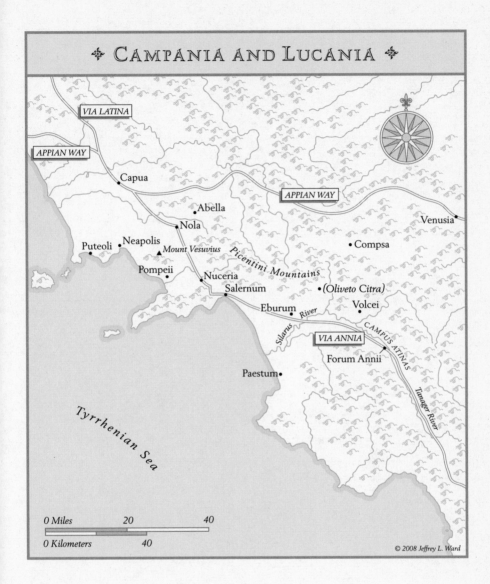

✤ CAMPANIA AND LUCANIA ✤

VIA LATINA

APPIAN WAY

Capua

Abella

APPIAN WAY

Nola

Venusia

Neapolis

Puteoli

• Compsa

▲ *Mount Vesuvius*

Pompeii

Picentini Mountains

Nuceria

Salernum

(Oliveto Citra)

Eburum

Silarus River

Volcei

VIA ANNIA

CAMPUS ATINAS

Forum Annii

Paestum •

Tanager River

Tyrrhenian Sea

0 Miles   20   40

0 Kilometers   40

© 2008 Jeffrey L. Ward

AUTHOR'S NOTE

I have used Roman place names wherever possible, with the exception of such common names as Italy and Spain.

I have translated all ancient Greek and Latin quotations myself unless otherwise noted.

INTRODUCTION

Lucius Cossinius was naked. Senator, commander, and deputy to the general Publius Varinius, Cossinius usually wore a full suit of armor and a red cloak, fastened with a bronze brooch on his right shoulder. But now he was bathing. A bath was a luxury in wartime, but no doubt hard to resist after leading two thousand men on the march. As he had approached, Cossinius could have seen the pool glistening on the grounds of a villa at Salinae—"Salt Works," located on a coastal lagoon near Pompeii. In the distance stood Vesuvius, still a sleeping volcano in those days, its hills green with pine and beech trees, its orchards overflowing with apples and with grapes that made wine good enough for a senator's table; its soil teeming with hares, dormice, and moles that the locals favored as hors d'oeuvres.

While Cossinius let his guard down, the enemy prepared to strike. Runaway slaves, gladiators, and barbarians, they were a rabble in arms, but they had already beaten Rome twice that summer. Their leader was as cunning as he was strong, as experienced as he was fresh, and he spoke words to steel the most timid soul. He was Spartacus.

There was probably only a moment's warning, maybe a centurion sounding the alarm or the shouts of the men. Cossinius, we might imagine, moved quickly out of the water and onto his horse before his slave finished rearranging his master's cloak. Even so, Spartacus's men burst into the grounds of the villa so fast that Cossinius barely escaped. Not so his supplies, which the enemy captured, and which would now go to feed the rebel force.

They hounded Cossinius and his men back to their camp. Most of the Romans were new recruits. Children of Italy's abundance, they had nothing but hasty training to prepare them for a savage foe, some of them giants, red-haired and tattooed, and buoyed by success. In spite of the curses and threats of their centurions, some Romans ran away; the rest stayed and were slaughtered. Everything they had now belonged to the enemy, from their camp down to their arms and armor. Lucius Cossinius was naked again, but this time he was dead.

It was the autumn of 73 B.C. After several months of rebellion, the fortunes of the Senate and People of Rome were heading toward low ebb. A city that had shrugged off Etruscan adventurers, weathered a Gallic invasion, stood up to Hannibal's charge, endured civil war, survived annual outbreaks of malaria, and fought its way to such power that it could think of itself as the head of the world, was afraid of a runaway gladiator.

What began as a prison breakout by seventy-four men armed only with cleavers and skewers had turned into a revolt by thousands. And it wasn't over: a year later the force would number roughly sixty thousand rebel troops. With an estimated 1–1.5 million slaves in Italy, the rebels amounted to around 4 percent of the slave population. To put that figure in perspective, the United States in the nineteenth century had about 4 million slaves, and yet Nat Turner's rebellion in 1831 involved only two hundred of them.

Rome had seen slave rebellions before but this one was different. Earlier revolts had either been relatively small or, if extensive, far off in Sicily, but this enormous army had come within a week's march of Rome. Not since Hannibal crossed the Alps had foreigners done so much damage to the Italian countryside. Earlier slave revolts coalesced around mystics and gang leaders, not gladiators and ex–Roman soldiers. Spartacus struck a chord in the Roman psyche. No other leader of rebel slaves was so well remembered or so feared. As a gladiator, Spartacus belonged to a group of men who were licensed to kill—to kill each other, that is: Romans had a lurid fascination with the arena but rebel gladiators aroused disgust and then dread.

Spartacus came from Thrace (roughly, Bulgaria), an area known to Romans for its fierce fighters and ecstatic religion, and for its alternation between alliance and rebellion. As a onetime allied soldier in Rome's service, Spartacus should have been a Roman success story. Instead, he had become the enemy within. Thracians, Celts, and Germans—barbarians all, in Roman eyes—made up most of his followers. Earlier slave rebels came from the citified Greek East; fairly or not, the Romans scorned their warrior prowess. They dreaded a fight against barbarians.

Timing made matters worse. When Spartacus began his revolt, Rome faced major wars at both ends of its empire. Mithridates, a king in Asia Minor (today, Turkey), had sparked a substantial war against Rome in 88 B.C. that had spread to Greece and Thrace and was still going strong after fifteen years. Meanwhile, in Spain, the renegade Roman general Sertorius ran a breakaway government whose Roman leaders had the support of a native resistance movement. Finally, at the same time, off the coasts of Crete, the Roman navy struggled to catch pirates who were plundering the sea lanes. Rome eventually defeated all these challengers, but in 73 B.C. that outcome was not yet clear.

By exploiting propaganda masterfully, Spartacus threatened to widen his base of support. He sounded themes that appealed not only to slaves but also to Italian nationalists and to supporters of

Mithridates. Although his message probably attracted few free men to his banner in the end, it was enough to frighten Rome.

Spartacus's was the most famous slave revolt in antiquity and arguably the largest as well. It was a revolt that absorbed southern Italy, caught Rome with its homeland virtually defenseless, led to nine defeats of Roman armies, and kept antiquity's greatest military power at bay for two years. How was it possible? Why did the rebels do so well for so long? Why did they fail in the end? And how could the world's only superpower have let such a problem persist in its own backyard?

It's a story that should have been in pictures, and, of course, it is. In 1960, *Spartacus* appeared, a Hollywood epic starring Kirk Douglas and directed by Stanley Kubrick. The film was a hit then and remains a classic. It was loosely based on a bestselling 1951 novel by Howard Fast, which he wrote after serving a jail term for contempt of Congress during the McCarthy era. An American communist who eventually left the Party, Fast was not the first communist to admire Spartacus. Lenin, Stalin, and Marx himself saw Spartacus as the very model of the proletarian revolutionary. German Marxist revolutionaries of 1919 called their group the "Spartacus League"; their failed uprising grew legendary. Soviet composer Aram Khachaturian wrote a ballet about Spartacus that won him the Lenin Prize for 1959.

Noncommunist revolutionaries admired Spartacus as well. Toussaint L'Ouverture, the hero of the Haitian Revolution, history's only successful mass slave revolt, emulated Spartacus. Giuseppe Garibaldi, who fought to unify Italy, wrote the preface to a novel about Spartacus. Vladimir Jabotinsky, the Zionist revolutionary, translated that novel into Hebrew. Voltaire, the French Enlightenment philosopher, judged Spartacus's rebellion as perhaps the only just war in history. Even anticommunists approved of Spartacus: Ronald Reagan, for example, cited him as an example of sacrifice and struggle for freedom.

But while Spartacus was the stuff of legend, he was no myth. He is, however, an enigma to us. Spartacus left no writings. His followers scratched out no manuscripts. Surviving ancient narratives come from Roman or Greek writers who wrote from the point of view of the victors. To make things worse, few of their writings survive. Still, they leave absolutely no doubt about it: Spartacus was real.

Plutarch (ca. A.D. 40s–120s) and Appian (ca. A.D. 90s–160s) provide the most complete accounts of Spartacus to survive from antiquity but they are short, late (one hundred fifty to two hundred years after the revolt), and come each with an ax to grind. Even shorter is the discussion by Florus (ca. A.D. 100–150), but his concise remarks are full of significance. These three writers relied on important but now mostly lost earlier works by Sallust (86–35 B.C.) and Livy (59 B.C.–A.D. 17). Almost nothing of Livy's discussion of Spartacus survives. We have a precious few pages' worth of selections from Sallust's account of the war.

Three other contemporaries of Spartacus comment briefly on his activities: the great orator Cicero (106–43 B.C.), the scholar and politician Varro (116–27 B.C.), and Julius Caesar (100–44 B.C.). Many other ancient writers over the centuries mentioned Spartacus, from the poet Horace (65–8 B.C.) to Saint Augustine (A.D. 354–430) but they add little. Even by the standards of ancient history, accounts of the Spartacus rebellion are meager.

However, there are archaeological finds, the results of topographical research, and experiments in historical reconstruction ranging from gladiators' contests—without real weapons, of course—to weaving vines into ropes such as Spartacus's men used to climb down Vesuvius. Coins, frescos, sling balls, and fortifications all record the rebels' path through the Italian countryside. The bones of a gladiators' cemetery in Turkey reveal training secrets and suggest the agony of death. Tombs, shrines, and towns; gold and iron; plaques and paintings, all take us beyond the stereotypes of barbarians in Greek and Roman texts. Finally, Roman slavery comes to life through graffiti, chains, auction buildings, slave quarters, and slave prisons.

The story of Spartacus is, first of all, a war story: a classic case study of an insurgency, led by a genius at guerrilla tactics, and of a counterinsurgency, led by a conventional power that slowly and painfully learned how to beat the enemy at his own game. The Spartacus War is also a tale of ethnic conflict. Spartacus was Thracian but many of his men were Celts; they were proud, independent, and fighting-mad. Tribal divisions turned the rebels into feuding cliques who ignored their chief. The march for freedom degenerated into gang warfare, and, as so often in history, the revolution failed.

The Spartacus story is also a love story and a crusade. Spartacus had a wife or mistress; her name is not recorded. A priestess of Dionysus, this unnamed companion preached a rousing message. She drew on the liberation theology that had fired Rome's earlier slave revolts and still fueled the anti-Roman war that had raged for fifteen years in the eastern Mediterranean. Spartacus had a divine mission.

The Spartacus War is also a story about identity politics. A rebel against Rome, Spartacus was more Roman than he cared to admit and certainly more Roman than the Romans could admit. He terrified the Romans not just because he was foreign but because he was familiar.

Spartacus was a soldier who had served Rome, and his behavior might have reminded Romans of their heroes. Like Marcellus, perhaps Rome's most red-blooded general, he thirsted to kill the enemy commander with his own hand. Like Cicero, he was an orator. Like Cato, he was a man of simple tastes. Like the Gracchi, he believed in sharing the wealth among his men. Like Brutus, he fought for freedom.

Like the most ambitious Roman of them all, he claimed to have a personal relationship with a god: like Caesar, Spartacus was a man of destiny. No sooner had he died than men began to dream of Spartacus's return. The human Spartacus fell to the power of Rome; the legend might topple empires still.

The Spartacus War is also a story about the complexity of slave revolts. We do not know if Spartacus wanted to abolish slavery, but if so, he aimed low. He and his men freed only gladiators, farmers, and shepherds. They avoided urban slaves, a softer and more elite group than rural workers. They rallied slaves to the cry not only of freedom but also to the themes of nationalism, religion, revenge, and riches. Another paradox: they might have been liberators but the rebels brought ruin. They devastated southern Italy in search of food and trouble.

In the end, the story comes back to Spartacus. Who was he? What did he want? Our answers must be based less on what Spartacus said, about which we know little, than on what he did. By necessity, we must be speculative. But we can also be prudent in our speculation because Spartacus's actions speak loudly. They fit the timeless patterns of insurgencies and uprisings, as shaped by the particulars of his case.

Rome was big, strong, and slow; Spartacus was small, hungry, and fast. Rome was old and set in its ways; Spartacus was an innovator. Rome was ponderous, while Spartacus was nimble. The Romans suffered so badly from Spartacus's ambushes, night moves, sudden turnabouts, and mobile flank attacks that eventually they gave up facing him in battle. They insisted on isolating his forces and starving them out before they were willing to risk combat.

The ancient sources describe a man of passion, thirsting for freedom and burning for revenge. Spartacus's actions tell a different story. He was no hothead but rather a man of controlled emotions. Spartacus was a politician trying to hold together a coalition that was constantly slipping out of control. Whether by nature or training he was a showman. His greatest prop was his own body but Spartacus used many symbols, from a snake to his horse, to form his image. A cult of personality helped attract tens of thousands of followers but at a price of luring them into the delusion of invincibility.

Spartacus was Thracian, and in Thrace warfare was the most honorable profession. The name "Spartacus"—Latin for "Sparadakos"—is plausibly translated as "Famous for His Spear." Thracians were masters of the horse, which made them fast, mobile, and utterly different from the Romans, who were born infantrymen with little talent for cavalry. And the Thracians had a genius for guerrilla warfare. They perfected light armor for foot soldiers and hit-and-run tactics, to which the heavy-armed Romans were vulnerable. And thanks to his service in an auxiliary unit of the Roman army, Spartacus had been schooled in conventional warfare, too.

When it comes to the Romans, our evidence is better, if still limited. The Romans were constrained by the enduring strategies of counter-insurgency. They had to locate, isolate, and eradicate an enemy that avoided pitched battle while harassing them via unconventional tactics. To do this required achieving superiority in intelligence, which in turn required local knowledge. Still, while the Romans never adopted a strategy of winning popular support, they displayed more savvy in dealing with locals than we might expect.

But the Romans had a lot more on their minds than Spartacus. In 73 B.C., Rome was a city of scars. Italy was a peninsula divided between Rome and its often-unwilling allies. Over the centuries Rome had conquered Italy's hodgepodge of peoples, including Greeks, Etruscans, Samnites, Lucanians, and Bruttians. Many tensions existed and two decades earlier they had exploded into a rebellion (91–88 B.C.). The Italian War (also called the Social War, that is, war of the *socii*, Latin for "allies") took three years of bloody battles and sieges before Rome restored peace, and only at the price of granting citizenship to all the allies. Especially in the South, some Italians remained bitter and unreconstructed. The Italian War was followed by a civil war between the supporters of Sulla and the heirs of his late rival, Marius. Sulla won and served as dictator, but after his retirement in 79 and death a year later, civil war flared up again in 77. Italy was at peace in 73 B.C. but stripped of legions, should trouble break out anew: they had been sent abroad to fight Rome's many enemies.

The Italian countryside included a large population of slaves, who often ran away and who sometimes rose in armed rebellion. In 73 B.C., Roman Italy was, in short, a bone-dry forest in a summer heat wave. Spartacus lit a match.

BREAKOUT

I

THE GLADIATOR

SPARTACUS WAS A heavyweight gladiator called *murmillo*. A man "of enormous strength and spirit," as the sources say, he was about thirty years old. *Murmillones* were big men who carried thirty-five to forty pounds of arms and armor in the arena. They fought barefoot and bare-chested, rendering all the more visible the tattoos with which Thracians like Spartacus proudly embellished their bodies. Murmillones each wore a bronze helmet, a belted loincloth, and various arm- and leg-guards. They carried a big, oblong shield (*scutum*) and wielded a sword with a broad, straight blade, about a foot and a half long. Called the *gladius*, it was the classic weapon of the gladiator. It was also the standard weapon of a Roman legionary.

Although we know nothing of Spartacus's record in the arena, we can imagine him locked in combat one afternoon. Fans that they were, the Romans have left masses of evidence about the games, and recent historical reconstructions enrich the picture. We know, for example, that Spartacus would have fought just one other man at a time, despite Hollywood's image of mass fights. Real gladiators fought in pairs, carefully chosen to make an exciting contest—but not a long life for the contestants.

A murmillo like Spartacus never fought another murmillo; instead, he was usually paired with a *thraex*. *Thraex* means "Thracian," but Spartacus did not represent his country in the arena, perhaps because his owner feared stirring up his slave's national pride. The thraex was also a heavyweight but he had to be quicker and more agile. His arms and armor were similar to the murmillo's but the thraex carried a small shield (*parmula*) that made him lighter and more mobile. And the thraex carried a curved sword (*sica*), like the one used by Thracians in battle.

Gladiatorial matches usually began with a warm-up with wooden weapons. Then the "sharp iron" arms were brought in and tested to make sure they were razor-sharp. Meanwhile, Spartacus and his opponent prepared to die—but not by hailing the sponsor of the games. The famous cry "Those who are about to die salute you!" was, as far as we know, a rare—and later—exception. Instead a match usually began with a signal from the *tibia*, a wind instrument like an oboe.

The contest unfolded with a combination of elegance and brutality. Gladiators attacked but rarely crossed swords, since their blades were too short. Instead they thrusted and parried with their shields, pushing an opponent back, drawing him forward, or—with the shield turned horizontally—hit him with the edge. The crash and boom of shields, rather than the metallic clank of swords, marked the sound of combat.

With his fifteen-pound scutum, a strong murmillo could hit harder, but a fast thraex could get in more blows in rapid succession with his seven-pound parmula. Knowing how much damage the curved sword of the thraex could do, Spartacus guarded his flank. Instead he tried to keep the battle on a vertical axis, constantly standing with his left shoulder and left leg forward, thereby denying his foe an opening while keeping up the pressure. He held his shield close to his body to prevent the thraex from rapping at it with his parmula and destabilizing it. Every now and then Spartacus would bring his shield forward in a sudden, powerful thrust to shift the thraex off balance.

Denied Spartacus's flank, meanwhile, the thraex might have ducked and lunged at Spartacus's unprotected right leg. He might even have attempted the more difficult move of leaping up, powering his right arm over the top of Spartacus's shield, and stabbing him with his curved sica. If these murderous maneuvers failed, however, they would have given Spartacus a sudden opening. The smart move for Spartacus would have been to feint, thereby tempting the thraex into thrusting toward him—only to find Spartacus ready to parry and deliver a deadly riposte.

Every so often during a fight, a glancing blow got through, leaving a man bleeding but not fatally wounded. Pumped up on adrenaline, he would have to keep fighting, however bruised, tired, and sweating he was, all the while continuing to think on his feet, always shifting his tactics. Although it appears that most bouts lasted only ten to fifteen minutes, there was no time limit; the fight went on until one man won. Meanwhile, each fighter had to close his mind to the noises of the crowd and the brass instruments accompanying the match and focus solely on combat. He also had to try somehow to keep the rules in mind. Gladiatorial bouts were no free-for-alls. A referee (*summa rudis*) and his assistant (*seconda rudis*) enforced the regulations. The most important rule was for a fighter to back off after wounding an opponent.

Let us imagine that Spartacus had driven his enemy off balance, knocked the man's shield out of his hand, and stabbed him in the arm. Spartacus would then withdraw from the wounded man. Whether to finish off the thraex was not up to a gladiator or referee; it was up to the producer (*editor*).

The producer, in turn, usually asked the audience. A decision about a fallen fighter was the moment of truth. If the crowd liked the losing gladiator and thought he had fought well, they would call for letting him go. But if they thought the loser deserved to die, they wouldn't be shy about shouting "Kill him!" They made a gesture with their thumbs, but it was the opposite of what we think today: thumbs up meant death.

In that case, the loser was expected to kneel—if his wounds allowed—while the winner delivered the deathblow. At the moment that the loser "took the iron," as the saying went, the crowd would shout, "He has it!" The corpse would be carried away on a stretcher to the morgue. There he had his throat cut, as a precaution against a rigged defeat. Burial followed.

Spartacus, meanwhile, would climb the winner's platform to receive his prizes: a sum of money and a palm branch. Although a slave, he was allowed to keep the money. After climbing down from the podium, he would wave the palm branch around the arena as he circled it, running a victory lap, taking in the crowd's approval.

It was an unlikely school of revolution. Yet fights like this steeled the blood of the men who would start the ancient world's most savage slave revolt.

Spartacus lived and trained in the gladiatorial barracks owned by Cnaeus Cornelius Lentulus Vatia. Vatia was a *lanista*, an entrepreneur who bought and trained gladiators, whom he then hired out to the producers of gladiatorial games. Vatia's business was located in the city of Capua, which sits about fifteen miles north of Naples. It is a part of Italy renowned for its climate, but Spartacus was not likely to appreciate the three hundred days of sunshine a year.

He had come to Capua from Rome, probably on foot, certainly in chains, likely tied to the men next to him. In Rome he had been sold into slavery to Vatia. Imagine a scene like that of the slave sale carved on a Capuan tombstone of the first century B.C., possibly marking a slave trader's grave. The slave stands on a pedestal, most likely a wooden auction block, naked except for a loincloth—standard practice in Roman slave markets. It was also standard to mark the slave by chalking his feet. Bearded and broad-shouldered, with his long arms at his sides, the slave in the relief looks fit for hard labor. And the artist uses a size imbalance to suggest a power imbalance, because he makes the slave smaller than the freedmen on either side of him.

Spartacus's first view of Capua might have been neither its walls nor temples but its amphitheater. The building rose up outside the city walls and just to the northwest of them, beside the Appian Way. The structure had the squat and rugged shape of what it was, one of Italy's first stone amphitheaters. Built in the Late Republic, it would have given Spartacus his first impression of the town.

Most of Spartacus's life had unfolded on the broad plains and winding hills of the Balkans but now his frame of reference was no wider than the walls of Vatia's establishment, with occasional glimpses of Capua. The city and the business had much in common. Neither was respectable in Rome's eyes and both depended on slave labor. Each occasionally offered a ladder of mobility to slaves. But there was one difference: outside the house of Vatia, the ladder sometimes led to freedom, but inside, it usually led to death.

Spartacus had taken the long route to Capua. In his native Thrace, young Spartacus had served in an allied unit of the Roman army. The Romans called these units *auxilia* (literally, "the help") and its men were called auxiliaries. These units were separate from the legions, which were restricted to Roman citizens. Although they were not legionaries, auxiliaries got a glimpse of Roman military discipline. Spartacus's later military success against Rome becomes easier to understand if we remember that he had seen firsthand how the Roman army worked.

As an auxiliary, Spartacus was probably a representative of a conquered people fulfilling their military service to Rome; that is, he was probably more draftee than mercenary. As a rebel he would display the eye of command, which might suggest that he was an officer under the Romans. In all likelihood, he was a cavalryman.

Almost all of Rome's cavalry were auxiliaries. None made fiercer horsemen than the Thracians. The Second Book of Maccabees (included in some versions of the Bible) offers a powerful image of a Thracian on horseback: a mercenary, bearing down on a very strong Jewish cavalryman named Dositheus and chopping off his arm. The unnamed Thracian had thereby saved his commander, Gorgias, whom Dositheus had grabbed by the cloak. That happened in 163 B.C. In 130 B.C. a Thracian cavalryman decapitated a Roman general with a single blow of his sword. Fifty years later the Romans still shivered at the thought.

According to one writer, Spartacus next deserted and became what the Romans called a *latro*. The word means "thief," "bandit," or "highwayman" but it also means "guerrilla soldier" or "insurgent": the Romans used the same word for all those concepts. We can only guess at Spartacus's motives. Perhaps, like many Thracians, he had decided to join Mithridates' war against Rome; perhaps he had a private grievance; perhaps he had taken to a life of crime. Nor do we know where he deserted, whether in Thrace, Macedonia, or even Italy. In any case, after his time as a latro, Spartacus was captured, enslaved, and condemned to be a gladiator.

In principle, Rome reserved the status of gladiator for only the most serious of criminals. Whatever Spartacus had done, by Roman standards it did not merit such severe punishment. He was innocent, as we learn from no less a source than Varro, a Roman writer in the prime of his life at the time of the gladiators' war. Knowing that he was guiltless would have added flames to the fire of Spartacus's rebellion. In any case, Spartacus had become the property of Vatia. The next and possibly last act of the Thracian's life was about to begin.

Capua was known for its roses, its slaughterhouses, and its gladiators. It was fat, rich, and a political eunuch. In 216, during the wars with Carthage, Capua had betrayed its ally Rome for Hannibal, Carthage's greatest general. After the Romans reconquered Capua in 211 B.C. they punished the town by stripping it of self-government and putting it under a Roman governor.

Yet Capua had bounced back, richer than ever. The city was a center of metalworks and of textiles. It was also the perfume and medicine capital of Italy as well as a grain producer and Rome's meat market, providing pork and lamb for the capital. Capua sits at the foot of a spur of the Appenines, Italy's rugged and mountainous spine. To the south lies a flat plain, hot and steamy in the summer when the fields are brown, alternately rainy and bright in the winter when the fields are green. Some of the most fertile land in Europe, this was *Campania Felix*, "Lucky Campania."

Lucky, that is, except from the point of view of its workers. Capua was in large part a city of slaves, both homegrown and imported. The number of slaves made Capua differ only in degree, not kind, from the rest of Italy. The 125 years of Roman expansion after 200 B.C. had flooded Italy with unfree labor. By Spartacus's day, there were an estimated 1–1.5 million slaves on the peninsula, perhaps about 20 percent of the people of Italy.

It was the heyday of exploitation in the ancient world, the zenith of misery and the nadir of freedom. Yet it was also an era of large concentrations of slaves, many of them born free, some of them ex-soldiers; of absentee masters, and of few or no police forces. Add to that the freedom given to some slaves to travel and even carry arms. Finally, consider the many possible refuges provided by nearby mountains. It is no accident that, within the space of sixty years, Sicily and southern Italy would explode into three of history's greatest slave uprisings: first in two separate revolts on the island (135–132 B.C., 104–100 B.C.) and then in Spartacus's rebellion.

In the countryside, masses of slaves worked on farms, often in chains, usually locked up for the night in prisonlike barracks. Others, employed as herdsmen, were left to fend for themselves or starve. Meanwhile, in town, slaves worked in every profession, from the shop to the school to the kitchen. In Capua, there were even slaves to collect the 5 percent tax owed when slaves earned their freedom. A lucky few made it to freedom and some prospered; some even went into the slave business, turning their backs on their humble origins. One Capuan freedman, for example, did not mind getting rich by manufacturing the rough woolen cloaks that were issued to slave field hands—issued once every other year, that is.

Coarse and rapacious, Capua was destined to become the center of gladiatorial games. Capua's sunny climate was considered ideal for training fighters. Thus Rome's impresarios came to scout talent. Julius Caesar himself would own a gladiatorial school in Capua.

And yet, by 73 B.C., not Capua but Rome—the capital—put on Italy's greatest gladiatorial games by far. Rome's cautious elite refused to allow gladiators to be housed there, though. Violent and dangerous, gladiators would have been foxes in the Roman henhouse. It was safer to keep them outside the capital. Capua was ideal: only 130 miles away, and connected to Rome by the most famous highway in the world, the Appian Way, as well as by another great road, the Via Latina.

After traveling one of those highways, or perhaps even before, in the chain gang along the way, Spartacus was introduced to his new colleagues. They were a motley group. Almost all were slaves, whether from birth, by civilian capture and sale, or as a result of becoming prisoners of war. Many were Thracians. Thrace provided Rome with a steady stream of slaves, thanks to the endless wars with Rome's bordering province of Macedonia and thanks, too, to the Thracians' burning passion for war.

Thracians loved hunting, drinking, and fighting. They were born brawlers with a reputation for brutality. Thracian cavalrymen, for example, fought "like wild beasts, long kept in cages and then aroused" when they defeated the Romans at a skirmish at Callinicus in 171 B.C. They returned to camp singing and brandishing on their spears the severed heads of their enemies.

Another people in the Roman world who were similarly spoiling for a fight were the Celts. The Celts "are absolutely mad about war," says the Roman writer Strabo. "They are high-spirited and quickly seek out a fight." And Celts made up the second large group of Vatia's gladiators. The sources call them Gauls, and surely some of them came from Gaul, or what is modern France. They might have been taken prisoner in one of several small Roman military operations in Gaul in the 80s and 70s B.C. They might even have been the sons of war prisoners taken in Marius's great victories in the West in 102 and 101 B.C. But most had been probably sold into slavery by civilians: the going rate for a Gallic slave was as little as an amphora (large jug) of wine. The Romans exported an estimated 40 million amphoras of wine (about 2.64 million gallons) to Gaul in the first century B.C. and got back in return perhaps as many as fifteen thousand slaves a year.

But some of Vatia's Celts may have come from the Balkans, a Celtic population center and scene of wars with Rome in the 80s and 70s B.C., and thus a rich source of slaves. The Scordisci, for example, lived on the plains south of the Danube, in what today is northeastern Serbia, and were Celts who had mingled with Thracians and Illyrians (another warlike people of the ancient Balkans).

If Vatia or his agents indeed had bought Scordisci, they had chosen the wrong Celts. Thracians and Scordisci shared a border and a hatred for Rome. In 88 B.C. the Scordisci and many Thracians supported Mithridates in his revolt against Rome. A joint army of Thracians and Scordisci invaded the Roman province of Greece in a major raid; both peoples later suffered in Roman punitive expeditions.

We probably ought to add Germans to the mix of gladiators in the house of Vatia. Germans too played a prominent role as Spartacus's soldiers. Many of Italy's slaves were German or children of Germans who, like Celts, had been captured in large numbers by Marius thirty years earlier; others had been sold into slavery by civilians. Besides, there was no clear distinction between Celts and Germans in 73 B.C.: boundaries blurred. In any case, both Greco-Roman writers and archaeologists agree that the ancient peoples of today's Germany were warlike, like the Celts and Thracians. "Peace is displeasing to [their] nation," wrote the Roman historian Tacitus, who stated that the Germanic economy rested on war and plunder. We don't hear of Germans until Spartacus's revolt spread, but perhaps a few of Vatia's gladiators were German.

Perhaps other ethnic groups from around the empire contributed men to Vatia's enterprise. Anatolia and the Black Sea region both provided Rome many of its slaves, and Vatia's establishment possibly included representatives of those lands. But one last important group to consider was not foreign at all: free Italians, even Roman citizens. Both poor and rich citizens volunteered as gladiators, whether out of desperation, boredom, or a search for adventure. In the first century B.C. such forays into the Italian underworld had already become fashionable.

And so we have the two hundred or more gladiators owned by Vatia: Thracians and Celts, with a likely admixture of Germans, Italians, and odd-lot others. Spartacus's colleagues were a multiethnic group. This was no accident. Roman authors advised mixing nationalities as a deterrent to solidarity. They recognized the deadly seriousness of a business that armed slaves.

Surprisingly, the Romans called a gladiatorial enterprise a game: in Latin, *ludus*. *Ludus* is also translated as "school," and indeed it trained beginners but, with few exceptions, there were no graduates. Most gladiators lived and died in the ludus where they started out.

Romans also described a ludus as a *familia*, a "family" or "household." As in any household, the ludus attended to the basic needs of food and shelter but it also offered medical care. Gladiators had to limit wine intake and eat a high carbohydrate diet, heavy on barley porridge. Like sumo wrestlers they were encouraged to put on fat around the middle, in their case as a protective layer in case of wounds. Like pampered racehorses, gladiators ate well. "Tell your masters to feed their slaves!" was the acerbic advice of a bandit in the Roman Empire as to how the Romans could stop crime. He would have been preaching to the choir had he addressed lanistae since they had to treat their gladiators well in order to succeed.

But a ludus was also a barracks and a prison. Gladiators were not free to come and go as they pleased. The best evidence comes from Pompeii, where two ludi from different periods have been excavated. Both stood at the edge of town. The earlier ludus was virtually a fortress, isolated by a raised, sloping sidewalk and additional steps, bringing the interior a full ten feet above street level—all unusual for Pompeii. Other security measures were found inside: an extra door and a sealed courtyard. Pompeii's second, later ludus was more open but it did contain a small jail, complete with iron stocks, and it may have held a guard post as well.

Vatia's ludus would probably have been built around an internal court, surrounded by stuccoed columns that were in turn covered with graffiti, such as these from Pompeii: Celadus advertised himself as "the one the girls sigh over." Florus reports that he won on July 28 at Nuceria and on August 15 at Herculaneum, both nearby cities. Jesus (sic) says, punning, that the murmillo Lucius Asicius stinks like cheap fish sauce (muriola) and is as weak as a lady's drink (also called muriola). Some gladiators record the name of their owner, while the gladiator Samus, who fought both as a murmillo and on horseback, says simply that he "lives here." The gladiators Asicius, Auriolus, Herachthinus, Philippus, and the "fearsome" Amarantus scratched their names and positions into the white stucco.

Ludus might mean "game" but life there was serious. A new recruit took the most sacred oath imaginable—and the most terrible:

he swore to be "burned" (perhaps tattooed, since tattoos were the mark of slavery), chained, beaten, and killed with an iron weapon. It was, says the Roman writer Seneca, a promise to die "erect and invincible," because facing death calmly was the height of the gladiatorial art. After his oath-taking, the new gladiator then followed a training schedule that was, in its own way, as pure and strict as a Spartan's.

Gladiators played such an important role in Roman culture that they received far better treatment than the average slave. Not that the Romans were simply positive about gladiators. Instead they considered gladiators to be both good and bad. To be forced to be a gladiator was demeaning; to volunteer as a gladiator was depraved; to become skilled as a gladiator was dangerous, but to die as a gladiator was sublime.

Gladiators didn't have friends. They had allies, rivals, bosses, hangers-on, punks, spies, suppliers, and double-crossers. The new gladiator learned whom to trust and whom to watch out for, who would cover his back and who would steal his food. He quickly took the measure of the men: the strong, the agile, the tough, the ruthless; the weak, the clumsy, the soft, and the kindhearted. A pecking order of leaders and followers would emerge, as brutal and as status-conscious as in any prison. One night a man shared a precombat meal with his comrades, the next day he killed his tablemate, and shortly afterward arranged for the victim's tombstone.

Maybe some gladiators deserted because life in the ludus was hard, but by Roman standards life there was not especially harsh. Discipline in the Roman legions, for instance, could be nearly as strict. Unlike gladiators, soldiers could not be tortured but they faced severe punishment for crimes ranging from theft and engaging in homosexual acts to loss of weapons and failure to keep the night watch. These punishments included whipping and execution by being clubbed to death.

Some of Vatia's slaves might even have liked the discipline. They could hardly have minded the rewards. Victorious gladiators got glory, cash, celebrity, and sex—which was better than what other slaves faced. And yet two hundred gladiators decided to break out of Vatia's ludus. By the standards of Roman slavery, gladiators were privileged. If it was ironic that they, of all people, should spark a slave uprising, it was also typical. Throughout history, privileged slaves have often led revolts, perhaps because they have high hopes. Did the gladiators explode because Vatia tightened the screws? Perhaps, or perhaps theirs was a revolution of rising expectations.

Hollywood made one of Vatia's trainers especially brutal, but we know next to nothing about Vatia and even less about the trainers. Even Vatia's name is uncertain, since the sources call him either Lentulus Batiatus or Cnaeus Lentulus. According to a plausible theory, "Batiatus" is a mistake; he was really Cnaeus Cornelius Lentulus Vatia, a Roman citizen from a rich and noble family known to have owned gladiators in Capua. The man was crude and thick-skinned enough not to mind having a job description—gladiatorial school owner (*lanista*, in Latin)—that Romans compared to butcher (*lanius*) or pimp (*leno*). Perhaps he kept his distance and left the management of the ludus to others, while he stayed in Rome. Maybe he never even met Spartacus before the revolt; who knows?

According to one ancient author, the gladiators decided "to run a risk for freedom instead of being on display for spectators." It was humiliating to have to fight to the death for the entertainment of the Roman public. A certain greatness of soul runs through the whole story of Spartacus, from Capua to his last battle. One ancient writer says that Spartacus was "more thoughtful and more dignified than his circumstances, more Greek than his race." Another says that Spartacus had the support of an elite few free-souled, prudent men—in a word, of the nobles.

There is a chance that Spartacus himself had been born an aristocrat. Straws in the wind: The name Spartacus is found in a Thracian royal family; the ancient sources say that there were a few "nobles" among the insurgents, which probably means slaves of noble birth or descent; two contemporary Roman writers admired Spartacus, which would have been easier for them if he were patrician. Even among gladiators, the glamour of a noble name might have helped Spartacus to draw in supporters.

As Spartacus and his allies gathered support for the revolt, they might have spoken of profit and vengeance as well as freedom and honor. They might also have pointed out that the time was ripe. They might have noted that Mithridates was still carrying the torch of Roman resistance high in the East and that Sertorius's revolt still smoldered in the West. And perhaps they knew of some of the many earlier slave rebellions against Rome: a dozen uprisings in Italy during the second century B.C., two massive uprisings in Sicily (135–132, 104–100), and an anti-Roman coalition of slaves and free people in western Asia Minor between 132 and 129 B.C. When in 88 B.C. Mithridates sponsored a massacre of Romans and Italians in western Asia Minor, he offered freedom to any slave who would kill or inform on his master. With so much revolt in the air, only a hermit could have remained ignorant.

Only thirty years before, Capua's slaves had risen in revolt—twice. Old-timers in town might still have talked about it. In or around the year 104, two hundred slaves at Capua rebelled and were quickly suppressed; no other details survive. Another Capuan revolt in 104 was more serious. Titus Minucius Vettius, a rich, young Roman in love with a slave girl but buried under debt, rose in revolt from his father's estate outside of Capua. He formed an army of 3,500 slaves, armed and organized in centuries like a Roman legion. The Roman Senate took this threat seriously. They appointed Lucius Licinius Lucullus to restore order; he was a praetor, a high-ranking public official who was combination chief justice and lieutenant general. Lucullus raised an army of four thousand infantry and four hundred cavalry but he beat Vettius by cunning, not brute force. Lucullus offered immunity to Vettius's general Apollonius (the name suggests a slave or freedman), who turned traitor. The result was mass suicide by the rebels, including Vettius.

The uprising failed but it left encouraging lessons to insurgents. Slaves could form an army, and one that was well organized and well armed. Rome was impressed enough that it used treachery instead of attacking the rebels head-on. It was striking too that Roman forces barely outnumbered the slaves. Perhaps Rome didn't send more troops because it couldn't send more troops. In 104 B.C., the Roman army was otherwise engaged.

The year before, in 105, an army of migrating Germans and their Celtic allies had humiliated the legions at the battle of Arausio (Orange) in southern France and killed tens of thousands of Roman soldiers. Not until 101 were the migrating Germans and Celts finally defeated. The two revolts in Capua circa 104, therefore, challenged a regime that already had enough trouble.

Now, in 73 B.C., the legions were abroad fighting Sertorius and Mithridates. At home a police force was all but nonexistent. A new uprising might succeed where the old one failed. Opportunity beckoned but something more basic may have inspired rebellion: survival instinct.

A gladiator's life expectancy was short. The best evidence comes from a cemetery at Ephesus, in Turkey, where 120 skeletons of gladiators have been excavated and studied. Almost all of them died before age thirty-five, many before age twenty-five. Between one-third and one-half of them died from wounds violent enough to cut or shatter their bones, and about one-third of those wounds were blows to the head. The other skeletons show no sign of bone damage, but the men might have died violently nonetheless, from disembowelment or a severed artery or an infected flesh wound, for example.

The Ephesus gladiators lived during the period of the Pax Romana (Roman Peace) in the second and third century A.D., when the games were a state monopoly. During Spartacus's era, in the Late Republic, the games were private enterprise, and that probably made things worse for gladiators. Sponsors were usually rich men in search of popularity, and the crowd loved bloodshed, so they might have tried to outdo each other in the number of gladiators they sacrificed. It would not be surprising if many gladiators died in their first match.

And that match might have been looming on the horizon. The gladiators' revolt began in the spring. It has been suggested that Vatia's men were being trained for the annual Roman Games, also known as the Great Games, which began on September 5. Gladiatorial contests were part of this two-week festival. With all Rome watching, the producer would have to give the crowd at least some blood. Some of Vatia's gladiators could expect not to be coming home.

Still, the life-expectancy argument can go only so far. Thracians, Celts, and Germans prided themselves on their contempt for death. They believed in the afterlife and they preferred to think of themselves as fearless fighters, not cowards. Spartacus had to convince them that there was a better fight waiting for them as fugitives than inside the ludus.

Gladiators wanted neither to flee nor to free others. But standing and fighting in Italy, killing Romans, stealing their wealth, and attracting supporters from the local slave population—*that* would have appealed to the men of the Familia Gladiatoria Lentuli Vatiae—Lentulus Vatia's Family of Gladiators.

And yet, this catalog of reasons somehow fails to explain Spartacus's success. Surely, his personal authority has to be added to the equation. When Spartacus spoke, men listened. It wasn't just his prowess in the arena, or his experience in the Roman army, or his possible reputation as a bandit. It wasn't simply his royal-sounding name or his communications skills—although those were surely considerable. Something else, some X factor, multiplied his authority. But what?

To answer that question, we will have to ask his woman.

2

THE THRACIAN LADY

I<small>N</small> 73 B.C. a Thracian woman announced a miracle. A prophetess, she preached the word of Dionysus, who took possession of her during ecstatic frenzies. The god, she said, had bestowed great power on a man. Like her, he was a Thracian who lived in Italy. He was her lover: Spartacus.

We know very little about the Thracian woman, not even her name. The surviving information, however, is tantalizing. She was Spartacus's messenger, perhaps even his muse.

Although nothing is known of her appearance, we can imagine the kind of ecstatic ritual that might have led to her prophecy, because a great deal of information survives about the worship of Dionysus. Popular in many places in the Mediterranean, Dionysus was the national god of Thrace. Thracian women danced for Dionysus, and wore long, ankle-length robes, barefoot with their upper arms exposed. Thracian women tattooed their arms with such patterns as geometric stripes, chevrons, dots, circles, and a fawn. A Bacchante (that is, worshipper of Dionysus) wore an ivy wreath in her hair. As she worshipped the god she typically held a thyrsus, a giant fennel staff topped with a pinecone. Beside her might have lain the tiny items that she used in her ritual: amber, seashells, knucklebone, and glass. But the most striking object would have sat in her right hand: a snake. Its body would have been curled around her upper arm and through her armpit, while its head would have extended downward toward the ground. Knowing that the snake was Dionysus's main companion and symbol, she probably felt no fear.

Plutarch is our sole source of information about the Thracian lady. He lived 150 years after Spartacus but he based his work on the now largely missing contemporary account of Sallust. What Plutarch says might not satisfy skeptics, but other sources make his account plausible.

We meet the Thracian lady in Capua but we can imagine the process that brought her there. Consider a scene on a tombstone of a slave dealer. The women are walking behind. They are modestly dressed in ankle-length tunics, their heads covered by shawls. Two children walk beside them. Ahead of them walk eight men, chained to each other at the neck, their bare legs showing between knee-length tunics. Leading the march is a man in a full-length, hooded cloak. He is a guard or slave dealer; the eight men are being led off into slavery. The women and children may be family, following two of the men into bondage.

The scene took place some time in the Late Roman Republic or Early Empire. The place is Thrace; the slaves were Thracians, sold into slavery in exchange for wine. But they may remind us of Spartacus and his female companion on the road to slavery in Capua in 73 B.C.

It may seem hard to believe that an enslaved gladiator was allowed to have a female companion. But gladiators could enjoy a stable family relationship, although as slaves they could not enter into a marriage that was valid in Roman law. Slave "consorts" and children are well attested in ancient sources. Owners might even have liked a gladiator to have a wife, as an anchor in the rough world of the ludus.

Spartacus's lady was a Thracian like him, and came from the same people as her man. Just which Thracian people that was is unclear. Plutarch says that Spartacus came from a nomadic people, by which he probably means a people whose wealth came from flocks that they pastured in the highlands in summer and in the lowlands in winter. That doesn't make Spartacus a humble shepherd but simply the product of an economy based on herding.

In any case, "nomadic" may possibly be a medieval copyist's error; the ancient text might have referred not to nomads but to Maedi (singular, Maedus). The Maedi were a Thracian tribe that lived in the mountains of what is now southwestern Bulgaria. Like Spartacus, they had a reputation for physical strength; like him, they fought alternately for and against Rome. Other Thracian peoples of this period provided hardy warriors, such as the Bessi and the Getae, and Spartacus and his lady may have belonged to one of those groups. Another possibility is the Odrysians, a people of southeastern Thrace, located between the Aegean Sea and the Rhodope Mountains. They were Roman allies who fought against Mithridates.

In any case, Spartacus's consort was Thracian. How she came to Italy, how she met Spartacus, and whether she too was a slave— these things are all unclear. Nor is it certain that she was with Spartacus in Rome, although that seems likely. But we do know that she cohabited with Spartacus in Capua and fled the city with him. And there is reason to think that the Thracian woman spread Spartacus's fame.

When Spartacus was brought to Rome to be sold into slavery, a remarkable event is supposed to have taken place. Plutarch records the story but he does not vouch for its veracity. While the Thracian was sleeping, a snake wrapped itself around his face. Or so the tale goes, even though modern experts explain that this is impossible.

Italy is home to a quite a few snake species but according to scientists, none of them would wrap itself around a sleeping person's face. Perhaps Spartacus woke up with a snake crawling close to or even on his face: unlikely but not impossible. The story could then have grown in the telling, either by Spartacus or others. Or maybe Spartacus said merely that he had dreamed the whole thing.

In any case, the Thracian woman interpreted the event as a miracle. Just as a snake had wrapped itself around Spartacus's face, so would he be surrounded by "a great and fearful power." The result would be—well, the manuscripts differ, with some saying Spartacus would have "a lucky end" and others saying "an unlucky end." The first version is attractive, considering the positive connotations of snakes in Thrace, not to mention the worthlessness of propaganda that predicted ruin.

The Thracian woman's words carried the weight of prophecy. Thrace had a long tradition of prophetesses and oracles, and Thracians set great store by women's religious authority. So did the ancient Germans, who believed that there was "something sacred and prophetic" about women. But anyone can grasp the timeless stereotype of the woman who speaks for natural forces: the siren, the sibyl, or the witch. Spartacus's companion might have been "a woman to make your heart tremble," as one seventeenth-century Englishman said of a woman who prophesized in public.

Seers played a proven role as troublemakers among slaves. They had incited one revolt in Sicily in 135 B.C. and led another in 104 B.C. The Roman agricultural expert Columella, writing around A.D. 60, might have had such events in mind when he warned managers to keep prophets and witches off the estate.

We don't know when the Thracian woman made her prophecy. Perhaps it only came later, when the revolt of the gladiators was under way. But if she predicted the future while Spartacus was still in Capua or even before, in Rome, then it might have been the spark that lit the rebellion. In the first century B.C. both rebels and Romans took seers very seriously.

For example, those bitter Roman political rivals, Marius and Sulla, shared a common devotion to seers. Marius brandished favorable predictions from various clairvoyants, and the most colorful of them was a Syrian prophetess named Martha. Supposedly, the woman first came to the attention of Marius's wife when Martha correctly predicted the outcome of a gladiatorial match! Marius brought Martha with his army on campaign.

Sulla did not let his rival outdo him. The most powerful man in Rome before his death in 79 B.C., Sulla often reported his dreams as omens and he proudly advertised the words of a seer from Mesopotamia (today, Iraq), that Sulla was destined to be the greatest man in the world. Sulla claimed the title of *Felix,* "lucky," because of the various gods who supported him.

But unlike Spartacus, neither Sulla nor Marius would have claimed Dionysus. In addition to being the god of wine and theater, Dionysus had a long political pedigree, going back to Olympias, the mother of Alexander the Great. More recently, Dionysus had been the symbol of Greek kings (especially Cleopatra's dynasty, the Ptolemies of Egypt), Thracian tribes, the poor and enslaved masses of southern Italy, and various rebels against Rome, from the leaders of the Sicilian slave revolts to mutinous southern Italian elites to Mithridates. A flexible figure, Dionysus stood for power, prosperity, patriotism, liberty, and even rebirth, depending on who wielded the symbol.

By associating Spartacus with a snake and god-given power, the Thracian lady gave him a new identity. She blended old notes of religion, nationalism, and class into a new song of rebellion. The snake made Spartacus a Thracian hero and linked him to Dionysus, who was known in his homeland as Zagreus or Sabazius.

Thracian culture glorified the image of a great heroic ancestor; Thracian art usually depicted the hero on horseback, often with a snake nearby. In Thrace, Dionysus worship was a fighting faith. For example, around 15 B.C. a Thracian revolt against Rome broke out; its leader, Vologaesus, was a priest of Dionysus.

To the downtrodden, Dionysus offered hope; to the Roman ruling class, he spelled trouble. They associated him with southern Italy and Sicily, where the god was especially popular, and where rebels had fought under the banner of Dionysus over the years. In southern Italy, Dionysus was linked to Orpheus, another mythological figure from Thrace. So-called Orphic writings were widespread, and they told a tale of the death and resurrection of Dionysus, a symbol of hope for the afterlife. As a Thracian and as Dionysus's chosen, Spartacus might find ready supporters in southern Italy: another reason for Dionysus to have worried the Senate. Even the most peaceful and law-abiding worshippers of Dionysus bothered Rome's strait-laced elite.

Worshippers of Dionysus met in small groups where they held their ceremonies and initiated newcomers. The Greeks called these rituals "orgies," the Romans called them Bacchanals; the reality was exuberant but no sexual free-for-all. Worshippers drank, danced, sang, and shouted at promises of liberation, rebirth, and immortality. Believers demonstrated their trust in the god by showing off their snake handling, by fastening their animal skins with snakes, by wreathing their heads with them, or by letting the snakes flicker their tongues over their faces without ever biting.

In 186 B.C. the Roman Senate claimed that Italy's widespread Dionysiac groups masked a conspiracy. In an atmosphere of fear and panic, the Senate launched a witch hunt up and down the peninsula and drove Romans out of the cult. After 186, only women, foreigners, and slaves were permitted to worship the god.

Dionysus was left to the powerless of Italy and they embraced him. In 185–184, the slave shepherds of Apulia—the heel of the Italian "boot"—revolted, and the sources hint that they claimed Dionysus as their patron. Between 135 and 101 B.C., two slave revolts in Sicily and one slave revolt in western Anatolia all invoked Dionysus. The god appeared again in the rebellion of Rome's Italian allies known as the Social War (91–88 B.C.): rebel coins showed Bacchus as a symbol of liberation. As mentioned earlier, Dionysus was a symbol adopted by Mithridates. The rebel king called himself the "new Dionysus," as had king Ptolemy IV (ruled 221–205 B.C.), and he minted coins showing Dionysus and his grapes on one side and the cap worn by a freed slave on the other.

There may be an echo of the Thracian woman's propaganda in the statement of a Roman poet that Spartacus "raged through every part of Italy with sword and fire, like a worshipper of Dionysus." The writer, Claudian (circa A.D. 370–404), lived nearly five hundred years after Spartacus, but he had an interest in Roman history, so his words may reflect a good source.

By invoking Dionysus, the Thracian woman stirred a chord among foreign-born gladiators and slaves as well as among Italians who remembered Mithridates' support during the Social War. Her message was, in effect, If you supported Mithridates' revolt against Rome, then support Spartacus!

As we have seen, we don't know whether Spartacus himself supported Mithridates when he deserted the Roman army before 73 B.C. and became a latro—that is, a bandit or a guerrilla. In any case, once he revolted against Rome in 73 B.C., Spartacus was no doubt glad to make common cause with Mithridates' supporters.

By the same token, there is no reason to think that Spartacus had ever served Rome with a whole heart. One historian has made a plausible guess about the details of Spartacus's military service. In 83 B.C. the Roman general Sulla prepared to cross from Greece to Italy in order to wage civil war. He recruited infantry and cavalry from Greece and Macedonia to join the forces he already had. Spartacus might have been one of those soldiers.

At the time, some of the Maedi had recently been defeated by Sulla, after which they had accepted Rome as overlord. It would not have been surprising if they sent a contingent of soldiers to fulfill their responsibility. If Spartacus and his fellow Thracians fought for Rome they could hardly have been happy about it. Sulla had invaded Thrace because of Thracian raids on Roman-controlled Macedonia, raids inspired by Mithridates' revolt. In Thrace, Sulla treated the natives virtually as target practice for his army. Those who escaped with their lives probably lost their property, since Sulla's men got rich from loot. This was the Rome that Spartacus served, deserted from, and finally revolted against.

Assuming that Spartacus was a young man of about twenty when Sulla recruited his soldiers in 83 B.C., the gladiator would have been about thirty in 73 B.C., when his revolt began. As a former Roman soldier who turned on Rome, Spartacus fit a pattern. Over the years, some of Rome's worst enemies had served in the auxilia. Take Jugurtha, charismatic king of Numidia (modern Algeria), whose armies humiliated the Romans for six years before the Romans finally captured him in 106 B.C. Years earlier, in 134 B.C., he commanded the Numidian cavalry in a Roman army fighting rebels in Spain—an education for him in Roman ways. Jugurtha put his lessons to good use during his war by bribing Roman politicians.

The worst turncoat was someone who lived after Spartacus, Arminius, also known as Hermann, a German tribal chieftain who not only served in a Roman allied unit but also won Roman citizenship and the rank of knight. That did not stop him from going home and giving Rome its worst defeat ever in Germany, the massacre of three Roman legions in the Teutoburg Forest in A.D. 9. It was a turning point in history. Without that defeat, Rome might have conquered Germany, and a Romanized Germany would have changed the course of European history. Never has a country raised a hungrier wolf in sheep's clothing.

Spartacus's feelings toward Rome and its enemies are likely to have been complex. Pride, rage, and shame are all part of what he may well have felt toward the Roman army. Solidarity, suspicion, and opportunism all may have marked his attitude toward Rome's enemies. These feelings were contradictory but Spartacus did not have to be consistent: as soon as the Thracian woman spoke, he had a god on his side.

By her prophecy, Spartacus's lady gave her man a holy duty. As a servant of Dionysus, Spartacus would be a liberator. He would be no mere theorist of freedom; he would have "great and fearful power." For a Thracian, power had a clear definition. A powerful man was a warrior, a hunter, a possessor of many horses, the father of many children, and a great drinker. In a word, he was a chief.

We don't know the dynamic among the different ethnic groups in the house of Vatia, but judging by their later actions, we might guess that each nationality stuck together. Spartacus likely began with his fellow Thracians. He had to convince them, first, to agree to overpower the guards and break out of the House of Vatia. To do that they would need weapons, but the weapons were kept under lock and key. So they would have to choose the right moment, either a time when they could steal the key or when the weapons were being distributed, say, on the eve of a match. They would fight—and how stirring to do so in the name of Dionysus Zagreus and Sabazius!

Celtic gladiators were probably a harder sell, since they were unmoved by Thrace's national god. But they too had a score to settle with the Romans; they too could see just how rich in loot the land around them was. And they would have appreciated Spartacus's authority, both human and divine.

They might have agreed to join Spartacus but it's not likely that they agreed to take orders from him. The Celts were as sensitive about status as any people in the ancient world. At feasts, for example, Celtic men sat according to rank. When the meal was served, the bravest man got the "hero's portion" of meat. If someone challenged his right to it, then, according to Celtic legend, the two men had to fight to the death. So the Celts did not challenge Spartacus to a duel but they did choose two leaders of their own, Crixus and Oenomaus.

We know nothing about the two men. Since they were Celts, they were probably proven warriors, possibly from noble families, and likely to be able to guarantee a large number of followers. Some sources make them Spartacus's equals; others say that he was commander in chief of the rebels. The distinction matters little, because in insurgencies, formal command structures count less than informal sources of power: charisma, power, persuasiveness, supporters, and a record of success.

Two hundred men decided to join Spartacus—no small achievement on his part. But because the plot was betrayed, most of them never managed to escape. Who leaked the information—a free person or a slave—is not known. We can only guess how Vatia or his agent reacted. He may have locked the doors, had the most dangerous gladiators chained, and called in armed reinforcement. Fortunately for the rebels, some of them reacted quickly. They would have to fight their way out. The only weapons in the house were locked up, so they had to make do with what they could get.

They went to the kitchen, rarely a pleasant part of a Roman house. It was usually small, smoky due to poor ventilation, dirty thanks to its packed dirt floor, and called to do double duty as a latrine. From here the gladiators took cleavers and skewers. Roman cleavers were big iron butcher knives that could sever a hand. Skewers, also iron, could easily prove fatal if aimed at soft tissue like the neck and, with enough force, could even kill a man through his chest. The guards, it seems, were well armed and in no short supply: of the two hundred conspirators, only seventy-four gladiators escaped, along with at least one woman, Spartacus's Thracian companion.

Still, the guards seem to have had their hands full with the gladiators left behind, as the rebels were able to stop on the road not far from the ludus. They had come across some carts loaded with gladiatorial weapons heading for another city. The fugitives got rid of the drivers and helped themselves to the arms. These weren't as battleworthy as the equipment of Roman legions but they were a major step up from kitchen utensils. Perhaps Spartacus now found a sica, the curved Thracian sword that had been denied to him in the arena. According to one ancient source, Spartacus wielded a sica in his battles.

The runaways were now free but freedom wasn't enough. As one Roman writer put it, "Not satisfied with having made their escape, they also wished to avenge themselves." The rebels' itinerary proves the truth of this analysis.

Capua sat at a crossroads. Highways ran south from the city to Puteoli (modern Pozzuoli) and north to the nearby temple of Diana Tifata and then up the Volturnus (modern Volturno) river valley. Italy's most famous road, the Appian Way, went north from Capua to Rome and south from Capua into the Apennine Mountains at Beneventum (modern Benevento) and, two hundred miles beyond, the Adriatic Sea at Brundisium (Brindisi). Finally, there was the Via Annia. This road ran south from Capua to Nola and Nuceria (Nocera), then past Salernum (Salerno) and into the mountains of Lucania (modern Basilicata) and Bruttium (modern Calabria), where it finally ended at Regium (modern Reggio di Calabria), 320 miles from Capua. The gladiators chose this road.

The selection says something about their goals. If their purpose had been escape, they would have taken a different road. For example, they might have headed north, on the overland route out of the peninsula. Or they might have gone into the Apennine Mountains to set up a camp of runaways—what in later days was called a community of maroons (from a Spanish word meaning "living on mountaintops"). We know of several maroon communities in Greek and Roman times.

They probably would not have gone to Puteoli, about twenty miles south of Capua. That crowded port offered boats and freedom but it was filled with arms of the law. Besides, Thracians, Celts, and Germans tended to be landlubbers and probably preferred to avoid the sea.

They likely walked along the Via Annia, probably keeping to the sand or gravel path at the edge in order to avoid the hard flagstones of the paved way. Dogs, wolves, and bandits were common sights on Roman roads, but armed and runaway gladiators were something new. We can imagine many travelers turning and running when they saw Spartacus's men. Those who held their ground lost their daggers and wooden clubs if not their lives.

Down the Campanian plain the gladiators went, through the neat, checkerboard pattern of subdivisions that the Romans imposed on the lands they ruled. They traveled past groves and shrines, inns and fountains, and some of Italy's richest farms, many of them belonging to absentee owners, administered by bailiffs, and worked by slaves. They no doubt stopped here and there to grab meat off a tavern's fire or to drink from a stream, keeping stones at the ready to fight off watchdogs. Perhaps already at the dawn of the revolt, they were shouting out to the field hands to join them, but few are likely to have answered the call. The seventy-four desperadoes probably looked more like bandits than freedom fighters. And they no doubt really were bandits to any rich person unlucky enough to come across their path. In any case, a slave needed some enticement before risking the long arm of the Roman law by joining a pack of rebels.

In a way, the gladiators did set up a maroon community, but it was a temporary one because they picked a place where they could not stay long. They chose Vesuvius. Today Vesuvius calls to mind the volcanic eruption that destroyed Pompeii in A.D. 79. But in 73 B.C. the volcano had not erupted for centuries. The countryside consisted of fertile, volcanic soil over which towered Vesuvius, the cherry on top of a rich cake.

The runaways would find plenty to eat. Vesuvius's woods were thick with game. The plain and the lower slopes of the mountain were filled with working farms: large slave-run estates that the Romans called "rustic villas." There was food and drink for the taking: olives, figs, and many other fruit or nut trees flourished, but the main product was the grape, either eaten fresh or made into some of Italy's most famous wine, the Vesuvinum—exported as far away as India. Ironically, Dionysus, Spartacus's patron and the god of wine, loomed large in the rites of local farm owners. His image appeared in the decoration of their dining rooms, household shrines, wine cellars, and even wine jugs. As for the thousands of slaves who did the real work, with a little coaxing they might have been ready to follow Dionysus's chosen men into freedom.

If Spartacus was already planning on going to Vesuvius when he was still in the House of Vatia, he must have had good intelligence. Vesuvius is about twenty miles south of Capua as the crow flies, a day's journey; it is not visible from the city. Perhaps Spartacus had seen the mountain in an earlier year, either fighting for Sulla in 83 B.C. or while raiding as a bandit—assuming he really did either of those two things. Or perhaps he had merely heard about Vesuvius and its attractions secondhand, perhaps from other slaves. Not only was Vesuvius a gateway to wealth but a fortress as well. For Thracians it had the added advantage of being sacred, since they worshipped the gods on mountaintops.

Standing alone and over four thousand feet high, Vesuvius made a dramatic pirate's nest. The mountain offers views northward of the Campanian plain toward Capua and southward of the valley of the Sarnus (modern Sarno) river and the rugged Lactarii (modern Lattari) mountains, on today's Amalfi Peninsula. The Apennine Mountains rise in the east and the Mediterranean Sea lies to the west. Cities such as Naples, Nola, Nuceria, Herculaneum, and Pompeii were all in reach. Whoever occupied the mountain would be able to see any attackers coming. Meanwhile, even on a sunny day on the plain, the peak of Vesuvius can be cloud-covered; it could protect the defenders with a thick mist.

After the heat and noise of Capua, the cool and peace of the mountain might have been welcome. Even in summer, Vesuvian nights can be chilly. The rebels would have to build fires and steal extra clothes.

It was probably not long after coming to Vesuvius that the gladiators faced a group of armed men from Capua, outfitted with proper weapons and armor. If Capua was like the city of Rome at the time, its police force would have been tiny. So the army sent against the gladiators might well have included men hired by Vatia, perhaps veteran Roman soldiers. The gladiators were unimpressed. They drove off the Capuans and seized their weapons. One ancient writer says the rebels were glad to throw away their gladiatorial weapons because they considered them "dishonorable and barbaric." Perhaps, but they might have been equally glad to add spears and breastplates to their stockpile, both of which were absent from a gladiator's armory.

It was probably just a small engagement but it might have been a turning point in the young revolt. We might speculate that news of the gladiators' victory echoed down the mountain, the sign that some were waiting for: the gladiators had the power to achieve something worth risking one's life for. In any case, it was around this time that local people began joining them.

The sources tell us that while they were camped on Vesuvius, Spartacus and his men accepted new recruits: "many runaway slaves and certain free men from the fields." One source claims that ten thousand fugitives joined the gladiators on Vesuvius, but running away was risky and the mountain was hard to climb, so "several thousand" is a safer estimate. Some of the slaves were probably Thracians or Celts, like the rebel gladiators, but they also included Germans.

The slaves worked on the estates that ringed Vesuvius. They were a hardy lot. Plowmen were ideally strong and tall; vineyard workers were supposed to be broad, powerfully built, and intelligent. Boys and even young girls looked after farm animals, but only the strongest young men were fit to be herdsmen. Leading cattle, sheep, and goats up mountainsides was difficult work, requiring strength, stamina, agility, and speed. Gauls were considered to be especially good herdsmen, particularly with horses, donkeys, and oxen.

Pasturage would have been a waste of the rich soil around Vesuvius: this was farm country. Ranches tended to be located farther south. In Campania, large estates or plantations predominated, typically worked by hundreds of slaves. These were the famous Roman *latifundia*, or "wide fields," to use a term invented in the empire. By day the slaves worked in gangs of, ideally, ten laborers or less. At night they were kept in barracks, often in chains. In fact, they sometimes worked in chains as well: in vineyards, for example, because viticulture required intelligent slaves—and brains could lead to trouble.

A privileged group of slave stewards managed the plantation. The key person was the *vilicus*, or bailiff. Since most owners were absentee landlords, the vilicus really ran the estate. His purview ran from settling disputes to leading prayers. He took care of the finances, organized the workforce, and oversaw its smooth operation. The *vilica*, a female official, was also essential: not only was she chief housekeeper on the estate but also a teacher and truant officer. She was handy enough to lead the senior slaves in making their own clothes. For all their power, the vilicus and vilica were slaves, and so, capable of revolting—and of freeing ordinary slaves from their chains. One of the leaders of the Second Sicilian Slave War (104–100 B.C.), for example, was a runaway vilicus. Tough and hardworking, farm slaves made good rebels, vilici fine leaders and organizers, and vilicae excellent quartermasters.

So much for slaves; what of the "certain free men from the fields" who joined the rebels? As recruits to Spartacus's cause, free men brought the perspective of Italian subsistence farmers. By the Late Republic (133–31 B.C.), the small farmers of Italy had been driven off the best land; in their place came latifundia and ranches. It was the great scandal of the Republic that Rome's greedy elite so mistreated the farmer-soldiers who had won the Roman Empire. But the smallholders didn't all disappear or move to the city. They stayed in the countryside, where they scraped by through farming marginal and inaccessible land. Around Pompeii, for example, there were many small farms here and there among the manors.

In order to put more food on the table, some small farmers joined the Roman legions. They became the shock troops of the civil wars between Marius and Sulla, and later, Caesar and Pompey, Antony and Octavian. Some won new land in reward. Sulla, for instance, gave about one hundred thousand veteran soldiers land in Italy, much of it simply taken from his enemies, the former supporters of Marius, who were evicted. Some of those Marians fled to Spain, to join the rebel Sertorius, but most stayed in Italy. Some worked as tenant farmers or day laborers for the new owners. Others turned to that classic activity of the Italian countryside—they became bandits, a word that is Italian in origin. So did some of Sulla's veterans who failed on their new farms because of bad harvests, hostile neighbors, or hard-driving creditors.

But few small farmers did anything so dramatic; most survived by doing seasonal and occasional labor for the well-to-do villa owners. They were the Roman equivalent of today's migrant workers. The Roman elite needed them and frowned on them. They are essential for harvesting grapes and cutting hay, says the Roman writer Varro; but you have to watch them carefully, says the statesman Cato the Elder, or they will steal your firewood.

Although poor, the small farmers were free men and native Italians; some of them no doubt looked down on slaves. But if they were desperate, angry, or adventurous enough, they joined Spartacus. And, in all probability, many were indeed desperate. Slave or free, it would have taken a hardy soul to climb Vesuvius and trust a band of professional killers. Surely most of the newcomers were young and probably most were men, but there were probably some women, too.

If a few free farmers joined Spartacus, even fewer elites would have backed an army of runaway slaves. Yet perhaps a small number did. Wealthy but diehard Italian nationalists, still bitter over defeat in the Social War, were not about to join a slave-led army but perhaps they turned a blind eye rather than playing an active role in resisting Spartacus. And then there were opportunists. Every society has people who say that money has no smell, as a Roman wit later put it. They saw no shame in doing business with runaway slaves and ex-gladiators if it could make them rich. The merchants who later traded with Spartacus's army might fit this category; the same is true of one Publius Gavius, a southern Italian who, although a Roman citizen, was convicted of spying for Spartacus in Sicily.

One possible index of Italian attitudes comes from the Mithridatic Wars. In 64 B.C., during the last stage of his struggle against Rome, Mithridates tried to incite an invasion of Italy by Celtic peoples of the Balkans. Not only did he promise assistance, he assured Celtic leaders that they would find willing partners on the Italian peninsula. Most of Rome's so-called allies in Italy, he told them, had really supported Spartacus, in spite of his degraded social status. But big talk is a politician's stock in trade, so Mithridates' claim deserves little credence. In any case, the Celts declined his invitation to invade Italy.

One group was conspicuously absent from the list of Spartacus's recruits: city dwellers, whether slave or free. This seems odd because cities like Pompeii and Nola were nearby. True, city walls made it hard for urban slaves to leave, but that isn't the only explanation. Urban slaves were a privileged group who generally enjoyed an easier life than rural slaves; some of them had a reputation for being soft and lazy. Urban slaves were isolated from their rural counterparts, and perhaps even frightened of the rough, tough country folk. We might wonder how many of them would have survived in the Italian outback. In short, they may not have wanted to join Spartacus. If so, it was a sign of things to come. Spartacus's revolt would remain overwhelmingly a revolt of the countryside.

But that was not yet clear on Vesuvius, where the rebels' numbers were growing and their character was changing. They were becoming an army. Their weapons were makeshift, their uniforms were homespun, and their experience was often minimal. But they trained, drilled, and practiced fighting together. No ancient source tells us this, but without such groundwork they could never have displayed the military virtues they did in the coming months.

We might wonder if they trained as much as needed, since temptation loomed. The ex-gladiators, former farmworkers, runaway slaves, Thracians, Celts, Italians, and miscellaneous others now devoted themselves to an alluring pursuit: crime. With runaway farm slaves and workers as their guides, they raided the rich villas of Vesuvius. They found food and drink, solid fare as well as delicacies such as ostrich eggs and vintage wine. There were more luxury goods than one man could carry: silver and gold, ivory and amber, glazed terra cottas and colored glass, earrings and bracelets, medallions and plates, silver table legs shaped like lion's paws and cameos of kings.

Writing fifty years later, the poet Horace marks a special occasion by telling his slave boy to bring the oldest vintage of wine. And then he adds, with a wink, "If roving Spartacus has spared a single jar."

Whatever the fugitives took they shared equally: Spartacus insisted on that. Whether justice or prudence motivated him is unclear. But more followers climbed the mountain.

What a change! Good old Vesuvius had given Campania every reason to love it. Consider a fresco at Pompeii: It shows Mount Vesuvius, green and fertile, and beside it Bacchus, the god of wine, covered with grapes. A large snake is depicted below. Then came Spartacus. The rebels from Capua had appropriated the gladiator, the vine, and Vesuvius: the very symbols of Roman rule in Campania.

Rome had to do something, if only because of the clout of the area's wealthy residents. The rebels spread terror, what the Romans called *terror servilis*, the fear of slaves; the gentry surely demanded action. Spartacus might have guessed as much, but if he did, he didn't let it stop him. Perhaps it was now that one of the rebels—maybe Spartacus himself—made the brave statement reported by one ancient writer: "If they come against us in force, it is better to die by iron than starvation."

They would not have to wait long. Perhaps as they waited, at night, around a fire under the stars, the Thracian lady heartened them with visions of the power that heaven had given to Spartacus.

VENGEANCE

3

THE PRAETORS

IN 73 B.C., six hundred and eighty-one years after the founding of the city of Rome, during the consulship of Lucullus (Marcus Terentius Varro Lucullus) and Cassius (Gaius Cassius Longinus), the republic was fighting wars at both ends of the Mediterranean. In Spain, Pompey ground down the renegade Roman commander Sertorius by taking out his strongholds one by one. In Asia Minor, Lucius Licinius Lucullus, the consul's brother, began an invasion of the homeland of King Mithridates, who had fought Rome on and off for fifteen years. In the Balkans, Gaius Scribonius Curio was the first Roman general, along with his legion, to see the Danube River. In Crete, Antony got ready to sail out against pirates attacking Roman shipping.

Given the big picture, the gladiators' revolt might have seemed minor. Capua had seen a slave revolt before, in 104 B.C., which had been crushed by barely the number of troops in a single legion—four thousand infantry and four hundred cavalry, for a total of 4,400 men—led by a praetor, a leading Roman public official. So the obvious policy in 73 was to send in the praetor.

In Rome, the Senate set public policy. Senators were all very wealthy men, and almost all members of a few elite families. They had automatically become senators, without election, after holding high public office, and they served for life. They were the oligarchy that ran Rome, except for those occasions when they were challenged by a general like Marius or Sulla. Once rare, those challenges had become more frequent. But in 73 B.C., the senators enjoyed a period of power.

The senators chose Caius Claudius Glaber to send against Spartacus. He was one of eight praetors that year, each of them at least thirty-nine years old, and each elected to an annual term. They were men of great expectations, since the praetors were the second highest-ranking of the annually elected public officials in Rome; only the two consuls stood higher. Who was Glaber? We hardly know. He never rose to the consulate and he had no known descendants. He was a plebeian with probably at most a distant link to the more famous members of the Claudius clan. His obscurity was another sign of how little attention Rome gave Spartacus.

Glaber led a force slightly smaller than the one sent against the rebels of 104 B.C.: three thousand men instead of 4,400 and, so far as we know, no cavalry. But the first revolt had been led by a Roman citizen who was a knight, no less, while the latest uprising was the work of barbarians and slaves. Apparently the Romans felt more confident in 73 than in 104.

The news from Capua was digested, analyzed, and classified. It was, to quote Caesar, "a *tumultus* of slaves." A tumultus was a sudden outbreak of violence requiring an emergency response. It was a serious matter but not organized war (*bellum*, in Latin).

As we know, Romans looked down on slaves. Their servile nature, said one contemporary, made slaves cruel, greedy, violent, and fanatical while denying them nobility or generosity of spirit. For slaves to behave courageously was against nature. For slaves to behave like free men was strictly for the Saturnalia, an annual celebration featuring role reversal—as a Roman officer once remarked in disgust when his men had to fight freed slaves. In revolt slaves were a nuisance but not a major problem. Or so the Romans told themselves, although the stubborn resistance of Sicily's slaves in two revolts (135–132 and 104–100 B.C.) should have taught them otherwise.

And then there were the gladiators and their leader. Doublethink runs like a red thread through Roman attitudes toward Spartacus. Fear and scorn, hatred and admiration, indifference and obsession— they were all there. For the Romans, gladiators were to be fed, trained, cheered, adored, ogled, bedded, buried, and even, occasionally, freed, but, never, never to be treated as equals.

As a slave and a Thracian barbarian, Spartacus was despicable to Romans. As a former allied soldier, he was pathetic. From their point of view, the Romans had offered Spartacus the hand of civilization by letting him into the auxiliary units of their army. Then, whether through bad behavior or bad luck, he ended up a slave. He had lost the chance that the army had given him (again, that is, from the Roman point of view). But in their mercy, as far as the Romans were concerned, they gave Spartacus another chance. They gave him the gladius—the sword.

To the Romans, a gladiator was not just an athlete or even a warrior: he was holy. And he was sexy. Whenever they went to the games the Romans took a walk on the wild side. The beasts were supposed to growl back at them; it made a better show. But Spartacus did more than growl. Like many a pro athlete, Spartacus was feared for the same reason he was adored: he was dangerous. Yet once he left the arena, a gladiator seemed almost harmless, even if he had taken up arms in revolt.

If this seems hard to understand, think of Spartacus as an athlete who rejected the love of his fans. We can forgive an athlete who misbehaves but not one who snubs us. Once Spartacus and his seventy-three companions left their barracks, they were no longer gladiators but *runaway* gladiators. In Roman eyes, they had shrunk from a fight, hence they were moral lepers: cowardly, effeminate, and degenerate. They had sunk from the glory of the arena to the shame of banditry. Spartacus could have been the pride of Rome; instead, it seemed, he was back where he began, a barbarian. From the Roman point of view, his men were not soldiers but runaway slaves, *fugitivi*. No wonder the Senate had little fear of him—at first.

Two other things are likely to have kept the Romans from making a bigger push against Spartacus: ambition and greed. Glory was the oxygen of Roman politics but there was little to be won in a police action against criminals. A slave war, says one Roman, "had a humble and unworthy name." Plunder might have served as consolation, but that was out of the question. All Italians south of the Po Valley were Roman citizens. Roman soldiers couldn't plunder their own country.

Because they were responding to a tumultus (emergency), the Romans did not hold an ordinary levy of troops on the Campus Martius (Field of Mars) outside the city. Instead they probably instructed Glaber to do what Roman commanders often did in an emergency: to recruit troops on the road, as he marched south.

Glaber's troops were probably not the best that Rome had, not by a long shot. Those were already fighting in Spain and in the East, where there were plenty of spoils and laurels to be won and top generals to lead the men. Italy had not been stripped of its good soldiers: Sulla's veterans, for example, represented a source of experienced troops. Sullan veterans were to be found at Pompeii as well as at Abella, and outside Capua, among other places. But they were not likely to sign up to help some nobody slap a few slaves back into irons. Glaber had to take what he could get.

So Glaber's army was probably no more than a militia. And yet no Roman army on the march was easily forgotten. The flash of mail armor and bronze or iron helmets as a long line of soldiers went by captured the eye. The clatter of the supply carts and the lowing of the oxen that drew them filled the air. And then there were the individual soldiers.

A standard-bearer, surrounded by trumpeters, carried the legion's symbol, a silver eagle on a standard (that is, shaft). Every century (a unit of 100 men originally, but by the Late Republic a unit of eighty men) also had its own standard, a spear decorated with disks and wreaths, carried by a standard-bearer in colorful dress: his helmet was decorated with an animal skin.

Meanwhile, six men called *lictors* marched in front of the praetor. Lictors served as attendants to all Rome's high-ranking officials. They were strong men; each carried the fasces, a bundle of rods tied with ribbons and symbolizing the power to command. Outside the city limits of Rome, the fasces were wrapped around an ax, signifying the power of life and death.

And so they marched, the praetor and his men, following the rebels to Vesuvius. They made camp, probably at the foot of the mountain. Glaber decided not to attack the enemy, who was on the summit. This may seem overly cautious, but the terrain favored the defenders. Only one road led up the mountain and it was too rough and narrow to deploy a legion. It was no place to test his new army. Instead Glaber decided to seal in the enemy and starve him out. He posted guards on the road to prevent a breakout.

It was not an imaginative or a self-confident plan but it might have worked, as long as the Romans had kept their guard up. Instead they handed the initiative to Spartacus. He decided to attack the Roman camp. Like any commander, Spartacus drew on his experience to put together a plan of battle. Rich and complex, that experience would serve him well, both at Vesuvius and later.

As a Thracian, Spartacus had a heritage of making war. In particular, Thrace specialized in light infantry, horsemanship, trickery, and unconventional warfare. Homer considered the Thracians a nation of horsemen; Thucydides respected their daggers; Romans feared their polearm. Thrace had invented the *peltast*, the quick and mobile lightly armed infantryman who fought at close range with a knife or at a distance with a javelin. They excelled at attacking or defending hills, using hit-and-run tactics, setting ambushes, setting or dousing campfires, making opportunistic raids on heavy infantry formations, and forming up in defensive mass against cavalry. Feints, ruses, tricks, and stratagems were all chapters in the Thracian war manual. And plundering was a national habit.

Spartacus was born and raised with the Thracian way of war but as an adult he added an additional string to his bow: Roman military doctrine. He combined Thracian speed and stealth with Roman organization and discipline. Single combat and swordsmanship did double duty for him, since Romans as well as Thracians valued these practices. Gladiatorial training may have added some new tricks to his sword handling.

At Vesuvius, Spartacus put all his military wisdom to use. Because of the dramatic changes to Vesuvius in the several eruptions since 73 B.C., we cannot reconstruct the topography in detail. But the overall picture is clear.

Nowadays, "Vesuvius" actually consists of two peaks: an active crater, called the Grand Cone, and a second peak, Monte Somma, which lies across a saddle to the north. Before A.D. 79 it seems likely that the Grand Cone and Monte Somma were joined and that there was only one peak. They shared a dormant crater at the top, about a mile in diameter; its northern and eastern rims are probably today the interior walls of Monte Somma, facing the Grand Cone.

Many scholars believe that Spartacus and his men camped in this crater. The surviving interior walls of Monte Somma are steep, forbidding, pockmarked, and precipitous. They are topped by a jagged series of crests. The highest point today is 3,700 feet. The walls are covered with broom, beech, locust trees, and lichen. In Spartacus's day they were covered with wild vines.

Nowadays often considered a nuisance plant, the wild grapevine, *Vitis vinifera sylvestris*, is the hero of the story. Unlike Spartacus, it was native to Italy, where it was a familiar sight. Spartacus's rural recruits "were used to weaving branches into baskets that they used for their farm work." This is nothing unusual for the Italian countryside; in fact until a generation or two ago, Italian country folk regularly wove baskets and containers in a similar way. We might also speculate that the sight of lava "ropes"—ropelike lava formations—on the wall of Monte Somma's extinct crater suggested the idea of using vine ropes on the mountainside. In any case, Spartacus's rural followers cut off the usable vines and entwined them into long and robust ropes. Wild vines grow long because they are left unpruned, which eased the rebels' task. Some other form of local vegetation with thinner branches probably served to bind the vines.

We don't know what time of day the following action took place, but dusk would have served well. The rebels let the ropes down a part of the mountain that the Romans had left unguarded because it was so steep and rocky. The soil here was crumbly and unstable. We should not think of the rebels using the vines for rappelling down the mountain. Vesuvius's slope is not vertical, and vines are not supple or strong enough to be coiled around someone's body. Rather, the vine ropes probably served as handholds and guide rails. One by one, the rebels climbed down—all except one last man. It was his job to stay and throw down the weapons that they had taken from their camp. The terrain was too uneven to carry weapons safely on the descent. Finally, having tossed all the arms down, the last man came down as well. Or so the sources say, but it seems more likely that a group passed the arms from man to man at the end.

We might guess that it was now nighttime. Since Thracians specialized in night attacks, Spartacus might have wanted to deploy this advantage. The fugitives had carried out their escape under the eyes of the careless Romans. Now they attacked.

Roman troops on campaign always constructed a defended camp to serve as a secure base both for attack and defense. Every camp was built on a standard pattern, usually a square, divided by streets, tent lines, and horse lines, and surrounded by a ditch and rampart. As a Roman army completed its march, a good campsite was chosen, surveyors carefully laid out the skeleton of the place, and then the men did the rest. The soldiers slept in leather tents, eight men to a tent. The commander's tent, known as the *praetorium*, served both as his living quarters and the army's headquarters. With three thousand men as well as animals, Glaber's camp probably covered about ten acres.

Because the Romans prided themselves on attacking the enemy, the camp's defenses were usually light. The ditch was normally only about three feet wide and deep, the rampart a low mound of earth topped with wooden stakes. Pickets were stationed outside the ramparts to warn of attack and to slow down the enemy. Of course, a dangerous and sly enemy required stronger defenses. But Glaber took Spartacus too lightly. The Romans, says one ancient source, "did not yet consider this a war but rather some raid, like an attack by bandits." Glaber seems to have ordered no special security.

One ancient source says the fugitives came from an unexpected direction; another, that they surrounded the camp; another, that they came from a hidden exit in a crevice. It is not clear that they outnumbered the Romans but they did have the advantage of surprise: the ancients all agree that the Romans were shocked—and well they should have been. Spartacus's men probably picked off the sentries and then fell on the men in their tents. Without time to get into formation, the Romans had no choice but to fight a series of melees, if they fought at all. The gladiators were big, agile, and fast enough probably to have cut to pieces any man who stood up to them.

Thracians, Germans, and Celts were all tall compared to Romans. Celts were known for their rapid and terrifying charges, accompanied by battle cries and songs. The Thracians' war cry had a special name in Greek, the *titanismos*. The Germans' battle cry was a "confused roar" caused by putting their shields to their mouths; if the Germans with Spartacus didn't have shields, they might have used animal skins instead.

Some of the Celts might have worn their hair long or had thick mustaches in the manner of Gallic nobles; some might have spiked their hair by washing it in chalky water, and then combed it up to make them look taller. It is possible that a few went into battle naked, except for a sword belt and torque, as a traditional Celtic sign of ferocity. Any women at the battle were prominently cheering their men on, as was the custom of Celtic, German, and Thracian women. Greek and Roman writers registered this practice with shock, and archaeology confirms it. In an immense mass grave of Gallic warriors in northern France, erected as a trophy of a battle in 260 B.C., one-third of the bones belonged to women: most of them, like the men, had fallen in the prime of life.

One thing seems likely: few of the insurgents went into battle without first drinking wine. This was standard procedure for both Celts and Thracians, and, for that matter, for most soldiers in the ancient world. The Romans faced attackers whose courage had been boosted by the fruit of Rome's best grapes.

Another likelihood is that all of them prayed before beginning their charge. Each no doubt called on his native gods but they all might have shared a prayer to the god who guided the star of the man who had started it all: Dionysus, the god of Spartacus.

The sources all agree that the Roman soldiers fled. Triumphant and perhaps even shocked at the ease of victory, Spartacus's forces took Glaber's camp. They promptly plundered it. No doubt they found food, clothing, weapons, and possibly letters from the Senate.

No casualty figures survive from the engagement. Some men surely were killed or wounded, most of them Roman. The rebels stripped the arms and armor from the dead. Experienced soldiers knew that they had to move quickly before rigor mortis made it difficult to undress a corpse. The gladiators probably suffered fewer casualties, but one of them might have been their third leader, Oenomaus, the Celt. We know that he fell in an early battle.

Part of Spartacus's success can be chalked up to Roman incompetence, but only part. Spartacus, Crixus, and Oenomaus were shrewd soldiers. Rather than attack the enemy head-on they went after his weak point. They came up with an ingenious plan that maximized their minimal resources. They executed the plan with daring and efficiency. Rugged mountainous terrain did not concern them; Thracians would have felt at home in that kind of country.

Spartacus and perhaps others had the advantage of knowing the enemy. True, when he had fought for Rome, Spartacus was an auxiliary, and auxiliaries did not receive Roman training. They used their own style of fighting, and they tended to have native commanders. But they benefited from Rome's impressive logistical and support system. Anyone with his eyes open would have seen just how well organized and disciplined the legions were in battle. Auxiliaries had ample opportunity to learn from the Romans. Nor are they likely to have underestimated the enemy.

Perhaps the most impressive things about Spartacus and his men were their cohesion and leadership. The rebels barely knew each other but they cooperated beautifully. Only the gladiators were in fighting trim, even if some of the runaway country folk were former soldiers, which is likely. As slaves or farmworkers the runaways were tough, and as oppressed people they had incentive to fight, but it takes more than that to win a battle. To take just one example, amateurs used their swords to slash rather than to make the more effective move, the thrust. New soldiers had to learn many such skills (and this happened to be a technique that gladiators could teach well). They also had to fight as a team. Leadership had molded the rebels into a victorious force. The three commanders surely deserve credit; the Thracian woman and her prophecies might also have played a role.

Glaber is never heard from again, at least not in our sources. Spartacus and the gladiators, on the contrary, might have now become household names around Vesuvius. They attracted many new recruits, in particular shepherds and cowherds from the surrounding area. They were "fast-moving brawlers" and the rebels armed them with weapons captured from Glaber's camp. At a guess, the new recruits included a number of Celts, who had a reputation as good herdsmen. They probably also included a large number of women, since Roman experts advised supplying herdsmen in the bush with women to cook for them and meet their sexual needs. Spartacus used herdsmen to serve as scouts and light-armed troops and—who knows?—some of those soldiers might have been women.

We might imagine that the rebels' base was now the Romans' former camp. There they could have lived in tents, a step up from the open air of the mountain. Glaber's praetorium was now Spartacus's headquarters, perhaps shared with Crixus. It was probably a busy place.

Basic food and supplies dictated continued raids around Vesuvius. But to keep on winning against the Romans, the rebels would have to forge weapons; they would have to train and drill; they needed to learn how to trust and communicate with each other. That was hard work—plunder and vengeance were easier and more fun. Spartacus and Crixus had to strike a balance between what their men wanted and what they needed.

Meanwhile, the news of Glaber's defeat arrived in Rome. The Senate appointed another praetor to replace him: Publius Varinius. He recruited troops on the road as he marched south. Around the same time or shortly afterward the Senate chose yet another praetor to advise and assist Varinius, Lucius Cossinius—unfortunately, he is only a name to us. Cossinius too, it seems, was told to raise an army on the march.

It was now autumn 73 B.C. The fugitives first encountered Varinius indirectly, via his legate Lucius Furius, at the head of two thousand men. A legate was a high-ranking officer, a member of the Senate, who was authorized to command in his superior's absence. A certain Furius had served as praetor in a corruption case in 75 B.C., and they may be the same man. If so, Furius was a better judge than general, because he was attacked by the rebels and they trounced him.

We don't know where the engagement took place, but most likely it was in Campania, like all the other fighting in this period between the Romans and the rebels. Like Glaber, Furius was probably surprised or ambushed by Spartacus's men. They had neither the training nor the equipment to face the Romans in regular battles.

The defeat of Furius was a bad omen for Varinius, but there was worse to come. Spartacus's scouts were closely watching the movements of Varinius's colleague Cossinius. It was now that the Thracian caught Cossinius bathing in a villa near Pompeii—the incident described earlier. Cossinius's humiliation, defeat, and death all followed fast. For the third time in a few months, a force of gladiators and fugitives had defeated an army led by a Roman senator.

But that was not all. Spartacus and his men managed to capture— or at least to raid—two more Roman camps: first, the camp of another of Varinius's subordinates, Gaius Toranius, and then the camp of Varinius himself. Unfortunately, none of the details of these events survive. But the result is clear: a blow to the morale of even the most seasoned soldiers. Varinius's men were overwhelmed.

Some of them were sick "because of the unhealthiness of the autumn." Some had run away after their recent defeats and had refused to return to the colors, despite a stern order to do so. As for the rest, as a Roman author reports, "the height of their disgrace is that they were shirking their duty."

Varinius decided to send a report to the Senate. It was both a way of asking for reinforcements and a way of covering himself if later he was blamed for failure. He gave this sensitive mission to Toranius, who could provide an eyewitness account. Presumably Varinius trusted Toranius either as a loyal friend or as a shrewd subordinate who knew that it would be dangerous to point a finger at his chief. Toranius served as Varinius's *quaestor,* a financial official with various civil and military responsibilities. The quaestorship was the lowest rung on the "ladder of honors." There were twenty quaestors, each elected to an annual term, and all granted entrance to the Senate afterward. They had to be at least thirty years old and they all came from wealthy families.

While Toranius was away, Varinius did not stand idle. Four thousand troops were willing to follow him to a position near the enemy, if not actually into battle. These troops probably represented the remnant of the various armies of Glaber, Furius, and Cossinius, as well as Varinius's own men. Varinius led his men and pitched camp near the enemy; he had the Romans fortify the camp with a wall, trench, and extensive earthworks. Gone was Glaber's overconfidence.

Meanwhile, the insurgents had their own problems. By this point, they probably numbered more than ten thousand people: some women and children but most of them men. They had more men than weapons. But the rebels were nothing if not inventive. Because they had no iron for spearheads, they hardened the wooden tips of their spears in the fire to make them look like iron—and to ensure that they could open severe wounds. Food was a bigger problem. The fugitives were running out of supplies, and foraging raids were no longer safe with the enemy close by.

The solution was another clever stratagem. In the second watch of the night—between about 9 P.M. and midnight—they all left camp in silence. Only a trumpeter remained behind. Meanwhile, to trick the enemy, they propped up corpses on stakes in front of the gates. They even put clothes on them and weapons in their hands, to make them look like guards. At the same time, they left camp-fires burning.

The trick worked so well that it was only in the light of day that Varinius suspected something. He noticed the silence. Not only was the usual clanging and banging of a busy camp missing, so were the rebels' special touches: they had been throwing stones at the Romans and taunting them with insults. Taunting the enemy, by the way, was a typical Celtic tactic on the eve of battle. Varinius sent a cavalry unit to a nearby hill to see if they could find the enemy. They were far away, but Varinius wasn't taking any chances. He withdrew in a de-fensive formation, in order to allow time to replenish his forces with new recruits. Apparently, he went to the city of Cumae, an old Greek city on the coast about twenty-five miles northwest of Vesuvius.

Whether Varinius got his reinforcements is not known. He did manage to boost morale, but only seemingly so: Varinius did not recognize the difference between bluster and self-confidence. Al-though his men now talked tough, they were still raw and defeated soldiers. After a few days, Varinius decided to throw caution to the winds and to accept his men's demands for a second chance: he led them against the enemy's camp, which his scouts had located. They marched quickly. As they approached the rebels, silence replaced the Roman soldiers' boasting.

They would have had to march quickly to catch the fugitives, who were constantly on the move. "They roved throughout all of Campania," as one Roman said. They went on raids in the southern Campanian plain, ranging north, east, and south of Vesuvius, over the rich farm country lying between the Apennines and the mountains of the Amalfi Peninsula. They devastated the territories of Nola and Nuceria. Whether the rebels moved as a single force or in separate units is unclear. Nor is the order of events known, but here is one plausible reconstruction:

Nola sits on the plain north of Monte Somma, in rich farm country. Lying as it does in the shadow of the mountain, Nola was directly in the rebels' path. They had special reason to hate it because of Nola's connection to Sulla. Ironically, Nola had fought hard against Rome in the Social War and later against Sulla. But after his victory, Sulla acquired a villa at Nola and no doubt seized land there for his friends.

Spartacus's men probably held Sulla's men in special contempt. The Sullans had a reputation for high living. Meanwhile, the men whose lands they had taken were forced into poverty—just the thing to make them join the rebels. The rebels might have enjoyed manhandling Nola.

Then the rebels turned on Nuceria, a city southeast of Vesuvius, on the road from Nola to Salerno. Nuceria was located high in the hills above the valley of the Sarno River. It was a prosperous community of farmers and traders. In 104 B.C. thirty slaves in Nuceria rose in rebellion but they were quickly foiled and punished. In 73, Nuceria's slaves had the chance to join Spartacus's men as they plundered their masters' lands.

From Vesuvius to Nuceria, the rebels had gone from strength to strength. Yet like the Romans, they too faced an autumn of discontent. In fact, the rebels staggered with success. Spartacus's men now had unrealistic expectations; the attempt to talk sense into them nearly broke the army in two. They were, says a Roman source, no longer willing to obey him.

What had happened is this: Crixus was in favor of attacking Varinius, while Spartacus wanted to avoid battle. That was a tactical difference, but a deeper, strategic disagreement divided them. Crixus wanted to widen the war in Italy. He wanted more loot, more revenge and, no doubt, more power. Spartacus did not think that the rebels were winning. In fact, in his opinion, the men were now in mortal danger. Their movements were aimless and ad hoc. Sooner or later the Romans would cut them off and wipe them out. To be safe, they needed to leave as quickly as possible.

And go where? Crixus might have asked. Spartacus wanted to take the army north to the Alps, where they would split up and head back to their respective homelands, be they in Thrace or the Celtic lands. Parts of Thrace and most of Gaul were still free. Gladiators, runaway slaves, and free Italians could all live there beyond the long arm of Rome.

It was an inspiring plan, and one that a follower of Dionysus might have relished: the Greeks, at any rate, believed that the god had traveled through the high and rugged Hindu Kush mountains (located between today's Afghanistan and Pakistan). Some even said Dionysus had been born there. Surely, the god would lead his follower Spartacus over the Alps.

It was, others no doubt replied, an impossible dream. But what was the alternative? The Alps were not easy to cross but they were not impassable, either. Hannibal had proven that. The Roman legions, however, were another matter. Spartacus knew the Roman army well, and he doubted the rebels' ability to defeat the Romans in a regular battle. If the rebels could not defeat a second-rate force like Varinius's, what would happen when the armies in Spain and the East came home, and the rebels had to fight veteran legions?

Spartacus understood the difference between guerrilla and conventional warfare. Guerrillas cannot defeat a conventional army by military means; they can only frustrate it. As long as the conventional army retains its will to fight, it will win in the end. And it was impossible to imagine the Romans losing their will in Italy. Eventually, the Romans would wipe out the rebels.

Spartacus was right but he was outvoted. He had only a small number of supporters, "a few farseeing people, men of liberal minds and nobility," as one Roman writer puts it. Crixus had behind him the majority of his fellow Celts as well as the majority of the Germans. Many of the Celts and Germans had been born in Italy, being the children of prisoners of war from 102 and 101 B.C. "Going home" might not have meant as much to them as it did to Spartacus. "Home" was Italy.

But a Roman writer gives Crixus's supporters lesser motives:

Some of them stupidly put their trust in the masses of new recruits flooding in and in their own fierce spirit, others were disgracefully heedless of their fatherland, and most of them had a naturally slavish temperament that longed for nothing except booty and bloodshed.

These comments are bigoted but they are not entirely inaccurate. From Thrace to Gaul, barbarian warfare put a premium on the acquisition of loot. It brought only limited wealth, since much of the booty was consecrated to the gods, but cattle, gold, and women were the coin of the realm, and Italy teemed with all three.

And military logic favored some of Crixus's points. After all, a reasonable person might have argued that if the rebels turned north now, they would have Varinius on their tail, and eventually he would force a battle. A reasonable person might also have pointed out the difficulty of crossing the Alps in autumn. The rebels would have to sit in northern Italy and fight off the Romans until the following spring, when they could go over the mountains again. Northern Italy was neither as rich nor as warm as the south. Why not build a base under the southern sun? After all, the Roman armies in Spain and Asia Minor were not likely to come back to Italy soon.

From the operational point of view, Spartacus was probably wrong. It was safer to defeat Varinius before heading north. But strategically, Spartacus was right. The rebels had to leave Italy, if not today or the next day then soon. And eventually they had to cross the

Alps. Spartacus was unable to win his case, but he did a signal service to his people even so: he held the army together.

Spartacus and his supporters might have quit. They might have worked their way quietly northward, avoiding Roman roads, and headed for the Alps. Or they might have used their loot to buy or bribe their way onto a boat heading east. But Spartacus was an armed prophet and did not want to be a general without an army. Dionysus's chosen one was not about to slink off.

The quarrel was settled by a compromise. As Crixus wanted, the fugitives would continue plundering and they would fight Varinius. But as Spartacus wanted, they would not fight him yet. Instead they would prepare carefully for the coming battle. It was inevitable, Spartacus said, that Varinius would rebuild his army. In preparation, the rebels needed to increase the number and quality of their troops. They needed elite recruits; the closest thing to that, Spartacus suggested, was to find shepherds. In order to find them, the rebel army would have to head into more open country, someplace more suited to grazing. In other words, they would have to go south into Italy's pasturelands.

Spartacus knew what he was doing. Roman herdsmen were slaves, tough, hardy, and independent. They were fighters, as they had to be in order to survive in the wild, where wolves and bandits were routine and bears were not unknown. Slave shepherds had made up the core of the great Sicilian Slave Wars. Herders had sustained the Lusitanian (Portuguese) rebel Viriathus in his eight years of guerrilla war against the Roman conquerors (147–139 B.C.) The current Roman rebel in Spain, Sertorius, drew many of his supporters from shepherds as well.

Spartacus knew one other thing, too: the margin of error. The Romans could afford bad generals and defeated armies. In fact, Roman history was littered with failure, from the Allia to the Caudine Forks to Cannae. The Romans could lose many battles as long as they won the last battle. And Rome's ironclad political system and profound population resources gave it the will and the manpower to go the distance.

The rebels had no room for mistakes. Spartacus knew that his men were good but also that they had been lucky. Roman incompetence allowed them the luxury of going on raids instead of drilling soldiers, of arguing with each other instead of fighting the enemy.

Rome could throw away praetors. The rebels needed a leader.

4

THE PATHFINDERS

I N AUTUMN 73 B.C., when Spartacus and Crixus struck their deal,
the army turned south. To avoid Varinius, they probably stayed
off the Roman road, which could be easily guarded, and headed for
the hills instead. They likely traveled on byroads along mountain
ridges, on the timeless paths of muleteers seated with their baskets,
on trails beaten through the woods by herds migrating to the mountains in summer and back to the plain before winter. Heavy-armed
legionaries and their supply wagons could not take that route, but
light-armed rebels could.

But the rebels could not find their way on their own. They
needed pathfinders, whether willing or coerced. Without local intelligence to point the way and to indicate food supplies, the fugitives would have been lost. Grizzled farmers, shaggy mountain
men, young girls on the way to draw water from a spring, slaves
barely free from their chains, fat landowners too slow to run from
the rebels: these would have been Spartacus's eyes and ears in the
Italian countryside.

The first example in our sources of one of Spartacus's guides is a prisoner. He came from the region known as the Agri Picentini, the fertile plains south of Salernum. But he could hardly have been the first local guide for the rebels, because they had already traveled over rough country. After leaving the vicinity of Nuceria, they had headed inland and passed by Abella (modern Avella), a small city about five miles northeast of Nola. Abella sits at the foot of the thickly wooded Partenio Mountains (modern name), in the upper valley of the Clanis (Clanio) River. It lies in green, well-watered farm country, famous for its hazelnuts and its high winds. Rainy and snowy in the winter, Abella was isolated and rural, its cool fresh air worlds away from the urban heat of Capua. But Abella had seen its share of history. An Italian city, it forged close ties with Rome. Roman roads, Roman land surveying, and late Republican rustic villas have all been found in Abella's farmlands. Abella stayed loyal to Rome during the Social War (91–88 B.C.) and, as a reward, was probably honored with the status of "colony" by Sulla. Now, as the sources say, Spartacus's men "happened upon the farmers of Abella who were watching over their fields." (The word for "farmers" can also mean "colonists.") Their meeting with the rebels was probably not a happy one for them.

Spartacus and his men now made for the southern Picentini mountains, about thirty miles away as the crow flies. Assuming they went through the backcountry, they would have crossed the hills of Irpinia and climbed into the Picentini, always heading south and east. They would have made their way through forests of oak and chestnut, past mountains nearly six thousand feet high, through gorges, and over torrents. It was neither an easy route nor a rich one; the fertile plains below around the Via Annia were visible here and there in the distance, but they were in the Romans' hands. No one could have eaten much on this march.

After leaving the Picentini mountains, the rebels' next goal was

the Silarus (modern Sele) river, about twenty miles southeast of Salernum. In ancient times, the Silarus marked the regional boundary.
Once they crossed it, Spartacus and his army would have left Campania for Lucania. About eight miles farther they would reach a pass
in the hills. Once they went over that, they would begin a new phase
of their revolt.

They would now be in the heart of Lucania, and so sailing on a
vast inland sea: green waves of hills broken by upland plains, thick
forests, remote towns, and craggy mountain peaks. Lucania's rugged
terrain stretched southward as far as the eye could see until the heel
of the Italian boot, where it dropped off into a fertile, coastal strip
bounded by the Ionian Sea.

Lucania was a land of woods, pastures, and slaves, a guerrilla's
favorite landscape. Like Sicily, it was populated by slave shepherds
and slave field hands. They were a rebel recruiter's dream. This was
Spartacus Country.

All of that lay before them, but first Spartacus, Crixus, and their
followers had to slip past the Romans. Surely the Romans had posted
guards on the bridge where the Via Annia crosses the Silarus. Enter
the Picentine guide. A Roman writer describes the situation concisely:
"and having hastily found a suitable guide from among the Picentine
prisoners, he [Spartacus] made his way hidden in the Eburian Hills
to Nares Lucanae and from there at first light he reached Forum
Annii."

This puts Spartacus's tactics in a nutshell. He made a quick decision that gave his men the advantage of local knowledge. The result
was a nimble, gutsy, and effective maneuver.

The Picentine was a man who knew the hills of the southern
Picentini mountains, north of the town of Eburum (Eboli). He might
have been a herdsman or, more likely, a ranch owner, since he was a
prisoner and not a recruit; a herdsman would probably have joined
Spartacus voluntarily. It should not have been difficult to intimidate

him into cooperating, given the dangers of captivity. Both Celts and Germans had a reputation for sacrificing prisoners of war as a way of honoring the gods. Reports of gruesome practices survive, such as cutting open a corpse to inspect the entrails, ripping fetuses out of their mothers' wombs, and drinking blood from dead people's skulls.

In any case, the Picentine took the rebels over the Eburine hills perhaps as far as the valley of the Middle Silarus river, where they could have crossed via an ancient ford. Then they swung south toward the town of Nares Lucanae. The Romans had no idea where the rebels were. Spartacus had run rings around Varinius, and he owed it all to his Picentine prisoner.

One wonders if that unwilling rebel was rewarded with a drink at Nares Lucanae. There was plenty of water there; the name of the place may mean "Lucanian Springs," and springs have been found at its site in the foothills of the Alburni mountains. The fingerlike peaks of that chain rise across the valley southeast of the Picentini. There was good pastureland between both sets of mountains and the sea, so the insurgents may have picked up some supporters from the vicinity.

At Nares Lucanae the rebels' route rejoined the main Roman road to Regium, the Via Annia. They traveled at night, no doubt to avoid detection. It was first light when Spartacus's men reached the little town of Forum Annii. The distance between Nares Lucanae and Forum Annii is about fifteen miles, a long way for even a light-armed force to cover in one night, especially if the group included women and children. But it was autumn, and the nights were getting longer; the chilly air might have hurried the fastest of them on to the prize ahead. Above all, they were determined to seize the offensive and achieve surprise. They did.

Spartacus and his men arrived at Forum Annii "unbeknownst to the farmers." Forum Annii was a farming community at the northern end of the Campus Atinas (modern Vallo di Diano). The Campus is a long, narrow, upland plain, green and fertile, watered by the Tanager (modern Tanagro) river running through it. It is closed in by hills, creating a constant play of light and shadow; in the west, the mountains roll in waves, sometimes ripples, sometimes breakers. An ancient area of settlement, the valley was very rich, with farms and villas spread over the lowlands and hills flowing with pastures. In a hill town north of the valley even today, the census lists 1,300 humans and 6,000 sheep; some of the latter are brought down from the hills and paraded around a chapel by their shepherds in an annual festival each June.

The population was probably made up mainly of Roman settlers and their slaves. There were native Lucanians, too, but they had been forced to make room for many Romans over the centuries, as punishment for choosing the losing side—something the hard-luck Lucanians had a knack for, from Hannibal to Marius to the Italian Confederacy of the Social War. The Roman settlers included both masters of large estates, primarily ranches, and small farmers. Some Late Republican tombstones depict the managers who ran the estates for their masters: men with a signet ring on a finger of their left hand and a pen and writing tablets clenched in their fist.

One autumn morning in 73 B.C., the fresh air of the valley was full of screams. Spartacus and his men had arrived. They immediately went on a rampage against his orders, raping young girls and married women. Anyone who tried to resist was killed, sometimes in the act of running away. Some of the rebels threw flaming torches onto the roofs of houses. Others followed local slaves to drag their masters or their treasures from their hiding places. "Nothing was too holy or too heinous for the anger of the barbarians or their servile natures," says one Roman writer. And no help was forthcoming from Varinius's army; it was nowhere to be seen.

Spartacus opposed the atrocities, either out of chivalry or a calculation that if farmers were well treated, some might favor the insurgents. Spartacus tried repeatedly to restrain his men, but it was a losing battle. Crixus's stance is unrecorded. Later events show that he wanted to loot Italy, but he also wanted to fight Varinius, and indiscipline would weaken the army.

And then there were the local slaves, of various national origins. Some of them had not waited to bring the rebels to their masters' hideouts, instead pulling out their quivering overlords themselves. It was a kind of offering to the insurgents and perhaps the local slaves were just trying to curry their favor. Or perhaps they were remembering the whips, chains, canes, stones, broken bones, gouged-out eyes, kicks, tongue-lashings, executions, or other punishments that Roman slaves are known to have suffered. Or perhaps they were thinking of minor humiliations, such as having their forehead tattooed with the master's symbol or having to pay the master for the privilege of having sex with another slave. Or perhaps they recalled some friend or relative among the slaves who had been sold off because he was sick or aged.

The rebels stayed at Forum Annii for that day and the following night. For the local masters it was twenty-four hours of savagery and slaughter. For the slaves it was liberation day. They surely poured in from the surrounding area, because Forum Annii was not a big place, and by daybreak, Spartacus and Crixus had doubled the number of fugitive slaves in their group. Some of the new recruits would have been farmers, but if Spartacus had judged his prospects correctly, most of them would have been herdsmen. By autumn they would have come down with their herds from the mountains to graze lower pastures, so they could have learned the news from Forum Annii.

At first light, the rebels broke camp again and made for a "very wide field," which sounds like someplace in the middle of the Campus Atinas. There they could see the farmers coming out of their houses, off to the autumn harvest. Those farmers never reached

their fields, because along the way they ran into a column of refugees from Forum Annii. The farmers hurried off to safety, perhaps
into the hills. The autumn harvest was left for Spartacus and his
hungry army.

They had outmaneuvered the Roman army, terrorized the master
class, and filled their ranks with new recruits and their bellies with
fresh produce, but the insurgents were still far from victory. On the
contrary, their rampage had opened the door to defeat. Like all military activities, foraging and pillaging require discipline. Excessive looting breeds just the opposite, a breakdown in discipline. The Romans
knew that soldiers who disobey commands while foraging would
disobey commands while fighting. Besides, looters were subject to
sudden enemy counterattack. Ever cautious, the Romans insisted on
discipline even for the simple acts of getting food and water.

Spartacus knew what a terrible precedent his men had now set.
He understood, as well, that wars are not won by raids. In his vain at-
tempt to stop the massacre, Spartacus had told the men to be quick.
Varinius, after all, would be coming.

After their success in the Campus Atinas, the insurgents had to
keep moving to evade the Romans and find new sources of food. The
new recruits had to be outfitted with weapons—probably makeshift
weapons. They had to take whatever rushed advice about fighting
they could get while the army was on the move.

They blazed the trail well, it seems, because by the time they
reached the Ionian Sea, the insurgents had finished off Varinius. We
don't know where and when. By the accident of survival, the sources
cast a spotlight on Spartacus's movements from the Picentini mountains to the Campus Atinas. Unfortunately, they grow dim again
for the six or so months following. The insurgents stormed through
Lucania; that much is clear, as is the outcome of the duel between
Spartacus and Varinius. Otherwise the narrative is mainly a matter of
educated guesswork.

The land drew the rebels ever southward. Not just the Campus Atinas but most of Lucania was good to plunder. It was rich in pastures, grain fields, vineyards, and woods, with large numbers of sheep, goats, and game animals. Lucanian horses were supposed to be small and ugly but strong—not perfect cavalry mounts, but they would do.

But where would the insurgents go and how would they get there? A look at the map can be misleading. It appears that Spartacus and Crixus had no choice in mountainous Lucania other than following the Via Annia, which ran southward through the Campus Atinas and down to Bruttium (modern Calabria). But in fact they had other options. A series of roads along Lucania's mountain ridges predated the Romans: most of them have been called "winding, narrow, and cramped" but the insurgents had seen worse.

After sacking the Campus Atinas, Spartacus's men could have, for example, followed the pass between the Monti della Maddelena and the Monte del Papa (Pope's Mountain), as they are known today, to the Roman colony of Grumentum. (Today, Italy's Highway 103 follows that route.) There in the high valley of the Aciris (modern Agri) river, they would have found a shepherd's paradise—and a recruiter's delight. Heading eastward, they then could have followed one of several routes to the Ionian Coast and the cities of Metapontum and Heraclea. From there, a coastal road led south to Bruttium and the city of Thurii.

For what it is worth, modern folklore has Spartacus traveling widely in Lucania. For example, the towns of Oliveto Citra, Rocca da spide, and Genzano di Lucania all claim to have been the site of one of Spartacus's battles. Castelcivita' has a cave of Spartacus and a bridge of Spartacus. Caggiano, Colliano, and Polla all boast that Spartacus passed through on his travels. But none of this is surprising, since southern Italy historically has been the land of brigands and Spartacus is the granddaddy of all outlaws. Nor do these claims prove that the insurgents passed through in autumn 73 B.C. rather than, say, a year later—if at all.

Also, for what it is worth, the ancient evidence for the months following the rebels' stay in the Campus Atinas refers twice to local guides. "They were very knowledgeable about the area," says one source about some of the insurgents. One local stood out for his pathfinding scouting skills. His name was Publipor.

All that survives about Publipor is one line in a lost history book. Yet of all the bit parts in Spartacus's saga, his might be the most intriguing. Among the insurgents' various pathfinders, Publipor was probably the best. "Of all the men in the region of Lucania, he was the only one with knowledge of the place."

Publipor means "Publius's Boy." He was a slave, the property of one Publius. Publipor was a common slave name, shared, for instance, by the great Latin playwright Terence, a freedman who had been called Publipor as a slave. Publipor was not necessarily a boy, since the Romans often applied the word "boy" to adult slaves. He might have been an adult and, given his expertise in Lucania's terrain, Publipor might well have been a shepherd.

Tens of thousands of slaves fought with Spartacus, but aside from the gladiators, Publipor is the only one whose name survives. We don't know why his local knowledge was important, but it surely was, since our source singles him out. Could it be that he did the insurgents the great service of showing them a spot where they could lie in wait for Varinius? Perhaps Publipor helped Spartacus stage one of his greatest coups yet.

The details of the fighting aren't known. But it is a good guess that the insurgents avoided pitched battle, preferring instead ambushes, traps, and hit-and-run attacks. Pitched battle was too dangerous because even if they outnumbered the Romans, the rebels could not match their equipment. They still had to rely on do-it-yourself arms and armor, as one source makes clear: "they were used to weaving rustic baskets out of branches. Because of a lack of shields then, they each used this same art to arm himself with small round shields like those used by cavalrymen." They stretched hides over the branches to cover the shields.

The insurgents captured standards from Roman centurions. Better yet, they took control of Varinius's lictors with their bundles of rods and axes—their fasces—that symbolized the praetor's power. And they also grabbed Varinius's horse; according to one source, they snatched it from under him, making his capture a very close call. Varinius escaped. But the real and immediate winner was the man to whom the standards and fasces were brought in triumph: Spartacus. It was now, it seems, that he really became "great and frightening," as Plutarch describes him.

The standards, the fasces, and the horse were better recruiting tools than a praetor's head on a pike (although the Celts, who were headhunters, might have disagreed). The standards were totems whose loss was immeasurable. The fasces was a sacred symbol, like a royal scepter or a bishop's crook. The horse was sacred to Celts, Germans, and Thracians. In the glow of these icons Spartacus was more than an adventurer: he became almost a king.

"After this," says one source, "even more men, many more, came running to Spartacus." "In a short time they collected huge numbers of troops," says another. The recruits came pouring in, usually barefoot, in coarse woolen cloaks, sometimes carrying their chains.

The numbers are difficult to reckon. The ancient sources vary greatly, ranging from estimates of 40,000 to 120,000 insurgents. To make matters worse, good ancient "statistics" tend to be approximations, while bad ancient "statistics" tend to be wild exaggerations. For example, the number 120,000—the high estimate for Spartacus's troops—appears often enough in ancient sources about this or that war to demonstrate that it was just a rhetorical maximum, the equivalent of "a huge number." To complicate things further, it is unclear whether ancient statistics about the insurgents include women and children.

The safest course is to follow the lowest figure, which gives Spartacus and Crixus about 40,000 men in spring 72 B.C. and even more by autumn. By ancient standards this was no small sum. It is more men than Hannibal had when he crossed the Alps, for example, and about the size of Caesar's army when he conquered Gaul. For that matter, the number of 40,000 men roughly equals the size of the largest army that the Romans would ever muster against Spartacus.

Around the time they defeated Varinius—we can't be sure of the sequence of events—the rebels found themselves at Lucania's land's end. The men who had washed their hands in blood in Capua now dipped their feet in the Ionian Sea. To be precise, they dipped them in a large inlet of the sea known as the gulf of Tarentum (modern Taranto). The turquoise waters of the gulf, about ninety miles long and wide, wash the arch of the Italian boot. The gulf's coastline, stretching roughly from Tarentum to Croton, includes some of the most fertile land in Italy. This was once Magna Graecia, "Greater Greece," a region of Greek colonies whose prosperity eventually outstripped that of the mother country. In its prime, Magna Graecia produced great generals, lawgivers, doctors, artists, and athletes. Pythagoras, one of ancient Greece's leading philosophers, built his school here. But the conquering Romans ended all that. The gulf coast was still lush and abundant, but power and influence had passed it by.

Because the land was a backwater, it was useful for Spartacus and Crixus. Far and remote from Rome, the Ionian coast made a perfect base for the insurgents. It had a mild climate and was well stocked with food. Its large slave population made it promising recruiting country. Its farms and towns had furnaces that could be used for melting down slave chains and reforging them as swords and spearheads. Its ports could attract merchants and pirates. Nearby loomed

rugged hills and dense forests to retreat to in case the Romans arrived. It was, in short, a place to build an army.

But this coastal area was not about to open its doors to the rebels;
they would have to break them down. And so the rebels attacked, inflicting "terrible slaughter," as one source says. They might have been
as brutal here as they had been in the Campus Atinas. One of the
places the insurgents went after was the city of Metapontum (Metaponto). Indeed, archaeology may show traces of their onslaught. A
stoa (portico) in town, used as a warehouse, was destroyed during
this period. Some see the hand of the rebels in this, and it certainly
isn't hard to imagine them crossing the moat and breaking through
the wooden palisade that was Roman Metapontum's main defense.
Perhaps the citizens had tried to stop them by using the catapult
balls that were being manufactured around this time in a nearby
villa. But that sounds rather grand for Roman Metapontum, a place
whose best days were behind it. Metapontum in 73 B.C. was more like
a small town than the great city it had once been.

In its heyday (circa 600–300 B.C.) Metapontum had been a success story, one of Greece's greatest colonies. Its fertile fields made
Metapontum a breadbasket, with ears of wheat proudly displayed on
its gold coins. But then came Rome and the familiar pattern of op-
pression, revolt, occupation, and punishment. The once-grand urban
space had shrunk to a small sector.

In Metapontum's countryside, meanwhile, the many small family
farms of the Greek period disappeared. The land had been handed
over largely to a few grandees, Romans or their local "friends." Me-
dium or large-sized villas now dotted the river valleys and the coastal
road or dominated the heights. Diversified agriculture was in decline,
and pasturage was prevalent, especially of sheep, cattle, and horses. In
other words, this was in large part ranch country and, therefore, slave
country: fertile ground for Spartacus's recruiters.

One of Roman Metapontum's few urban renewal projects was

the temple of Apollo, which was revived and expanded. In the form he was worshipped here, Apollo was, for practical purposes, equivalent to Dionysus, and the religion was very popular in the city and its countryside. The message of the Thracian woman, therefore, might have fallen on willing ears at Metapontum.

About twelve miles south of Metapontum lay Heraclea, in the rich soil between the valleys of the Siris (modern Sinni) and Aciris rivers. It was a center of agriculture and crafts and a well-known market town. Unlike Metapontum, Heraclea had played its cards well with Rome. Over the centuries it maintained its autonomy—and on such favorable terms that it even hesitated to accept Roman citizenship when it was offered after the Social War. We hear nothing about Spartacus going to Heraclea, which may reflect the reception he expected to get there. But the people of Heraclea couldn't be sure that Spartacus wasn't coming and so they took precautions.

We might conclude this from a small, gray vase that had been buried under a private house in Heraclea. The vase was filled with a gold necklace and over five hundred coins, all of them Roman silver. The necklace is decorated with garnets and glass beads, with delicate gold terminals in the shape of antelope heads. The coins date from circa 200 to circa 70 B.C.; most of them come from a twenty-year period, 100–80 B.C. Nearly half of the coins are small change, which is odd, considering the value of the necklace: one scholar takes this as a sign of haste, as if whoever filled and buried the vase had no time to separate good money from bad. Were these objects interred in a hurry at a sign of Spartacus on the horizon? Or perhaps it was their own slaves whom the Heracleots feared. The city was a center of the Dionysus cult.

South of Heraclea the coastal plain narrows sharply between the sea and the foothills of the Pollino Mountains (modern name). This range marked the southern boundary of Lucania. Beyond lies the southernmost region of Italy: Bruttium. Like Lucania, Bruttium is mountainous, and its people were similarly tough. Bruttium was destined to play a big part in Spartacus's revolt. That role began here, just beyond the last foothill of the Pollino massif along the coast. A vast plain opens up here, wider, greener, and lusher than even the country of Metapontum or Heraclea.

This is the Plain of Sybaris, almost a world unto itself. About two hundred miles square, the plain is cut off on the north and west by the peaks of the Pollino, towering and snowcapped for most of the year; on the south by the steep twisting hills of the Sila Greca; and to the east by the sea. The grand sweep of its fertile soil lies under the hot sun, watered by the Crathis (modern Crati) and Sybaris (modern Coscile) rivers. The climate was mild enough to make the place famous for an oak tree that didn't lose its leaves in winter.

The golden plain was the California of antiquity, and its San Francisco was a Greek colony planted there circa 700 B.C.: Sybaris. The city's luxury was so legendary that even today, *sybarite* is still a synonym for *hedonist*. Gastronomy was the preferred vice, and why not, when the land was so bountiful that the Sybarites supposedly ran wine rather than water through their clay pipes! In addition to its wine, Sybaris was famous for its olive oil and its wool. Grain was cultivated on the plain, while fig and hazelnut trees were grown on the hillsides. Wood and pitch were brought down from the thick forests of the Sila mountains. The sea teemed with fish, including the much-prized eel. Sybaris's bustling seaport attracted traders from a wide variety of Mediterranean ports.

Sybaris had been totally destroyed in a war with its neighbors in 510 B.C., but the plain was too fertile to leave fallow. In 444 B.C. a new Greek city, Thurii, was founded in its place. In 194 B.C. it was Rome's turn. The Romans founded a colony at Thurii and renamed it Copia, "Abundance." But most people continued to call it Thurii. Supposedly there was so much good land here that the Romans had trouble finding takers for all the lots. But nature abhors a vacuum. By 73 B.C.

the valleys of the Crathis and Sybaris contained a number of Roman villas, some large, but most midsized. Roman senators and knights and a veteran of Sulla are among those known to have owned property here. While herding took place, agriculture remained a major activity in this fertile country.

Another of Thurii's resources was a cadre of discontented slaves. Around 70 B.C. a property holder in these parts armed his slaves and sent them to loot his neighbor's farm and murder the inhabitants, in an attempt to take over the property himself. About ten years later slave insurgents were active in the area. In 48 B.C. the Roman thug Milo was sent to Thurii to raise a revolt among the shepherds in the vicinity.

But the people of Bruttium were famous for waging guerrilla warfare: it was "their natural disposition," says one Roman writer. In addition, Thurii had for centuries been a center of Orphic religion, a cult with Dionysiac overtones that offered a natural opening to the Thracian woman and her prophecies. It was, in short, promising recruiting ground for the insurgency. No wonder Spartacus and Crixus looked with wide eyes at Thurii in late 73 B.C.

Once they crossed into Bruttium, the insurgents fanned out into the hills. No doubt they went after Roman farms. Then, when they had found food and recruits, they turned on the city of Thurii itself. Until now, Spartacus and Crixus had damaged the territory of various cities but they had not conquered and occupied any urban spaces. Their supporters consisted of "slaves, deserters, and the rabble," as one ancient writer puts it. "Rural people, mainly slaves but also some free" would be a more impartial description.

At Thurii they finally conquered a city. Thurii was not big, but it was walled. The insurgents were making wicker shields, not siege engines, and they could hardly have stormed the town. Nor did they have the time to surround the city for months to starve it out. The most likely explanation of their success is that Thurii's walls were in a state of disrepair and so easily breached. Either that or someone within the city, perhaps a group of slaves, opened the gates to the rebels. The result might well have been a slaughter.

It may have been around this time that the insurgents raided the city of Consentia (modern Cosenza), the capital of the Bruttians, an inland town located on the Via Annia about fifty miles south of Thurii. Consentia sat in a rich territory of farms and pastures with the prospect of additional supplies and supporters.

From Metapontum to Thurii and perhaps beyond, the insurgents had brought fire, death, and freedom. Yet they were also building an army. At Thurii they could finally settle down to train. Among their urgent needs were weapons and discipline. Spartacus addressed both necessities by laying down the law: whatever merchants might offer, his people could not buy gold and silver; only iron and bronze for weapons were allowed. Crixus presumably backed up Spartacus. Another source of arms-grade metal was the runaway slaves' own chains, which were melted down and reforged into weapons. It is hard to say which is more striking, Spartacus's strictness or the traders' willingness to take a chance on dealing with the fierce insurgents. Were these "merchants" really pirates, as some suggest, or were they simply gamblers who saw big profits in risky business?

Arms don't make an army. The newcomers needed training. By winter 73–72 B.C., the summer's raw recruits had become old hands, and they no doubt passed on practical experience. Still, there was no substitute for a professional. Ex-gladiators and veterans, whether of Roman or other armies, played the most important role as drill instructors, we might guess.

Spartacus surely knew that building an army takes a first-rate management team. We might imagine him choosing carefully his battalion and company commanders. Any prior military experience was surely invaluable. Veterans of Marius or former soldiers captured in Rome's border wars probably shot to the front of the pack. But organizational skill is a necessity in a commander, and slave foremen had that skill in spades. Nor can the moral factor in leadership be discounted. As an astute judge of character, Spartacus might have chosen some men without prior military experience to lead units of his army.

And although Spartacus hated Rome, he didn't hesitate to borrow from it. He modeled his army on the legions, at least in some respects. "They attained a certain level of skill and discipline that they had learned from us," said Caesar of the insurgents. Like the renegade Vettius, a Roman who led the slave rebellion in Capua in 104 B.C., Spartacus might have organized his soldiers in centuries, eighty-men units that were the companies of the legions.

The insurgents designated their units by Roman insignia. The victorious rebels had captured Roman battle flags, silver eagles, and fasces. The eagle was the symbol of a legion, while the flags stood for cohorts (six hundred men each) and centuries. The fasces were the insignia of a Roman praetor, consul, general, or governor.

We might imagine the insurgents proudly carrying Roman flags and eagles into battle to taunt the enemy. As for the fasces, Spartacus accepted them as symbols of his own office, presumably to be carried by his bodyguard. It was a sign of the world turned upside down, but it was also a symbol of discipline. The fasces represented the power to punish. An effective commander must be not merely inspirational but stern. Few soldiers enjoy punishment, but most accept it as the price of victory. Punishment builds discipline; discipline wins wars.

Perhaps Saint Augustine had Thurii in mind when he wrote, centuries later, "from a small and contemptible start in petty crime, they [the insurgents] attained a kingdom." The language is imprecise, because although he held sway in a corner of Italy, Spartacus was not a king. The leaders of the earlier Sicilian slave revolts took royal titles but Spartacus did not. He had the favor of Dionysus, as the Thracian lady announced, and he probably inspired religious awe in some of his followers, but he had no throne.

A paradox lay at the heart of Spartacus's enterprise. His men had just thrown away their chains; they did not want new ones. They were herdsmen used to independence, field hands drunk on newly found freedom, and gladiators trained to kill each other. They barely shared a common language, Latin, and it belonged to their enemy. With women and no doubt children present among them, they resembled a caravan as much as an army. Most men probably felt closer ties to their family than to their fellow soldiers. No one knew if they would bow to Spartacus's commands. Freedom built his army and freedom could destroy it.

All he could do was try to make things work. And so tens of thousands of marching feet now echoed on the Plain of Sybaris. They meant something shameful for the Romans, honorable for the men: slave legions. As one Roman writer put it, even a slave is a human being, and if a slave takes up arms, he may become as free as a Roman citizen. But, as he adds, for a Roman to have to fight such a man is to add insult to injury.

As improbable as the slave legions were, even more improbable was the group of mounted knights riding beside them. As was also the case in Germany, fighting on horseback brought a warrior high status. During their travels the rebels had captured wild horses that roamed the southern Italian countryside. To their good fortune, they were in horse country. Even today, wild horses are seen in the mountains of southeastern Campania, in Lucania's high valley of the Agri River and in the Pollino Mountains on the border between Lucania and Bruttium. Celts, Germans, and Thracians were good enough tamers to train them. And so was born the insurgents' cavalry.

They would need it. The Romans had not forgotten them. Neither the beatings they had suffered at the rebels' hands nor the ruined farms and lost investments in slaves had escaped their attention. So the Romans chose new commanders for the new year, with more soldiers at their disposal to break up the rebellion.

The mountains ringing Sybaris are covered with snow in the winter. When it melted in spring 72 B.C., torrents of water would run down into the riverbeds of the plain. The yellow flowers of the broom plant would set the hillsides on fire. Rome's legions would march south on the peninsula's paved roads; the insurgents would slip through the hills in an attempt to fight on terms of their own choosing. And all Italy would hold its breath.

5

THE STOIC

I T WAS A war without glory. In 72 B.C. Rome needed men to fight against Spartacus. About 150,000 Roman citizens, all from Italy, were already in arms abroad, well above the average figure of 90,000 Romans in arms between 79 and 50 B.C. But the recruiters would have to find many more soldiers. Cato volunteered.

Marcus Porcius Cato—Cato the Younger—had the bloodlines to make him Rome's "Mr. Conservative." His great-grandfather Marcus Porcius Cato "the Censor" (234–149 B.C.) championed Roman simplicity over Greek culture and coldly insisted: Delenda est Karthago, "Carthage must be destroyed." Cato the Younger's uncle was Marcus Livius Drusus, known as "the patron of the Senate" for his proposed constitutional changes, which were an attempt to co-opt challengers to the old guard by bringing them into the elite. Drusus's bold plan only got him assassinated but it was a lesson in courage for young Cato, already an orphan, who was raised in Drusus's household.

In 72 B.C. Cato was twenty-three years old. He was a patriot, but not too idealistic to forget his family. Cato idealized his older half brother, Quintus Servilius Caepio, son of his mother's first marriage. Caepio was chosen as a junior officer against Spartacus, serving under one of the consuls for 72 B.C., Lucius Gellius, so Cato followed Caepio into the army. Cato's family owned land in Lucania, which made them well aware of the danger posed by Spartacus and might even have made Cato one of Spartacus's victims.

The young soldier Cato displayed the toughness for which he would become famous. He was, for example, a pedestrian for all seasons. Regardless of the weather, he never rode: there were no litters for the young follower of the Stoic philosophy. The Stoics preached austerity. Simplicity, they taught, bred self-control; self-control led to virtue, and a virtuous man was a good man. Cato always traveled on foot; indeed, he sometimes walked the streets of the city of Rome barefoot. He would have needed all his energy for Spartacus in 72 B.C. The ex-gladiator led the Romans on a chase for nearly all of Italy's seven-hundred-mile length. The Romans wanted to hit the rebels hard. Spartacus dared them to reach a moving target.

By late 73 B.C. the Roman Senate, as one source claims, was no longer merely ashamed but afraid. No more praetors: it was time to dispatch the two consuls. They would have four new legions, about twenty thousand men, raised in the final months of 73 B.C. The consuls-elect sent out "searchers" (conquisitores), that is, recruiting officers to Italy's various towns. They preferred volunteers but did not hesitate to pull out the census lists and force men to do their duty.

Though the Romans hated to admit it, they no longer faced a police action but rather a war. But to fight Spartacus, they had to find him. He would not make it easy. As the Romans came south, Spartacus would go north. He planned to march up Italy's mountainous spine, keeping his mobile forces out of the heavy-armed Romans' reach. He would stop from time to time to forage, to loot easy targets, and to pick up new recruits. But mainly he would keep moving, heading ever northward. A few of the rebels rode on horseback or in carts, but the vast majority walked. No doubt they were often hungry, tired, and cold; surely most of them were barefoot and dirty; certainly they lost men to desertion, illness, and death. They kept going.

Their audacious goal was the Alps. Spartacus sought safety for his men across the mountains where they could head for their Celtic or Thracian homelands. In northern Europe, out of Rome's reach, they had a fighting chance. Italy would be their graveyard.

Meanwhile, if the Romans did find him on the march, Spartacus would fight them, but not by the books. Not for him to line up the men in methodical ranks and march them into a killing zone of Rome's choosing. He would not send men armed with branch-and-rawhide shields and wooden spearheads against a wall of iron. Spartacus knew that irregulars could not beat the legion at its own game, not even a legion as soft as one of the new units of 72 B.C.

Still, the sources state that Spartacus fought at least one if not several pitched battles against the Romans this year. It is plausible that he dared to do so under the right circumstances. Hill country and mountains provided favorable terrain for the insurgents. Ambush, trickery, surprise, speed, and psychological warfare all offered promising lines of attack. Superiority in cavalry gave Spartacus a way to harass the enemy's flanks and to neutralize Roman light-armed troops.

The events of the Spartacus War of 72 B.C. exploded onto Rome's consciousness. They shocked the city and marked the turning point in the rebels' fortunes. But with the exception of an episode or two at the year's end, most of the year's activities survive in only the sketchiest form. Hence the narrative must be even more speculative here than elsewhere.

At the start of the campaign season in spring 72, the Romans learned that the rebels had split into two groups: one led by Spartacus, the other by Crixus. Both men were on the move. Crixus's group remained in southern Italy but not in Thurii. It headed to Apulia (today's Puglia), a wealthy agricultural region of gently rolling hills and one stark mountain. Spartacus's forces, meanwhile, turned northward.

Like the Romans, we cannot be sure just what the two groups were up to. Was the split tactical or strategic, friendly or hostile? Plutarch said that Crixus left because of his "arrogance and presumption." Perhaps, but irregular armies break up as easily as volcanic soil. Crixus and Spartacus had already disagreed the year before over whether to stay in Italy and loot. Meanwhile, ethnic differences, rival ambitions, and the natural jealousies of former gladiators made common cause difficult. A friendly divorce made political sense.

It was sound tactics as well. The rebels needed food. They had no commissariat to feed forty thousand soldiers plus an unknown number of women and children. The prospects were better for two smaller groups, foraging in separate locations, than for one large group descending on a single spot.

Spartacus had the big battalions. The sources say that he began the campaign season with thirty thousand men, while Crixus had only ten thousand. This seems right, however much ethnic ties bound his fellow Celts and their German allies to Crixus. Spartacus's supporters followed him not because he was Thracian but because he was Spartacus. By now the rebels had taken his measure. They recognized a winning general and a favorite of the gods as well as a giant gladiator. His vivid gestures moved them. His austerity hardened them; his generosity helped them. His care for innocent civilians might have left them cold, but it underscored the quality that sums up Spartacus: righteous.

Spartacus's authority was neither formal nor forced; it was moral. As Napoleon said, "in war the moral is to the material as three to one." No wonder three-quarters of the army followed Spartacus.

But where did he tell them that they were going? They couldn't stay in the plain of Sybaris. When the Romans came they would force a battle, and the insurgents would want to fight in the hills, where the terrain was better suited for ambush, trickery, and surprise. Sybaris is ringed by hills, but if they camped there the rebels would have run out of food in short order. To the south lay the sea, but they had no ships so they had to go north. Italy had plenty of fertile land, plenty of loot, and plenty of slaves to recruit. Let the Romans chase them.

Every chase comes to an end, however, and Spartacus knew it. His plan was probably to lead his people to safety out of Italy, over the Alps, to Gaul or Thrace or—after dividing the army—both. The rebels could hardly have been sanguine about so daunting a task, and a prudent commander might have kept the plan to himself. We might speculate that Spartacus did not level with the army as they marched north. Perhaps he floated the notion that they were simply spreading the revolt and searching for loot in another part of Italy. Later, when they were caught between the Romans and the Alps, they would surely find it easier to accept the unacceptable. So Spartacus might have reckoned.

After their forces split, Spartacus and Crixus had every reason to keep the door open. Each man should have hoped for the other's success, if only to keep the Romans busy. Spartacus was too shrewd to burn his bridges. As an experienced soldier, he would have known the risks of his long journey. He had to retain the option of returning to the South and reestablishing contact with Crixus. Meanwhile, Crixus had no interest in hurrying Spartacus out of Italy and freeing the Romans to concentrate on him. Crixus might have encouraged Spartacus to take his time gathering supporters among the downtrodden of central and northern Italy. Both sides likely kept in touch via messengers.

Rome surely knew little of this in spring 72 B.C. The consuls were Lucius Gellius and Gnaeus Cornelius Lentulus Clodianus. They held the highest regular office in Rome, each already having held the second-highest office, the praetorship. Ambitious Romans aimed for the consulship soon after their term as praetor. Lentulus had been praetor in 75, so as consul in 72 he knew that his career was on track. But Gellius had waited two long decades since serving as praetor in 94. In 93 he held office as a Roman official in the East and got egg on his face when he waded into a dispute among Athenian philosophers. Now, in 72, his time had finally come. Was he ready for it? Neither he nor Lentulus was known for previous military commands. And Gellius was not young: he was at least sixty-two years old. No wonder that Gellius received a high-level assistant, another praetor of 73 B.C., Quintus Arrius. He had been slated to take over the governorship of Sicily in 72 B.C. but the Spartacus War got in the way, and Arrius was reassigned to Gellius's staff, with the rank of propraetor.

Arrius was a self-made man whose life's ambition was to be elected consul, an honor that had previously eluded his family. As praetor, he was well on his way. Chances are that Arrius would rather have been governor of Sicily than fight Spartacus. Governors could squeeze the locals and raise the equivalent of today's campaign contributions. Law and politics, not war, were Arrius's forte. Still, Arrius was "a vigorous man," said Cicero, who also once compared Arrius to a boxer. Given the assignment to fight the rebels, Arrius would surely work hard for the victory needed to advance his career.

Even so, the Roman government ought to have been able to do better. Spartacus was too big a threat to give the job to anyone less than an expert general. But Rome faced the crisis with mediocrities. It had happened surprisingly often in the past, in spite of serious threats like Hannibal.

Either in Rome or in the field, the Romans got the news that the insurgents had divided. Lentulus's assignment was to deal directly with Spartacus, while Gellius would attack Crixus first and then join the campaign against Spartacus. Lentulus had the much tougher job so we might imagine that he planned to nip at Spartacus's heels while avoiding battle until Gellius arrived. As it turned out, Gellius came with a dose of good news: the first Roman victory of the war.

With Arrius's assistance, Gellius crushed Crixus's army. The struggle took place in Apulia near Mount Garganus (modern Gargano). Sometimes called the spur of Italy, Mount Garganus could be dubbed the sore thumb. It juts into the Adriatic about ninety miles north of Barium (modern Bari). It is not a peak but a rugged and thickly forested peninsula attached oddly to Apulia's undulating countryside. The rocky heights of the Gargano Peninsula reach 3,500 feet; the limestone terrain is pockmarked by caves; in Roman times the area was famous for its oak forests. In short, Garganus was natural guerrilla country.

Mount Garganus would have made a good base for rallying the slaves of Apulia to revolt. The region's slave shepherds had risen up against Rome before, so the rebel cry might have fallen on ready ears. If things ended up badly, an escape route by sea beckoned. At the end of the Garganus promontory there were several harbors, should the rebels have sought help from pirates, as they would shortly afterward. But Crixus failed to use these natural features to his advantage.

The Romans outgeneraled Crixus: they took him by surprise. The rolling hill country beside the Garganus promontory was well stocked with farms, no doubt tempting Crixus to sally out on a plundering raid. Perhaps this is where the Romans caught him. Or perhaps they trapped him in an upland meadow on the promontory itself.

It was typical for a consul's army to consist of two legions. The "paper" strength of a legion in the first century B.C. was 6,200 men; the real strength was about 5,000 men. That is, when the legion was newly formed; in time, after losing men in combat or to illness or desertion, a legion's strength was probably about 4,000 men. When a consul took office and raised an army of two legions, therefore, it probably comprised about 10,000 men. A legion was only as strong as its subunits. The basic tactical unit of the legion was the cohort. Each legion consisted of ten cohorts, nominally of 480 men each; each cohort was comprised of six centuries, nominally of eighty men each. Light-armed troops and cavalrymen added to a legion's numbers.

The commander of each legion was called a legate. Below him stood six junior officers called military tribunes. Cato's brother Caepio was a military tribune in one of Gellius's two legions; Cato no doubt served on his staff. The lowest rank of officer was a centurion, commander of a century. The centurions were often the unsung heroes of the legion, because small-group leadership can make or break an army.

These armies consisted almost entirely of infantrymen, with only small groups of cavalry, light-armed, or specialist troops. They were inexperienced and far from the best Rome had, but they were much better armed than the insurgents, and they could be far more confident about food and housing.

We know next to nothing about the battle. In the absence of evidence of creativity on the part of Gellius or Arrius, we might expect that they lined up their army by the book. Each legion was deployed in a three-line formation, with four cohorts (a paper strength of 1,920 men) in the front line and three cohorts (a paper strength of 1,440 men) in each of the two rear lines. The insurgents probably had to organize themselves more hastily. Given their reputation as horsemen, the Celts should have possessed a good cavalry, but they might have lacked time to deploy it properly, and the Romans might have outnumbered it.

The heart of the Roman army consisted of the heavy infantrymen, that is, the legionaries. Each legionary was protected by body armor, typically a mail coat, and a bronze or iron helmet. He also carried a big, oblong shield (*scutum*). His weapons were a javelin (*pilum*) and a short sword (*gladius*). Some of Spartacus's and Crixus's men had similar arms and armor, stripped from the enemy dead, but many of the rebels had only primitive weapons and light protection.

Both armies no doubt advanced with war cries to hearten themselves and frighten their opponent. The Roman light-armed infantry
usually tried to soften up the enemy by shooting arrows and slings,
some of which had an effective range of perhaps one hundred yards.
After absorbing any losses, the insurgents probably raised the rebel
yell and blew their war trumpets. Roman armies typically advanced
by banging javelins on shields and shouting war cries. As the legions
closed in, at a distance of about fifty feet, they would have begun
throwing their javelins. They shouted, accompanied by the "threatening rumble" of the commander's horn, followed by the strident call
of the trumpets. Then, with their banners flying, they charged the
enemy at a run.

Sometimes the Romans would make such an intimidating show
of discipline and equipment that the enemy would turn and run
away. But on this day it would come down to a hard fight. Legionaries would hack and thrust at the enemy with their swords, while the
other side would reply with sword or spear.

Ancient battle lives in the imagination as a climax: a collision, followed by dozens of disorderly, individual fights that go on until one
side prevails. Real battle was probably episodic. Like boxers, the two
sides combined, broke apart, regrouped each in its own corner, and
then hit each other again. Finally, one army would collapse and run.
Such a typical Roman battle lasted two to three hours, but episodes
of hand-to-hand fighting probably each lasted only fifteen to twenty
minutes before exhaustion set in.

The only detail of the battle of Mount Garganus to survive is the
report that the rebels "fought extremely fiercely": a conventional
statement but it might be true. Celtic warriors were known for their
ferocity and tenacity in battle. We might imagine the bravest legionaries circling the enemy's flank or trying to stab their way into the
enemy lines. Eventually they succeeded, but probably at a price.
The insurgents perhaps forced the Romans to fight many "rounds"

of battle before a decision was reached. It was enough to do the rebels honor but not to avoid a massacre. According to one source, two-thirds of Crixus's men died. Among the fallen was Crixus himself. This too fits the picture of Celtic warfare. Celtic warriors were supposed to group themselves around their chiefs in battle. It was a disgrace to abandon one's chief and it was unthinkable for a chief to do anything but fight to the finish. Germans behaved similarly, to judge by the women of the Cimbri tribe who stood in the rear of one battle on chariots, and killed the fleeing warriors rather than let them run away.

It was the first defeat after a string of victories for the insurgency. How can such a reversal of fortune be explained? Not by the prowess of Gellius and Arrius. As events later in 72 would show, they had not created a victory machine. The cause of defeat probably lay with Crixus. He was Spartacus's equal in courage but not in common sense. That Crixus shared Spartacus's taste for discipline and austerity is doubtful; that he lacked due diligence when it came to scouts and pickets is apparent.

Meanwhile, Spartacus marched north. He was somewhere in the Apennine Mountains in north-central Italy. The rebels had marched from a land of olive oil to one of butter, a zone that was cooler, rainier, and greener than the south. There was plenty of fresh water and herds of sheep and goats, but there were also wolves and bears. As a landscape, the Apennines are vertical, narrow, and difficult, all of which worked in the insurgents' favor.

Even so, the Romans wanted to fight Spartacus. Roman doctrine called for offensives and Crixus's fate boded well for success. Still, Spartacus's army had reason for optimism. The men had fine leadership; past victories should have raised their morale; and their cavalry force should have been better than the Romans'. Their leader shared the men's risks; he looked heroic and was physically courageous; he was charismatic and had a flair for the bold gesture; he could be inspiring on the battlefield. The insurgents were nimbler and tougher than the enemy, quick and violent enough to shock an inexperienced foe, and superior in numbers.

The Romans, nonetheless, found the enemy and forced him to fight on what looked like auspicious terms. The consul Lentulus, thanks no doubt to good intelligence, was able to block the road ahead. Meanwhile, Gellius, conqueror of Crixus, had marched up from Apulia in rapid pursuit of the main rebel army. Spartacus was trapped.

One plausible theory locates the confrontation in a mountain pass in the Apennines northwest of Florence. The little village of Lentula lies at the foot of Mount Calvi (4,200 feet) in a valley that runs north toward Modena (the Romans' Mutina). Local tradition insists on a direct connection between the village name and the consul Lentulus, just as it points out that Spartacus later made his way to Mutina. The theory is unproven, but the rugged terrain around Lentula would have made a fine site for the battle.

Spartacus now showed what made him a great battlefield commander. It is possible for a good general to rescue his army from encirclement as long as he is decisive, agile, and calm. He also has to be sure of complete loyalty and obedience on the part of his troops. Caesar had these very qualities, and he saved his army at the battle of Ruspina (modern Monastir in Tunisia) in 46 B.C. Finding himself surrounded, Caesar arranged his army in two lines, back to back, and had them each push the enemy back. That give him the breathing space to launch two coordinated charges, and he broke through to freedom.

In the Apennines in 72 B.C., Spartacus achieved even more, and by different tactics. Admittedly, the Thracian's situation was less desperate than Caesar's. Spartacus outnumbered the enemy: he had 30,000 men while each consular army had a maximum of about 10,000 men. Gellius's army might, in fact, have been even smaller, due to losses suffered in the battle with Crixus. Unlike Caesar, Spartacus had time and space to attack each of his enemies in turn. Like Caesar, though, Spartacus could never have succeeded without commanding his men's trust. We can only imagine what he might have said in a prebattle speech to rally his troops. But the message was clear as a bugle: attack!

The mere fact of the attack might have surprised the Romans; they might have expected to see the beleaguered enemy assume a defensive position. Spartacus went after Lentulus's army first; one source claims that the rebels struck with a sudden rush. A cunning commander like Spartacus might have positioned part of his forces behind hills and then had them pour out to shock the enemy. He probably used his cavalry to good effect. A well-timed cavalry attack could break the enemy's formation, particularly the light infantry, who wore little protection. The Romans typically counterattacked against cavalry by means of arrows and slings, but they didn't always do the job. A quick and sudden cavalry charge, for example, could prevent archers and slingers from inflicting much damage. If the legions held firm, they might have stopped a cavalry charge by massing in a dense formation, almost a shield wall with room for thrusting with their pikes. Horses will not crash into a solid object or what looms like a solid object. The difficulty, however, was standing firm, because the sight of a cavalry charge was enough to terrify inexperienced troops. In a later battle the Romans appear to have taken additional precautions against Spartacus's cavalry, which suggests bitter experience.

In any case, once he had softened up the enemy with such tactics, Spartacus probably sent in his infantry. They surely struck with all the fury that made Celts, Germans, and Thracians famous. We might guess that individual cases of valor paid outsized dividends. Let just a few of the enemy break into the line, or allow a strong cavalryman to gallop by and sweep up an enemy soldier, or have an enemy soldier issue a successful challenge to single combat, and a wavering army might turn and run.

However the rebels attacked, the Romans' response was to panic and flee, disgracing the tradition of the legions. The insurgents' attack was no doubt terrifying, but a disciplined army would have held its ground. The Romans usually were disciplined: they had long experience fighting barbarians; they had often defeated much larger armies. But in 72 B.C. neither their training, their trust, nor, apparently, their commander was enough to make the legionaries stand firm. One source says that Spartacus defeated Lentulus's legates and captured all of the army's baggage. Another says that the Romans abandoned the field in great confusion. Another says that Spartacus "thoroughly destroyed" Lentulus' army. Then he turned on Gellius's forces and defeated them, too; no details survive.

The captured baggage offered Spartacus tools: mess tins, cooking pots, satchels, baskets, iron hooks, leather thongs, spades, shovels, saws, hatchets, axes, scythes, and wheelbarrows. There were weapons, too, both what could be taken from prisoners or stripped from the dead and what was carried as baggage: from extra arrows and spears to shield covers and neck guards. Cloaks and sandals were probably precious finds. But the greatest treasure was food, carried in wagons drawn by pack animals.

Under Gellius and Lentulus, Romans ran in disorder from the battlefield. Hannibal had crushed Rome's soldiers at the battle of Cannae in 216 B.C.; in the Apennines in 72 B.C., Spartacus humiliated them. The Carthaginian killed tens of thousands of Romans. The Thracian caused far fewer casualties but he made his point. He now proceeded to hurt Rome's pride further.

In a speech delivered fifteen years later, in 57 B.C., Cicero still remembered Spartacus's insult. Nothing, said Cicero, could have been "more polluted, deformed, perverted or disturbed." What Spartacus did was to give gladiatorial games for slaves—a spectacle that

Rome usually reserved for the free. Spartacus added a bitter twist by reversing roles: he made the slaves spectators and the Romans gladiators.

The occasion was Crixus's funeral games. The news of his comrade's death and defeat had reached Spartacus, perhaps via a messenger, perhaps from the survivors of Crixus's army. To have a pair of gladiators fight at the grave of a great man was an old Italian custom—barbaric to us but in ancient times, a sign of great honor and respect. Spartacus did not have merely one pair of gladiators fight: rather, he commemorated the fallen Celt by a spectacular ritual. Spartacus called up three hundred (or four hundred, according to another source) Roman prisoners and had them fight to the death around a pyre—a symbol, at least, of Crixus, assuming that his corpse had not been recovered. This was a gladiatorial offering on the grand scale. It was all but human sacrifice: glorious to the memory of the dead, humiliating to the Romans who were about to die, and ennobling to the reputation of the host.

What a morale boost for the men! By attending a gladiatorial game, they declared their freedom. In Rome, funeral games were reserved for victorious generals and for praetors and consuls. By awarding this honor to Crixus, Spartacus asserted equality. He also laid claim, at least implicitly, to being Roman. He wielded Roman symbols as well as if he had been born in Rome itself.

As a gladiator Spartacus had been a man of the lowest social order. As an impresario, Spartacus reached a high status in Roman eyes. Thus, as a Roman writer says, Spartacus had in effect purged himself of all his prior infamy. Meanwhile, he gave Rome a black eye.

After defeating the consuls' armies, Spartacus and his men continued northward through the mountains. As they came down from the Apennines, they were greeted with the magnificent view of the broad plain of the Padus (modern Po) river. They crossed into the province of Cisalpine Gaul, "Gaul on this side of the Alps," as the Romans called northernmost Italy. The province stretched to the Alps; in this era, most of its inhabitants were still not Roman citizens.

Their scouts might have told the rebels that trouble awaited them. About ten miles north of the Apennines lay Mutina. One of about ten Roman and Latin colonies in the province, Mutina was the base of the governor, the proconsul Gaius Cassius Longinus. As provincial governor, Cassius had a standing, garrison army to draw on, consisting of two legions (about ten thousand men). It is plausible that he was assisted by the propraetor Cnaeus Manlius.

Cassius had been one of the two consuls the year before, 73 B.C., and earlier had served as mint master and then praetor. It was a successful career, befitting his old and eminent family, but Cassius is best known for his son, also named Cassius, the famous murderer of Caesar. The son had a lean and hungry look, as Shakespeare later put it, and the father might have been equally keen. He was the only card that Rome had left to play between Spartacus and the Alps. Cassius threw down the gauntlet. "As Spartacus was pressing forward toward the Alps," says one writer, "Cassius . . . met him."

Only the barest details of the battle survive. The insurgents crushed the Romans, inflicting many casualties, and Cassius barely escaped with his life. He never played a major role in public affairs again.

The road to the Alps was now open, but Spartacus did not take it. Instead he and his army turned back south. Spartacus's strategy is a mystery. He supposedly had aimed for the Alps and beaten every army that had stood in his way, only, when he had the opportunity to cross the Alps, to turn around and head back to southern Italy. If he had wanted to cross the Alps, why didn't he do so? Many theories have been proposed, but the best explanation was already hinted at in the ancient sources. Spartacus's own men probably vetoed him. In the past, they had never wanted to leave Italy; now success might have gone to their heads and aroused visions of Rome in flames. Perhaps Spartacus had held back the truth and told his men, as they marched north, that they were simply spreading the revolt and searching for loot in another part of Italy. Then, when they reached the plain of the Padus River, and he tried to persuade them to cross the Alps, it was too late to change their minds.

The last straw might simply have been the sight of the Alps. As anyone who has ever looked up from the plain toward the rock wall of the Italian Alps knows, the mountains are overpowering. Most people in Spartacus's army had probably never seen the Alps before. Many of them had never left southern or central Italy.

Other factors may have played a role. There is an outside chance that Spartacus received news from Thrace that gave him pause. The proconsul, Marcus Terentius Varro Lucullus, had won great victories over the Thracians, who had allied with Mithridates. It now looked more difficult than ever for Spartacus and his army to find safety in Thrace.

And perhaps Spartacus had caught what the Japanese would later call "victory disease." Spartacus was "elated by his victories," says one Roman writer, in what is perhaps just a plausible guess. Perhaps he had acquired a foolish belief in his own invincibility. Perhaps he too forgot the Roman habit of responding slowly but inexorably to those who attacked Rome. He might have allowed himself a luxury that no general can afford: hope.

It is such a surprising turn of events that some scholars conclude that Spartacus had never planned to cross the Alps in the first place. But ancient writers took this plan seriously and they were in a better position than we to know Spartacus's motives. Admittedly, they might have engaged in a certain amount of guesswork, since it's not clear if the Romans debriefed captured rebels well. But I prefer their guesses to ours.

And so the rebels headed south again. They had a new goal, they said: Rome. "Terror," says one ancient writer, "spread through the city of Rome, just as it had in the time when Hannibal had threatened its gates." No doubt Romans were terrified, but we might wonder if they had good reason to be afraid. Could Spartacus really threaten a city that was too well fortified for even Hannibal to launch a serious attack? Ten years earlier, in 82 B.C., during the civil war between Marius and Sulla, an army that tried to take Rome fought all night long. It was obliterated by morning. How could Spartacus think of success?

For one thing, he traveled light. He burned unnecessary supplies, slaughtered the pack animals, and killed all prisoners of war. This last act might also have been meant to terrify the enemy. For another thing, Spartacus had a sizable army.

Spartacus began the campaign season with thirty thousand men, enough to outnumber each of his various foes to date but not enough to attack Rome. Each victory boosted Spartacus's reputation and so might have swollen his ranks. New recruits might have come from central and northern Italy, while the survivors of Crixus's defeat might have made their way to Spartacus. He surely would have accepted most of them gladly.

According to ancient sources, after defeating Cassius, Spartacus turned away "many deserters who approached him." Just who these "deserters" were is an interesting question. The prospect that they were legionaries is intriguing but more likely they were slaves performing support duties for Roman troops. Turning them away was not only a gesture of contempt but perhaps also a cold psychological assessment of their unreliability and potential for espionage.

Spartacus could not have afforded to turn away good men because the Romans were about to attack him again. The two consuls, Gellius and Lentulus, had regrouped and joined forces. They now had an army of four legions or about 20,000 men, minus any losses already suffered and not replaced. If Spartacus enjoyed anything like the 3 to 1 advantage that he did against the first army that he had faced that year, he would have commanded about 60,000 men by the time he faced the joint consular army in late 72 B.C.

With all the ifs, ands, and buts in the previous paragraphs, the conclusion is clear: we don't know how many men Spartacus had. But an
educated guess of 60,000 soldiers at the peak of the revolt in late 72
B.C. seems sensible and even conservative. In fact, 60,000 is the lowest
estimate in the ancient sources for the size of Spartacus's army at its
height; other figures are 90,000, over 100,000, and 120,000. In addition to the soldiers there was an unknowable number of civilians:
women, children, and perhaps even old men.

The showdown between Spartacus and the joint consular army
took place in Picenum, in north-central Italy. Once again, details are
lacking. But the sources state that this was a pitched battle. Evidently
his string of successes gave Spartacus the confidence to fight the Romans on their own terms. A vignette survives from either this or the
earlier battle fought by the consul Lentulus; which one is uncertain.
The report is as follows: "And at the same time Lentulus [left] an
elevated position which he had defended with a double battle-line
and at the cost of many of his men, when from out of the soldiers'
kit bags, officers' cloaks began to catch the eye and selected cohorts
began to be discernible."

That seems to mean that Lentulus took up a defensive position on
a hill, where he divided his troops into multiple lines. Caesar would
do something similar in Gaul. Although they had to attack uphill,
the enemy inflicted heavy casualties on Lentulus's men. Apparently,
Lentulus called for help, but he didn't ride off until it became clear
that the reinforcements were nearby. Or so this fragmentary sentence might be reconstructed.

The brief sentence speaks volumes about the conditions of ancient battle. Isolated on a hill, Lentulus had to rely on the naked
eye to see the legion coming to his aid. The legion didn't appear
all at once but rather as a patchwork. First the purple cloaks of the
commanders appeared, then a few separate cohorts became visible. The phrase "out of the soldiers' kit bags" should mean that the

reinforcements were marching near where Lentulus's men had left their baggage.

The scene shows the insurgents at their best. They isolated an enemy unit. They executed the difficult maneuver of attacking uphill, a move in which their lighter armor increased their mobility. Although the rebels did not destroy Lentulus's men before reinforcements arrived, they inflicted heavy losses. Presumably Lentulus expected the reinforcements to defeat the enemy, but that did not happen. Either the rebels on the hill remained strong enough to turn on the reinforcements and overpower them or Spartacus sent fresh troops against the reinforcements, which would speak well of his command and control of the battlefield.

The Romans lost the battle and once again, they ran from the field. Spartacus had reason to be pleased. But he also had cause to reevaluate the attack on Rome. As one ancient account says, "he changed his mind about going to Rome, because his forces were not appropriate for the operation nor was his whole army prepared as soldiers should be (since no city was fighting with him, but only slaves and deserters and the rabble)."

Rome's stone walls were over thirteen feet thick and in places over thirty feet high. The circuit of walls ran nearly seven miles and enclosed one thousand acres. Spartacus had no siege engines nor experts to man them. He had few if any soldiers with experience of laying siege to a city or taking a city by assault.

Nor had Spartacus's experience of battle in 72 B.C. been entirely encouraging. He had won every engagement, but his colleague Crixus's army had been destroyed and Crixus was dead. The Romans, meanwhile, refused to accept defeat. No matter how hard Spartacus hit the Romans, they kept coming back. There was no reason to doubt that they would return. It was far more prudent to prepare for the next battle than to open a new front that was unlikely to bring success. And so the army returned to southern Italy, probably to Thurii.

There the insurgents had yet another encounter with a Roman army, possibly under the propraetor Manlius. They defeated the Romans and reaped a rich load of booty. It was a happy end to their journey, yet the men had reason to wonder just what they had achieved.

They had made a punishing trip of about 1,200 miles, which could hardly have taken them less than four or five months, considering the marching rates of ancient armies and the time needed to stop, forage, and fight. They had fought four battles, mourned their colleagues' defeat in a fifth, and amassed loot. They had buried old comrades and attracted new ones.

They might glory in their status as the dominant army in Italy. It was an astonishing truth that most would have ascribed to the gods and perhaps, above all, to Dionysus. Yet the rebels were only as strong as their ability to beat Rome's next army. That army was sure to come, even if vain rebels and pessimistic Romans both failed to see it in the distance.

By summer's end, Italy had seen two big stories in 72 B.C. One was Spartacus's Long March and the other was Rome's disgrace. A rabble in arms had defeated a regular army.

One of the few to have served with distinction was Cato—but he also served with disdain. At the year's end, Cato's commander offered him a military honor, such as a crown, a neck ornament, a golden armband, or one of the other decorations handed out to Rome's best legionaries. Cato, however, refused. Family pride might have caused him to balk at accepting honors amid military disgrace.

Cato's great-grandfather Cato the Censor had once sneered at a commander who awarded his soldiers crowns just for digging ditches or sinking wells—prizes, the Censor said, that would have required at least the burning of an enemy's camp back when Rome had standards. Cato's uncle Drusus had once rejected honors himself, no doubt aware of the malicious remark that they would have dwarfed the man who wore them. Malice might have come Cato's way too if he had received honors while his brother hadn't, and the sources don't mention honors for Caepio. So Cato declined the proffered honors.

Few Romans could have bemoaned the nation's defeats more than Cato. Austere, public-spirited, and uncompromising, he lived for virtue. Most Roman politicians, including his allies, eventually fell short of Cato's lofty standards. Cicero, a friend who felt Cato's sting, once wrote in exasperation that Cato thought he was living in Plato's Republic instead of the sewer of Romulus. In 72 B.C., Cato had abundant reasons to be displeased.

RETREAT

6

THE DECIMATOR

IN THE AUTUMN of 72 B.C. a new general took command of the legions. Determined to restore discipline, he revived a brutal and archaic form of punishment. Fifty Roman soldiers who ran away from battle and disgraced the legions were caught, condemned, and executed by their own army. Each of them was clubbed to death by nine of his fellow legionaries, men with whom they might have changed places, since the victims were chosen by lot. Five hundred men were caught shirking their duty; one out of every ten was selected for execution, which is why the procedure was called *decimation* (analogous to our word *decimal*, that is, one-tenth). Rome's new general wanted his men to fear him more than they feared Spartacus. His name was Marcus Licinius Crassus.

A marble bust survives that is probably a portrait of Crassus; it is revealing. Stare directly and you see the picture of resolve: the skin of his face tightened, lips pursed, jaw clenched, eyebrows drawn down, neck muscles tensed. In profile, however, his jowls, a double chin, and the crows' feet around his eyes are all apparent. Not only vigor but caution and suspicion are etched into his features. The bust was found in Rome, in the family tomb of the Licinii, one of Rome's most prominent families, but there are other copies, proof that they depict an important person. The style fits the end of the Roman Republic. The scholarly consensus is that the bust is Marcus Licinius Crassus.

Crassus took command at the order of the Senate and to the applause of the People. Bold politics, the choice made poetic justice. In his own way, Crassus resembled Spartacus. Not that Crassus wanted to overturn Rome: far from it. Like Spartacus, though, Crassus was unconventional. He wanted to rise to the top of Roman politics but he would beat his own path. Unwilling or unable to win the approval of the old nobility, Crassus courted the common people and made deals with new politicians. The *optimates*, literally, the best men, as Rome's conservatives called themselves, did not approve. Given a choice, the Senate's old guard would never have turned to a man like Crassus. Spartacus forced their hands and made Crassus the man of the hour.

Crassus came from one of Rome's most eminent families but its luster was no brighter than a decadent age could produce. Crassus displayed good generalship against other Romans and great initiative in exploiting the misery of others. He was known as a man of selective vice rather than strict morality. For example, he beat a charge of seducing a vestal virgin by proving that he was merely greedy and not impious, since he was interested in her property rather than her chastity.

In his early forties—he was born circa 115 B.C.—Crassus was one of Italy's richest but least luxurious men. Frugal and severe, he felt more at home in the Rome of brick than the Rome of marble. With a private fire brigade at his disposal, he pounced on men whose houses were on fire and talked them into selling fast and cheaply before they had nothing left to sell. Yet he wouldn't treat himself to a vacation home. It wasn't comfort that Crassus wanted but political power, which was why he amassed wealth in the first place. A good general but no military genius like Pompey (or, later, Caesar), Crassus saw that the path to political success lay in buying votes. He doled out money, giving loans to the rich, handouts to the poor, and favors to the influential. Crassus made himself popular even though he lacked none of the scathing arrogance of the Roman nobility.

In 72 B.C. his popularity paid off. As best we can reconstruct it, the Senate and People of Rome agreed to award Crassus a special command against Spartacus, with virtually unlimited power (what the Romans called proconsular imperium), even though he was a private citizen. This was a rare distinction, since commands were usually reserved for officeholders. What made things even sweeter was that Pompey held a similar command in Spain against Sertorius. Pompey was Rome's leading general and its most ambitious politician. Crassus considered Pompey his chief political rival, but now Crassus had matched him. To add to his triumph, the disgraced consuls Lentulus and Gellius were Pompey's allies.

Crassus in command would drive his men hard. He was a tough man but he had not had an easy life. Before his thirtieth birthday, Crassus saw his father's severed head hanging from the speakers' platform in the Roman forum. The proud old man had committed suicide rather than surrender to Marius when the latter took Rome. Crassus himself was too insignificant to be executed but two years later, in 85 B.C., danger loomed as the civil war reignited, so he ran for his life.

Crassus fled all the way to Spain. Sheltered by a family friend, Crassus spent eight months in hiding from the pro-Marius provincial government. He lived in a cave. Finally, the news that the leading Marians were dead brought Crassus out and into action.

He raised an army of 2,500 men. As Crassus later said, a Roman wasn't really rich unless he could raise his own legion. His men were picked troops, chosen from among friends and family supporters. He requisitioned ships, sailed with the men to North Africa, and tried to join forces with the anti-Marian proconsul there, Quintus Caecilius Metellus Pius, but the two men quarreled. Undaunted, Crassus voyaged to Greece, where he joined the leader of the anti-Marian forces, Sulla. He returned to Italy in 83 B.C. with Sulla and his soldiers, possibly including, ironically enough, that Roman auxiliary Spartacus. In spring 82, Sulla sent Crassus to raise more troops in central Italy, which Crassus did with great success. He also captured the city of Todi, where he was accused of taking more than his fair share of the spoils—if true, it contrasts with Spartacus's later fairness in dividing the spoils equally.

Young Crassus had his rendezvous with destiny outside the walls of Rome, in the last of a series of bloody battles up and down the Italian peninsula. Sulla attacked the Marian forces at Rome's Colline Gate in the northeastern part of the city walls. The struggle commenced in the late afternoon of November 1, 82 B.C. and it went on into the night. The Marians pinned Sulla's center and left wings against the walls. Only Sulla's right wing was victorious, but that decided the battle, because it crushed the enemy's left wing, drove it in flight, and pursued it for two miles. The commander of Sulla's right wing was Crassus.

From what little we know, Sulla was the architect of victory in the Battle of the Colline Gate. Crassus merely executed the plan, but he did so with vigor and guts. It was enough to make his fortune. With Sulla triumphant, Crassus put down his sword for a decade and devoted himself to moneymaking and politics.

When Sulla came to power he named about five hundred wealthy and prominent supporters of Marius as outlaws. The Romans called this "proscription" because the names were inscribed and posted in a public list. The outlaws were hunted down and killed. Their property was confiscated and men like Crassus gobbled it up at cut-rate prices. By the time of the Spartacus War a decade later, Crassus's portfolio included estates in the Italian countryside and real estate in the city of Rome; mines, perhaps Spanish silver mines; and large numbers of slaves, some of whom he may have rented out. Born rich, Crassus had become superrich.

His moment came in autumn 72, when Rome entrusted Crassus with a special command to fight Spartacus. Why Crassus wanted the command is no mystery. It could have made his career. Up to then, he had advanced more slowly in politics than a man of his ambition would have wished. He had served as praetor at some point, it seems, but he had not held Rome's top office, the consulship. A special command opened the door to military glory, which would have put political preeminence within reach. Defeating Spartacus would have given Crassus a card to play against Pompey. Then, too, Crassus had his economic interests at stake. Since he owned large, slave-run estates in southern Italy, he fit the profile of Spartacus's victims. Putting down the rebellion would not just bring Crassus glory but save his investments.

Nor is there any doubt why the Roman people wanted Crassus. He was victorious, popular, and filthy rich. Thanks to his wealth, Crassus should have been able to pay at least some of the soldiers out of his own purse, perhaps as a long-term loan to the treasury. Rome's military budget was already funding armies in Spain, Thrace, and Asia Minor, and a navy off Crete.

Crassus had the proven ability to raise troops. The current emergency demanded a knowledgeable chief of recruitment who could fill the ranks quickly. As a former general for Sulla, moreover, Crassus should have been able to talk some of Sulla's veterans back into service. Many of them were no longer young, but unlike raw recruits, experienced soldiers don't run when the enemy charges. The sentence

"Everyone who had a soldier's heart, even if his body had grown old" survives in one ancient source about the Spartacus War. We don't know just what the sentence refers to, but how intriguing to think of it as Crassus's recruiting slogan.

Crassus was no Alexander the Great but he knew how to fight. Crassus had learned about unconventional insurgents in Spain, a land that had resisted Rome fiercely for two centuries.

When he was around twenty, in 93 B.C., Crassus had seen his father Publius celebrate a triumph over the Lusitanians (Portuguese), men known as masters of irregular warfare. Publius had spent three or four years (circa 97–93 B.C.) as governor of Hispania Ulterior, today's Portugal and western Spain. Young Crassus lived with his father there and he may have served on his father's staff in that war. The details of Publius's campaign do not survive. Since he won a triumph, he must have scored one or more successes, but we may doubt whether he matched the enemy's speed and cunning. Against the Lusitanians the Romans rarely did.

The Lusitanians had a reputation as raiders and rustlers. Their greatest leader, Viriathus, had bedeviled the Romans with eight years of guerrilla warfare (148–139 B.C.). Viriathus was too shrewd to fight a pitched battle as the Romans wished. Stymied, the Romans attacked civilians in the towns that supported Viriathus and finally resorted to having him assassinated. The leaderless Lusitanians made peace, but it did not last. Again and again the Lusitanians revolted, which led to Roman reprisals. In the decade before Publius's governorship, for example, two Roman generals celebrated triumphs over the Lusitanians. More recently, Lusitanian light infantry and horsemen formed the core of Sertorius's insurgency on the Spanish peninsula (80–72 B.C.). Both Viriathus and Sertorius excelled at speed, mobility, deception, ambush, night attacks, and the other tricks of unconventional warfare.

The Lusitanians imposed slippery and devious warfare on Rome.

Around the time that Publius was fighting Viriathus, Rome faced a more static conflict in the neighboring province of Hispania Citerior, or Nearer Spain. Siegecraft was the main tactic there, and endurance vied in importance with deceit. This war offered lessons in brutality for Crassus.

Publius's colleague Titus Didius, governor of Hispania Citerior from 98 to 93, spent nine months besieging a rebellious Spanish town in order to put an end to its people's banditry. In the end, he talked the town into surrendering in return for a land grant, but once he had them in his power, Didius ordered a massacre. He herded the women and children into a canyon along with the men and had them all slaughtered.

Rome's greatest siege in Spain had taken place at Numantia. A fortified city, Numantia had fought Rome for the better part of twenty years, between 154 and 133 B.C. The Numantines inflicted defeat and humiliation on a half-dozen Roman commanders. Finally, in 134 B.C., Rome entrusted the war to Scipio Aemilianus, the man who had conquered Carthage in 146 B.C. Scipio first raised a new army and trained it hard. Next he cut off Numantia's food supply. Then he encircled Numantia with a huge wall, patrolled by Roman troops stationed in seven different forts. Then Scipio waited. Slowly, the city starved; when it reached the point of cannibalism, Numantia surrendered. Fifty survivors were paraded in Scipio's triumph; the rest were sold into slavery. Numantia was razed and its territory divided among its neighbors.

Scipio's policy was as blunt as it was brutal. It had required 60,000 Roman and allied soldiers to defeat 4,000 defenders of Numantia. Even so, Crassus might have looked back to it as a model as he prepared to fight Spartacus. Like Scipio, Crassus held a special command. Like his father, Publius, he faced a quick and shifty foe. To take on Spartacus in battle was to risk being outfoxed like a half-dozen Roman commanders before him. Why not lead Spartacus into a trap instead, where the Romans could lay siege to him? Why not outfox the fox? Call it the Numantine solution.

It was also a classic recipe for counterinsurgency: location, isolation, and eradication. After finding Spartacus, Crassus had to herd him into a place where the Roman could cut him off from support and supplies. Then Crassus could kill him.

Executing the plan required thorough knowledge of southern Italy's terrain. Luckily Crassus possessed just that. In 90 B.C. his father, Publius, back in Italy, had taken on Rome's rebel allies by fighting a battle in Lucania. In his mid-twenties at the time, Crassus is likely to have fought alongside him. Although Publius lost the battle, Crassus learned about the land. Crassus's Lucanian connections extended to the city of Heraclea, where his father had granted Roman citizenship to an important resident. South of Lucania lay Bruttium, another province in which Crassus had a hand, since he had grabbed an estate there from a Marian after Sulla's victory in 82 B.C.

Crassus took over command from the consuls Gellius and Lentulus either in late summer or early fall of 72 B.C. By November or thereabouts they were back in Rome presiding over Senate meetings. According to Plutarch, an angry Senate had stripped them of their command but not their office. Another possibility is that the consuls made a deal to step down voluntarily in exchange for support from Crassus for their campaign to be chosen censors—in other words, they agreed to be kicked upstairs.

The two consuls proved to be better legislators than generals. They passed a law enabling commanders to reward conspicuous bravery with Roman citizenship. Crassus's new legionaries already were Roman citizens, but the troops in Cisalpine Gaul were not. The new law gave them an incentive for valor if Spartacus returned.

Crassus raised six new legions: about 30,000 men. He commanded them as well as the remaining troops of the four legions previously commanded by Gellius and Lentulus: perhaps another

16,000 men. Crassus then counted around 45,000 legionaries. This was an enormous army, about the same size as the army that Caesar would later use to conquer Gaul. It was more than twice as large as any force that the Romans had sent out yet against Spartacus. If Spartacus had about 60,000 men, then he continued to outnumber the Romans, but that probably did not bother Crassus unduly. Roman military doctrine emphasized quality over quantity, and Romans often went into battle outnumbered, especially against those they considered barbarians. Besides, Crassus had no intention of doing battle against Spartacus until he had first worn down the Thracian.

Meanwhile, the appointment of Crassus energized the war effort. Many elite Romans, especially his friends and allies, joined to fight for the hero of the Colline Gate. Crassus drew his supporters from the rank and file of the Senate rather than its leadership. The names of five of his officers in the Spartacus War are known: Quintus Marcius Rufus, Mummius, Caius Pomptinus, Lucius Quinctius, and Cnaeus Tremellius Scrofa. Quinctius came from a humble background, while Rufus and Pomptinus both belonged to families that, as far as we know, had not held office before. Tremellius Scrofa came from a just-miss family: it had produced six Roman praetors but no consuls.

Only Mummius had a famous name. One Lucius Mummius Achaicus had been consul in 146 and sacker of Corinth; we don't know, however, if Crassus's officer Mummius came from the same branch of the family. Even if the blood of Achaicus flowed in the veins of this Mummius, it did not carry the great ancestor's talent. Mummius embarrassed Crassus with a great mistake at the campaign's start.

Once again the Roman army marched south. At Eburum, the Picentini mountains look like tabletops, rising in an abrupt sweep from the plain. It was here, we might imagine, beside these hills, that

Crassus's men laid out their camp. Eburum lay on the Via Annia, from which Crassus could control the valley of the Silarus river and the passes into Lucania. It was the key to Picentia, which was, in turn, the doorway between Campania and Lucania. Picentia stood at the edge of civilization, as it were. South of it lay Spartacus country, too mountainous and rugged for Crassus's new army to cross through safely. Picentia made an excellent base because the rich territory between Salernum and Paestum was fertile enough to feed Crassus's men—today it produces Italy's most famous mozzarella—and wide enough to allow them to train.

Spartacus, for his part, seems to have moved northward from Thurii into northwestern Lucania, perhaps back into the fertile Campus Atinas, where his men had rampaged a year earlier. It was harvest time again, as it had been during their attack the year before, and food would have drawn Spartacus's men there. In addition, the Campus Atinas offered other advantages to a shrewd commander like Spartacus: it was a good spot for his army to intimidate Crassus while his scouts inspected the new Roman forces. Crassus, meanwhile, put the pressure on as well. He sent two legions to circle around Spartacus and follow him. Their route, for example, might have taken them north into the valley of the upper Silarus river, then eastward and back south into the territory of Volceii (modern Buccino). This route bypassed the Via Annia while following well-beaten and relatively level paths.

Crassus entrusted command of the two legions to Mummius. According to one source, these were the legions formerly under Gellius and Lentulus, and not the new units raised by Crassus. Crassus gave explicit orders: Mummius was to follow Spartacus closely but not to fight, not even in a skirmish. Evidently, the plan was to pressure Spartacus without risking a defeat against his battle-hardened troops. Unfortunately, instead of obeying orders, Mummius took advantage of the first good chance to join battle. Perhaps he occupied the high ground or perhaps his scouts said that the enemy had its guard down. In any case, Mummius lost. As the sources put it, "Many of his men fell, and many saved themselves by dropping their weapons and fleeing." In the ancient world, dropping one's weapons to save one's life earned a man great shame: it practically defined cowardice. The fugitive soldiers slunk back in disgrace to the Roman camp in Picentia.

If the Romans had stood firm in close order, they would have formed a wall against which the enemy charge might have broken. Instead the Romans obligingly turned and ran. For the rebels, it was barbarian warfare at its best.

Crassus planned to turn the fiasco into what is nowadays called a teaching moment. No more defeatism: that was the rule of the new imperator. He began by treating Mummius harshly—precisely how is not known. Next, Crassus had new weapons issued to the men who had thrown theirs away, but only on the condition that they formally promise not to lose them again. Then he struck.

Crassus chose the first five hundred runaways to have returned to his camp—"tremblers," to use the old Spartan term employed by Plutarch to describe these men. These five hundred soldiers perhaps belonged to one legionary cohort (battalion). Crassus divided the men into fifty groups of ten men each, and had one man chosen by lot from each group. These fifty men were forced to undergo decimation.

Decimation was an ancient Roman military punishment that had gone out of use until Crassus revived it. According to traditional procedure, the executioners survived but were forced to camp outside the defenses of the main camp. There they were fed barley instead of wheat, like animals. The sources don't tell us how long Crassus's men underwent this disgrace. It was a symbolic humiliation but also dangerous, since they were left unprotected and exposed to rebel raids.

Crassus had defined himself in his men's eyes. As one ancient source says, he had made himself more fearful than the enemy. It was a high standard of military discipline. The act of decimation probably took attention away from Spartacus and focused it on Crassus. Perhaps now someone remembered that Crassus's grandfather had earned the nickname Agelastus, "he who does not laugh." Stickler or tyrant, Crassus was indisputably in charge.

Perhaps to underline that point, Crassus now took the offensive. He led his men out against the enemy. Spartacus retreated south through Lucania. One of our sources implies that Spartacus and his high command reached this decision on their own, without a blow being struck. Apparently they had taken Crassus's measure and concluded that they could not match him. Better to draw the Romans into the mountains of Lucania than to risk fighting them on the Picentine plain.

But it is hard to imagine Spartacus persuading his huge army simply to give up after their victory over Mummius. Besides, it would have taken nearly supernatural foresight to gauge the change in the Roman army. Surely the rebels had to bleed first before they awakened. That brings us to a different source and a more plausible account, at least more plausible in parts.

In this version, Crassus's army quickly encountered a detachment of about ten thousand men from Spartacus's army, camping on their own. Just what the men were doing is unclear; perhaps they had been sent to follow the Romans, perhaps they had gone off in search of supplies, or perhaps they represent yet another factional split in the rebels' camp. In any case, the Romans attacked them. With their vast numerical superiority, Crassus's men won a great victory. The sources say that they killed two-thirds of the enemy and took only nine hundred prisoners. The numbers strain credulity but if they are true, they suggest that the rebels had guts. No one seems to have run away.

It was a big defeat for the insurgency, the biggest since the death of Crixus. Worse still, the Romans now had a commander who could keep up the pressure. Crassus now turned on the main rebel force. We might guess that the two armies met somewhere in northern Lucania. Spartacus commanded the rebels, while Crassus led the Romans. According to the sources, these two great generals now met in battle for the first time. High drama, but unfortunately the sources are stingy. After crushing the enemy detachment, Crassus marched on Spartacus "with contempt." Crassus "defeated him and pursued him vigorously in flight." Another source says, "Finally . . . Licinius Crassus saved the Romans' honor; the enemy . . . were beaten by him and fled and sought refuge in the tip of Italy."

This reads like the stuff of official reports. But no one as cagey as Crassus would have then treated Spartacus with contempt. Furthermore, if Crassus won a splendid victory over Spartacus's entire army, it is impossible to explain Crassus's next move, which was to hold back and try to cut off Spartacus's force, rather than to engage it in battle.

It's more likely that Crassus and Spartacus fought a skirmish. It did not lead to a major defeat but it was enough to make the point: Crassus had built a new Roman army. What Spartacus had warned his men all along was now coming true. The men had spirit but Spartacus knew the odds. He understood Rome's overwhelming superiority in pitched battle. Earlier Roman soldiers had turned and fled but Crassus's men would fight. Against previous Roman commanders there had always been room for ambushes and other tricks. Crassus, however, would not be easily fooled. In addition to the fact of defeat, Spartacus's scouts might have discovered other evidence of the changes that Crassus had brought. They might have noticed, for instance, that unlike the earlier legions they had scouted, Crassus's men marched in good order and did not dare engage in undisciplined foraging or looting. These Romans knew how to fight. It was better to draw them deeper into the Lucanian hills than to risk a battle on the plains.

Besides, Spartacus, we might imagine, was still looking for a way out. The rise of Crassus offered a golden opportunity. His men had preferred taking their chances against Lentulus and Gellius to undertaking a passage over the Alps. Faced with Crassus, however, they might have been willing to reassess matters.

So Spartacus led his men toward the other exit from the Italian peninsula. He marched them to the sea. Assuming they had enough of a head start on the enemy, they could have taken the Via Annia south toward the city of Regium. Down the road they went, past the cities of Atina, Nerulum, Consentia, and Terina until they finally reached the Tyrhennian Sea.

As it hugs the mountainside near Italy's southern tip, the road turns a bend and presents the traveler with a sudden panorama below: Sicily, rising majestically in the hazy blue sea. Only the narrow Strait of Messina separates Sicily from the Italian mainland. Sicily is the largest island in the Mediterranean, yet two of its three sides are visible from this point. An ancient traveler might have stood in wonder at the thought of the wealth and fertility that lay before him on the island.

Sicily was Rome's first overseas province and remained its most important. Famous in antiquity for its fertile soil, the island provided much of Rome's grain; it was rich in cattle as well. Lush and abundant, Sicily was a great prize. It fed the legions, and Spartacus might have reasoned that it could also feed his men. Then too, Sicily had long been a goal of Italy's runaway slaves, who sought refuge there. In addition, the island seemed ripe for subversion. By stirring up the embers of the slave revolts that had convulsed the island a generation before, Spartacus could threaten Rome's food supply and further shake the pillars of the social order. By transferring his men there from Italy he could save them from Crassus, even if only temporarily.

It surely occurred to Spartacus that Crassus could follow him across the strait. But Sicily might give him a respite to find ships and move on, perhaps to North Africa, which lay only ninety miles south of the Sicilian coast.

So Spartacus and his men might have reasoned when they reached the vicinity of Regium in late 72 B.C. All they had to do was cross a narrow body of water.

7

THE PIRATE

As THE PIRATE ships drew near to Syracuse, capital of the
Roman province of Sicily, the helmsmen took their bearings
from the rays of sunlight reflected off the golden shield on the front
of the temple of Athena—that is, if the corrupt Roman governor,
Gaius Verres, hadn't already looted it. If he had, well, never mind,
men like these, who knew how to ride the rough winter waves, could
find their own way to one of the most famous cities in the ancient
world. They traveled in four fast ships, small, sleek, and stripped for
action. The pirates tended to stay clear of Roman naval harbors but
today they were at ease. The night before they had run a squadron
of the Roman fleet ashore about twenty miles to the south and had
lit the night sky with their flames. They were pirates, captained by a
man named Heracleo.

That day they sailed into the turquoise waters of Syracuse's
Great Harbor, perhaps admiring the marble buildings of the old city
to starboard. They sailed right up to the quays. Then they held water
and, before the astonished and terrified eyes of the townspeople—

watching from a safe distance—they waved wild palm roots. It was the visual equivalent of blowing a raspberry. The pirates had captured the roots the day before from the Roman fleet. Roman sailors normally ate grain, not wild palm roots, but Verres, it seems, had sent his ships out undermanned, underfed, and poorly led. By waving the roots, Heracleo and his men taunted the Romans with their incompetence and shame. Then the victorious pirates sailed out of the harbor.

The details, like most involving Verres, may be exaggerated. The source is Cicero, who successfully prosecuted Verres for extortion in 70 B.C. and then laid it on thick when he published his speeches. Yet if the scene in Syracuse was extraordinary, the sight of pirates wasn't. Pirates were the hijackers and kidnappers of the ancient world and this was their heyday.

For a moment in late 72 B.C., Heracleo or men like him held Spartacus's fate in their hands. Pirate ships could carry the rebels across the Strait of Messina so they could reap all the strategic advantages offered by Sicily. What is more, the pirates might have done so with gusto, since they shared a common enemy in Rome. Driven to the toe of the Italian boot by a Roman army, Spartacus came up with possibly his most daring and ambitious move yet.

Pirates had terrorized the coast of Italy since 75 B.C. and other parts of the Mediterranean for many decades before that. They captured Roman celebrities: two praetors in their purple togas; Mark Antony's aunt; and most famous of all, Julius Caesar. He was kidnapped as a young man around 75 B.C. and held for forty days until he was ransomed. He then returned with a force of marines, rounded up his former captors, and had them crucified—just as he had promised them he would.

From a distance of centuries the pirates excite our admiration, but these pirates were no Robin Hoods. Their primary source of income lay in the slave trade. At first the Romans had been silent partners who were glad to buy free people from the eastern provinces snatched up by pirate slave traders. Eventually, however, the complaints of Roman friends and neighbors grew too loud. Beginning in 102 B.C., the Senate sent commanders out to suppress the pirates, but they had little success.

Spartacus surely knew much of this. Perhaps he also knew that after Rome turned on them, the pirates turned on Rome; they fought for Mithridates in the East and for Sertorius in the West. It made sense for Spartacus to seek help from them now, at the end of 72 B.C., as he and his men camped on the Italian side of the Strait of Messina. The rebels sat within sight of Sicily on a narrow strip of land between the mountains and the sea. Having reached the strait, the insurgents had traveled practically the entire length of the Italian peninsula, from the foothills of the Alps southward. But they had come to the end of the line.

It was, moreover, winter. Southern Italy does indeed have winter. The west coast, facing the Tyrrhenian Sea, suffers harsher conditions than the east coast, on the Ionian Sea; the rebels in Bruttium would have missed the mild winter around Thurii. Along the strait, the average temperatures in December and January range between 48 and 58 degrees Fahrenheit; rain is common and it can be windy. Some days the turbulent sea sends waves crashing against the shore of the strait. The mountains climb up rapidly from the coast; in the higher elevations, it snows. It was a difficult time of year to travel or fight, making the pirates' navigational experience especially valuable.

The pirates whom Spartacus met on the strait originally came from Cilicia, on Anatolia's Mediterranean coast, one of the main breeding grounds for pirates. Crete was the other. Whether Heracleo was one of the men whom Spartacus met on the strait is not known but he was certainly a typical pirate: a commander of small, speedy ships who looked down on the Romans but not without a healthy dose of fear. After all, the usual pirate raid was not as easy as Heracleo's Syracusan romp. Nor did every Roman governor leave the barn door as open as Verres did then; but even Verres sometimes rose to the occasion.

Thanks to Cicero, Verres survives in venom-soaked ink. According to the orator, Verres left Sicily defenseless while blackmailing wealthy natives with trumped-up charges of stirring up slave revolt. Cicero never mentions Spartacus but refers instead to the "great Italian war" or the "war of the Italian fugitives," thereby downplaying the seriousness of the problem facing Verres.

Fortunately, evidence in other writers and hints in Cicero's own work paint a more accurate picture. Verres was probably not caught flat-footed by Spartacus's approach toward the island. Verres knew all about the danger; indeed, one source says that the Senate extended Verres's governorship to three years instead of the usual one year so that, as an experienced administrator, he could put Sicily on a protective footing. That did not stop Verres from looting public and private artworks and shaking down wealthy landowners, but he did keep a lid on rebellion.

Cicero's contemporary the historian Sallust states flatly: "Gaius Verres strengthened the shores closest to Italy." As provincial governor, he had two legions at his disposal. Verrres might have ordered them to build shore defenses and establish guard posts on the coast. They no doubt sought help and local knowledge from the people of the main Sicilian city on the strait, Messana (modern Messina). It may not be coincidence that Messana was the one Sicilian city treated well by Verres, perhaps because he anticipated the danger.

Meanwhile, Verres claimed to have clamped down hard on the island's slaves. He said that he investigated charges of trouble brewing on various places all over the island, from near Lilybaeum (modern Marsala) and Panormus (modern Palermo) in the west to Apollonia (modern San Fratello) in the northeast and Imachara (near Enna) in central Sicily. Some of these places had been rebel strongholds in the earlier revolts. He ordered that slave suspects be arrested and tried, including farmhands, shepherds, farm managers, and master herdsmen. None of this impressed Cicero, who accused Verres of being lenient when he should have been harsh and harsh when he should have been lenient. Cicero charged Verres with taking bribes to release guilty slaves and with extorting money from innocent masters whom he threatened to arrest on trumped-up charges: he planned to accuse them of slackness toward their potentially rebellious slaves. Worst of all, Verres had a man crucified in Messana as a runaway slave and spy for Spartacus when, in fact, he was a Roman citizen, as a simple inquiry could have shown. The man in question was Publius Gavius, who came from either the city of Compsa (modern Conza) in Lucania or Consentia in Bruttium. A Roman citizen was exempt from the cross; even if guilty, he had the right to a lesser punishment.

Why a Roman citizen supported Spartacus is an interesting question. Was Gavius one of the "free men from the fields"—that is, a poor but free person—who joined the rebellion? Was he an elite and unreconstructed anti-Roman, so dogged in his Italian nationalism as to support a rebel slave general? Or did he simply work for Spartacus in exchange for pay? We can only guess at the answer or at the possibility that Gavius was innocent.

Verres, it seems, indeed denied Gavius his rights as a citizen, but no one can unravel the rights and wrongs of Cicero's other charges. The one sure conclusion is that some Sicilians genuinely worried about the spread of Spartacus's revolt to the island. That is no surprise, since the ancients had long memories. In 72 B.C., many Sicilians had lived through the Second Sicilian Slave War (104–100 B.C.). Thirty years before that had come the First Sicilian Slave War (135–132 B.C.), and now the wheel might seem to have turned ominously again. The root causes of rebellion no doubt remained. Each war, after all, had broken out against a background of abuse and humiliation of slaves and the toleration of armed gangs of slave herdsmen who eventually turned on their masters with a vengeance.

The slave uprisings had ravaged the island. Each had lasted about four years and involved tens of thousands of rebels. Each broke out in the rich farmland of the island's interior and spread. In each revolt, gangs of rebel herdsmen played a prominent role. Each time, urban slaves joined rebels from the countryside, as did most poverty-stricken free Sicilians.

Rome responded slowly and badly each time. After several humiliating defeats in the first revolt, the consul Publius Rupilius laid siege to the two main rebel cities and each time found a traitor to open the gates. Then he engaged in mopping-up operations around the island. After a series of incompetent generals failed to put down the second rebellion, the consul Manius Aquilius rose to the occasion. He killed the rebel king in single combat, which would have won him Rome's highest military honor had his opponent been a free man and not a slave.

Now another rebel, Spartacus, was waiting for the pirates. Their swift ships would carry him across the strait to break the chains of Sicily's slaves. Ancient Sicily teemed with agricultural wealth. Its soil was much more fertile than Bruttium's. As the hungry rebels watched the sun set behind Sicily's hills night after night, and then saw its afterglow shining in the clouds, they might have dreamed of a new life on the island. The pirates could provide that, but naturally, they presented a bill for their services. Any losses, should the Romans fight them at sea, would be expensive to replace. The pirates also demanded payment in advance. Spartacus apparently understood this, and he gave them gifts. "Gift" was a flexible word in the ancient vocabulary, meaning, among other things, bribes.

The plan was that the pirates would ferry two thousand men across to Sicily. This represented just a small portion of Spartacus's army but it probably was the best thing under the circumstances. Pirate ships were small and could not carry large numbers of men. The two thousand could serve as an advance party. Assuming they had been carefully chosen, they would have been elite fighters, skilled at stealth and able to make contact with Sicilian slaves. As soon as they had established a base, they could bring more men over from Italy. Meanwhile, the bulk of Spartacus's army could go to ground in Bruttium's hills.

But it was not to be. As the sources state succinctly, "Once the Cilicians had made an agreement with him [Spartacus] and taken gifts, they tricked him and sailed off." Had Verres or Crassus been in touch with the pirates and outbid Spartacus? Did a dawning awareness of Rome's military might scare off men like Heracleo despite their sympathy for the rebels? Or did the pirates simply behave like pirates?

In any case, they left. Spartacus's Sicilian expedition seemed to be over before it had begun. Yet once again the Thracian displayed his strength of character. He neither despaired nor panicked but instead changed tactics with seeming effortlessness. His followers might have been less calm. If ever Spartacus needed his Thracian lady to inspire their faith, it was now.

Between Sicily and the Italian mainland lies a body of water that is one of the world's more dramatic and dangerous because of its fast current and treacherous riptides. "The narrowness of the passage," writes the Greek historian Thucydides, "and the strength of the current that pours in from the vast Tyrrhenian and Sicilian mains, have rightly given it a bad reputation." The Strait of Messina is about nineteen miles long. About nine miles at its widest, the strait is narrowest at its northern end; on the Italian side sits a narrow piece of land called Cape Caenys (the modern Punta Pezzo), in the modern city of Villa San Giovanni. Here, where the strait is not quite two miles wide, you can almost feel Spartacus's frustration.

Looking across the strait from Cape Caenys, a person might have read the fortune of the rebellion in the landscape. Sicily lies ahead, seemingly close enough to touch. To the north sits the island's end, Cape Pelorus (modern Peloro), a narrow, low-lying spit of soil. A mile or so southeast of the cape the mountains of Sicily begin to rise gently, like a body slowly waking up. They climb in stately measure ever southward, toward Mount Aetna (modern Etna), the great volcano that stands just out of sight.

A harsher landscape lies on the Italian side. At Cape Caenys, the last stretch of the Apennines tumbles down to the sea, in steplike ridges cut by gullies and crossed by zigzag roads. Above, a massive hill rises like a closed fist. Traveling only about a mile, the land rises sharply from sea level to two thousand feet. These are the foothills of the Aspromonte Mountains (modern name). *Aspromonte* means "harsh mountains" or "white mountains," the latter referring to snow or perhaps to bare rock. It was hostile terrain, in either case.

The Via Annia from Capua reached the strait about three miles south of the narrows at Cape Caenys, at the ancient Statio ad Statuam (modern Catona). The favorable current made this the crossing place of choice in ancient times. Nowadays, there is an hourly car ferry to Sicily nearby. Rowboats cross the strait here, and in summer swimmers race across. But swimming was out of the question for men who would emerge on the Sicilian shore naked and dripping and into the arms of Verres's soldiers, if they would emerge at all. An inexpert swimmer might find it rough going. A current of six knots or more (depending on the tides) flows through the strait, often accompanied by sudden waves and whirlpools. Besides, it was not summer but winter. The gray-green water of the winter strait is too cold for swimming.

The ancients personified the dangerous seas of the Strait in the myth of Scylla and Charybdis. Charybdis was a sea monster whose huge mouth swallowed and spit out water, creating killer whirlpools. Scylla was a doglike beast that sat on a huge rock on the other side of a strait and killed passing sailors. According to myth only the greatest of helmsmen could pick his way between Scylla and Charybdis. The Greeks and Romans placed these two creatures in the Strait of Messina. The real strait posed more manageable challenges, which Spartacus decided to face. He told the men to build rafts.

The decision to construct rafts was risky but rational. If it was not easy to cross the strait by raft, neither was it impossible. Legend says that the prehistoric settlers of the island, the Sicels, did so. Thucydides, a Greek historian and hard-nosed former admiral, considered this tradition credible, as long as the Sicels had waited for the wind to die down before they made the crossing. More recently, a Roman general and consul had managed the crossing by rafts. Lucius Caecilius Metellus, victor in a battle in Sicily against Carthage, came to Messana in 250 B.C. in order to cross back to Italy. He had captured 120 elephants from the enemy and he wanted to bring these exotic imports back to Rome to march them in his triumphal parade. An ancient writer explains how Metellus ferried them across the strait:

A number of huge jars, separated by wooden stays, were fastened together in such a way that they could neither break apart nor yet strike together; then this framework was spanned by beams, and on top of all earth and brush were placed, and the surface was fenced in round about, so that it presented somewhat the appearance of a farmyard. The beasts were then put on board this raft and were ferried across without knowing that they were moving on the water.

Spartacus's men used what look like similar raft-building techniques, maybe as a result of recruiting local helpers. The fish-rich waters of the strait surely employed many boatbuilders. A contemporary source describes the rebels' rafts: "When they placed large, wide-mouthed jars under the beams, they tied them together with vine branches or strips of hide."

Building rafts required finding jars, timber, vine branches, and strips of hide, and that would have taken foraging in turn. Houses, shops, cellars, warehouses, farms, and forests might all have been scoured for supplies. It seems unlikely that the rebels did this at their leisure or with their full attention. Some of their manpower had to be devoted to finding food and the rest had to handle security, in case there were a raid by Crassus.

Where Spartacus launched his rafts is not known. The currents favored the ferry crossing at the Statio ad Statuam, but the Romans knew that, and they surely lined the opposite shore. Cape Caenys offered a narrower crossing and perhaps a chance to surprise the enemy on the beach in Sicily. The dangerous currents there would have made it risky to depart from Cape Caenys, but Spartacus was a risk taker. A launch from Cape Caenys would help explain what happened next, but of course it is not possible to be certain. An ancient source picks up the story: "They tried to launch rafts of beams and large, wide-mouthed jugs tied together with brush and branches in the very swift waters of the Strait—in vain." Moreover, "The entangled rafts were hindering the provision of help."

Nature, it seems, kept the rebels from crossing. In the fast and shifting currents the rafts got caught on each other, and no one was able to repair that tangle. Surely they lost boats and provisions and perhaps some men drowned, too. Metellus had done better, but he no doubt chose the least dangerous place to cross the channel. He enjoyed superior logistical support to Spartacus and could get more experienced helmsmen. Few if any of the rebels had experience steering ships, but they might have persuaded or forced locals to help. Besides, Metellus might have crossed in summer or, if not, he could have waited for a day of good conditions to make the crossing, a luxury surely denied to Spartacus.

Spartacus's attempt to cross the strait failed. He now had to turn his army around to force his way back through Roman Italy. The opposing general whom he would face, Crassus, had worked wonders

AMPHITHEATER. The arena at Avella (ancient Abella) in Campania is one of Italy's earliest surviving sites of gladiatorial combat. (Barry Strauss)

MARBLE RELIEF OF GLADIATORS. A pair of *provocatores* fights on the left. To their right stands a *murmillo* like Spartacus; all that is visible of his opponent (extreme right) is a small, rectangular shield, which probably identifies him as a *thraex*. (Erich Lessing/Art Resource, NY)

SLAVE SALE. This close-up of a first-century B.C. tombstone from Capua shows a slave on the auction block. (Barry Strauss by courtesy of the Museo Campano)

VESUVIUS. The rugged outline of the mountain that sheltered Spartacus and his followers rises in the distance behind the forum of Pompeii. (Barry Strauss)

BACCHUS AND VESUVIUS.
A Roman fresco showing a grape-covered god of wine alongside Mount Vesuvius and a snake, symbol of fertility. (Scala/Art Resource, NY)

THRACIAN WOMAN. This Thracian worshipper of Dionysus has tattoos on both arms. She is brandishing a sword. (Erich Lessing/Art Resource, NY)

THRACIAN HORSEMAN. A gilded, silver plate from Thrace showing a hunter on horseback, a heroic image of Thracian manhood. It is dated to the fourth century B.C. (Erich Lessing/Art Resource, NY)

CELT FIGHTING ROMAN. A long-haired, mustachioed Celt wields a sword against a legionary in this stone relief from Rome. (Erich Lessing/Art Resource, NY)

LEGIONARIES. This Roman sarcophagus depicts warriors about to sacrifice to Mars. Note the long shields, the body armor, and the plumed helmets. (Erich Lessing/Art Resource, NY)

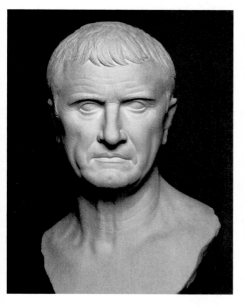

CRASSUS. The scholarly consensus is that this marble bust represents the general who defeated Spartacus. (Ny Carlsberg Glyptotek, Copenhagen)

POMPEY. This marble bust shows Crassus's rival, the general whose troops killed 5,000 fleeing followers of Spartacus. (Bildarchiv Preussischer Kulturbesitz/Art Resource, NY)

MELÌA RIDGE. A view, looking westward, of the rugged mountain ridge that is plausibly where Crassus and Spartacus fought in the winter of 71 B.C. (Barry Strauss)

CATO THE YOUNGER. A bronze bust of the austere stoic who fought against Spartacus in 72 B.C. (Erich Lessing/Art Resource, NY)

STRAIT OF MESSINA. A view westward from mainland Italy (foreground) to Sicily (distance) across one of the narrowest parts of the channel. (Barry Strauss)

APPIAN WAY. The great highway at Minturnae, which lies northwest of Capua. Here the road might have been lined with crosses holding Spartacus's defeated followers. (Barry Strauss)

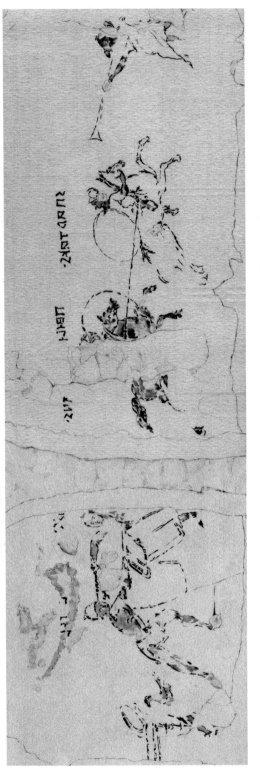

SPARTACUS FRESCO. On the far right, a trumpeter signals the clash of two gladiators on horseback. The rider on the right is labeled "SPARTAKS" (read right to left), which is Oscan for "Spartacus." To the riders' left stand two gladiators in combat, with a small structure to the left of them that may possibly be an altar. (Jon Reis, Courtesy of the Istituto Poligrafico e Zecca dello Stato, Rome)

with his legions but he had not yet turned them into force that could hunt down and destroy Spartacus's army. On the contrary, it seems that Crassus had done nothing to stop Spartacus at the strait. Instead he held back and left the job to Verres. The governor of Sicily either had Neptune on his side or good strategy.

One ancient source, Cicero, gives credit elsewhere. The orator praised Marcus Crassus, "that bravest of men, whose courage and good judgment saw to it that the fugitives were not able to tie rafts together and cross the Strait." Cicero speaks of a great effort made to stop the rebels from crossing. He offers no details, however. Did Crassus attack Spartacus on the beach? Spartacus had cavalry to defend his position; Crassus's behavior in the next month shows reluctance to take Spartacus head-on.

Besides, the circumstances of Cicero's comments raise suspicion. He made them in 70 B.C. while prosecuting Verres for alleged misbehavior as governor of Sicily. Cicero aimed all his rhetorical power at Verres, ridiculing the governor's arrogance for claiming the credit for stopping Spartacus. Cicero won the case and Verres was ruined, but what if Verres was right? The weight of the evidence says that he did as much as any Roman to win the battle of the strait by deploying his forces opposite the most advantageous point for crossing the water.

In fact, it is hard not to suspect Crassus actually of encouraging Spartacus to try to cross the strait. Crassus surely was in contact with Verres and knew of the governor's efforts to stop the rebels from landing on the island. Scouting reports that the enemy was building rafts might not have worried Crassus, given the season. All in all, Crassus might have been confident that Spartacus would fail.

Crassus would not have wanted to risk attacking the rebels on the strait. The narrow coastal strip offered little room for the pitched battle that he desired. Besides, if challenged, Spartacus would send his men into the hills rather than agree to fight such a battle. His cavalry would harass the Romans while his infantry laid ambushes in the many hills and gullies of the region. On top of all that, it was winter, and no time for fighting. Rather than risk such engagements, Crassus had a different plan: to squeeze the rebels between the strait and the mountains.

Spartacus had no choice now but to retreat. No doubt the need to leave Italy was clearer than ever but the Strait of Messina would not be the exit. The Thracian would have to come up with a new strategy. That, however, lay in the future; at the moment, his priority was feeding the army. There was food about a dozen miles to the south, in the city of Regium, but the town was walled and no doubt well defended. The next easiest alternative was to head north on the Via Annia, but the Romans surely had that road well blocked. So Spartacus and his followers took the least desirable escape route and climbed into the Aspromonte Mountains.

If any of Spartacus's marching men turned and watched the sun disappear behind Sicily's hills, we do not know. But if they did, they might have paused and thought about what might have been.

8

THE FISHERMAN

IT WAS A winter morning in the mountains, three thousand feet above sea level, in early 71 B.C. Normally it was silent here in winter, when even the herdsmen had left for lower ground. On this day, however, on a ridge about half a mile wide, two armies were about to meet. In one, tens of thousands of rebels stood in their ranks, weapons ready, and, we might imagine, hearts warmed by wine, ears impatient for the command to have their mouths let loose the roar that signals the start of their charge. The Roman army was not surprised; its scouts had watched the enemy from a series of signal towers.

The Romans waited behind a defensive network of deep trenches lined with sharpened poles, wooden palisades, and, as an obstacle in the forefront, an embankment topped by a dry-stone wall at least twenty-five feet high. The Romans' positions closed off three sides of the ridge, blocking even the mule paths by which the rebels might have outflanked them. The Romans had left only the southern approach open, forcing the attackers to charge at them from that direction. As they advanced, the rebels were funneled into a narrow space.

Like a fisherman who drives big fish into his nets, Crassus had set his trap well.

Suddenly the Roman counterattack began, a torrent of arrows and acorn-shaped lead missiles, forged in field furnaces nearby by the methodical defenders. The barrage blunted the rebels' charge. Many of the attackers reached the fortifications and fought ferociously, but they could not break through. Eventually, Spartacus's men had no choice but to run away or die.

It was a good day for Rome and it had just begun. The rebels would attack again in the evening, and once again they would fail. Afterward the Romans claimed an immense body count, saying that twelve thousand dead insurgents cost Rome only three dead and seven wounded. Ancient battles often produced lopsided casualty rates but this sounds like propaganda. Uncertainty is frustrating to the historian but it is best to be clear: both these figures and the very details of the engagement are speculative. Indeed, our knowledge of the events in this chapter is unusually tentative, and for several reasons. The sources contradict each other even more than usual. Perhaps that is not surprising in the case of events that took place in the dead of winter, deep in the mountains of a remote corner of Italy.

Besides, for Romans the domestic political stakes were almost as high as the military ones. Crassus had gambled everything on a defensive line in the mountains. The massive fortifications symbolized the man who had made his fortune in real estate. He would defeat Spartacus by outbuilding him. Some said that Crassus gave his men the construction job just to keep them busy during winter, the off-season for warfare. That sounds like false modesty. Crassus cared too much about his command to fill it with make-work projects. He knew that the campaign in Bruttium would make or break him.

Crassus wanted to defeat Spartacus, but if he couldn't, he had to control the way the story was told to the Roman public. To do so he needed influential friends, and surely he obtained them. A man who could buy armies could afford the rewards that would cement friendships. We might suspect the hand of his publicists, for example, in the assertion in the sources that the Romans had got their courage back thanks only to Crassus's policy of decimation. The campaign in Bruttium proved to be intensely controversial. We will never know precisely what happened there, but we can pick our way cautiously through the evidence.

In spite of exaggerated casualty figures, a Roman victory that day is a reasonable assumption. The Romans had earned success. Crassus and his men had spent weeks if not a month or two preparing a killing field. The Romans could have ended the rebellion that very day if they hadn't faced a general of the Thracian's skill. But we are getting ahead of ourselves.

For Spartacus the story began on the day that he marched his men from the Strait of Messina toward the Aspromonte Mountains. He could not take the Via Annia near the coast, as the Romans surely would have blocked it. Besides, Spartacus had to feed his army. To do that required going inland on raids and in pursuit of new supporters. This was herding country, known for its cows, sheep, and swine. It was terrain for hunting hare and boar. As the rebels traveled northeast from the strait over the highland plains of Aspromonte they probably got some of what they wanted by charming slave herdsmen—and the rest they took. Wherever they went, the rebels ravaged countryside.

Archaeology may provide evidence of the damage they did. About twenty-five miles north of Cape Caenys, in an olive grove near the Tyrrhenian Sea, a treasure recently turned up. There, buried and protected by two large slabs of stone, lay a clay lamp and a group of silver objects: pitchers, cups, a ladle, a teaspoon, and a medallion with a bust of Medusa. A graffito may refer to the name of a wealthy Roman landowning family. The objects date to the period circa 100–75 B.C. and it is tempting to associate them with Spartacus. They were buried in an isolated spot in ancient times, far from the center of the nearest town. Perhaps a landowner buried them to keep them from the rebels or a rebel might have buried them himself after looting them.

Having turned away from the coastal highway, Spartacus headed for another road located in the center of Bruttium, about equidistant from the Tyrrhenian and Ionian coasts. Migrants over the centuries had traveled down this road from the Serre Mountains (modern name) to the north, and with good reason. The road takes advantage of a remarkable landscape, a ridge high up on the crest of the Aspromonte Mountains. From a distance it looks like a tabletop in the clouds. As a traveler comes onto the plateau, he feels as if he has stepped onto an isthmus. Today called the Dossone della Melìa, that is, the Melìa Ridge, it lies between three thousand and four thousand feet above sea level. The ancient highway ran along the ridge on a north-south axis. In the eighteenth century it was called the Via Grande or "Great Way"; the modern road follows its path. Adding to the ridge's strategic importance, roads branched from it eastward and westward, via high mountain passes (about three thousand feet high), to the Ionian and Tyrrhenian seas.

The city of Locris sat at the eastern end of the lateral road, on the Ionian Sea. A former Greek colony, Locris had long been firmly in the Roman orbit. At the western end of the lateral road the plain of Metauros (modern Gioia Tauro) stretched along the Tyrrhenian Sea. Exceptionally rich, the plain was known for its olives and grapevines. Crassus's fortifications cut it off from Spartacus and his raiders.

Whoever controlled the Melìa Ridge controlled the crossroads of southernmost Italy. No wonder that Crassus chose to make his stand here. The sources say that the nature of the terrain suggested to Crassus the plan to block off the peninsula. The Locrians might well have provided detailed intelligence about the lay of the land.

The heart of Crassus's fortifications stood on the Melia Ridge near the modern Highway 111, which runs on an east-west line about fifty miles northeast of Regium (by modern roads). Here the Italian peninsula is only about thirty-five miles wide from sea to sea. Plutarch writes that Crassus built his wall across the peninsula for a length of three hundred stades, that is, about thirty-five modern miles. That is an exaggeration; in fact, the main section of the Romans' defensive works covered only half a mile. But Plutarch is right in implying that Crassus effectively blocked off the entire thirty-five-mile width of the peninsula.

As Spartacus proceeded northward, his scouts warned him of trouble ahead. The Thracian is said to have responded with scorn, no doubt skeptical that the Romans could stop him in what amounted to his natural habitat, the mountains. Many scholars seem to feel about the same way. They doubt that the Romans made their stand here. Great engineers though they were, not even the Romans could have found it easy to build a thirty-five-mile-long walled trench—through the mountains, no less. Besides, if Crassus had cut off Spartacus about fifty miles northeast of Regium, he would have left the rebels in control of a large territory to the south, about a thousand square miles in size, roughly equivalent to the American state of Rhode Island or the English county of Hampshire. One might well ask, left to rule such a kingdom, why would Spartacus need to leave?

Some historians turn Crassus's plan into a modest project: no thirty-five-mile-long set of fortifications, no willingness to give up a thousand square miles to the enemy. In their view, Crassus went toe to toe with Spartacus from the outset by marching ever southward, practically up to Spartacus's camp on the strait. The Romans fortified the ravines in the steep hills above the coast to cut the rebels off, no more than a mile or two away. The result was a line of fortifications no more than a mile or so long. While his men were negotiating with pirates and building rafts, Spartacus could see the Romans right nearby.

But Spartacus is unlikely to have sat back and let Crassus corner him. In order to build his trap, Crassus would have had to work far from his enemy's eyes, not under his nose. So, while Spartacus camped on the coast, Crassus's men were dozens of miles away and three thousand feet higher up in the hills.

Yes, an instant thirty-five-mile-long defensive system strains credulity but only if we fail to take into account the lay of the land. In fact, most of the thirty-five-mile width of the peninsula is impassable, so it required little fortification. East of the Melia Ridge the land dips down toward the Ionian Sea via a series of rocky glens, while west of the ridge there lie vast and impenetrable gorges. The only places that could be easily traveled were the two coastal strips and the Melia Ridge—the latter, only about a half-mile wide. Since the Romans occupied the coasts and since Spartacus took readily to the mountains, Crassus could reasonably expect to block him on the Ridge.

The thousand square miles behind Spartacus were no gift. The territory in question is poor, mountainous, and largely infertile, unlike Sicily and its abundance. Nor was it harvest season. The rebels would have found it difficult to live off this land for long. It is not surprising to read in the ancient sources that Spartacus's men were beginning to run out of food, nor that one reason Crassus decided to build the fortifications was precisely to deprive the enemy of supplies.

Archaeological evidence tends to support this scenario, although it doesn't prove it. On the Melia Ridge there are a series of old trenches and walls, and in the hills nearby are the ruins of three lead-smelting furnaces whose internal walls are sprinkled with lead oxide. The Romans used furnaces to make sling bullets. Without scientific archaeological excavation, these sites cannot be securely dated. But they do fit the description in the sources of a system of trenches—while also casting well-founded doubt on Plutarch's claim that the Romans cut a trench from sea to sea. In addition, the ruins have been surveyed by a local historian in southern Italy—an amateur who, as often happens, knows the terrain better than the professionals. The opening paragraphs of this chapter follow his plausible if still unproven reconstruction.

The origin of place names is notoriously difficult to pin down, but even so, several places in and around the Melia Ridge have evocative names. A section of the ridge is known as the Plains of Marco, leading down into Marco's Ridge (Marcus Licinius Crassus?); to the west there is a town of Scrofario (Crassus's lieutenant, Scrofa?); to the east are hamlets of Case Romano and Contrada Romano ("Roman Houses," "Roman Neighborhood") and a place called Torre lo Schiavo ("The Slave's Tower").

Perhaps the most intriguing place name is the heart of the Melia Ridge, today covered by a huge forest of ferns with scattered groups of beech trees: "Tonnara," that is, "tuna trap." The slopes to the west of Tonnara are called "Chiusa" or "Chiusa Grande" ("Enclosure" or "Great Enclosure"). *Tonnara* refers to the traditional Mediterranean practice of catching tuna by blocking their migration route with complex systems of fixed nets. Ancient fishermen regularly practiced tuna trap fishing off the coasts of southern Italy and Sicily. "Tonnara" would make an appropriate name for the place where the insurgents were trapped on their trek northward.

Spartacus had failed to break out and he had taken casualties, but he had no reason to despair. Far from being trapped, he might have reasoned that he now had Crassus locked in an encounter that could destroy either one. Help, he knew, was on the way. His cavalry had not reached him yet; no doubt they were still scouring the countryside for food and supporters. Once they arrived, the horses might provide the punch to allow him to break through. Meanwhile,

if Spartacus could not survive indefinitely on the Melia Ridge, neither could Crassus.

Spartacus's main problem was logistical; he needed to feed his
army. He would find little food on the ridge. In the summer it was
good grazing ground for cattle, and the humidity made it rich in
mushrooms. It was winter, however, so the army depended on raids
down in the valleys.

Crassus's main problem was political. Rome wanted him to crush
the enemy, but Crassus preferred strangulation, and that took time.
Spartacus increased Roman frustration by prolonging the struggle.
He distracted, exasperated, and delayed the enemy. As the sources
say, Spartacus "annoyed the men in the defensive works in many
ways from place to place; he constantly fell upon them unawares
and threw bundles of wood into the trenches that he had set on fire,
which gave the Romans nasty and difficult work" as they hustled to
put out the fires.

It was effective psychological warfare while Spartacus waited for
his cavalry, but the struggle in the mountains took a toll on his own
men. It was the crowning misery of months of trouble since November, when Crassus had come onto the scene. Back in the summer,
when they had defeated two consuls and the governor of Cisalpine
Gaul, the insurgents could never have guessed that it would come to
this. Even a few weeks earlier, although things were difficult, at least
they faced the possibility of escaping to Sicily. Now they were fighting for their lives in the chilly clouds of Italy's forgotten mountains.
Conditions were miserable, food was in short supply, and it would be
surprising if some men weren't deserting. The Thracian decided to
shock them out of their funk.

"He crucified a Roman prisoner in the space between the two
armies," the sources report, "thereby showing to his own men the
sight of what they could expect if they did not win the victory." There
was nothing subtle about this gesture, but it was no exaggeration.

The Romans did not plan to issue pardons. They regularly crucified runaway slaves. Besides, it was an age of massacres, from Sulla's proscription of the wealthy and his execution of thousands of prisoners of war to Mithridates' massacre of tens of thousands of Italian traders and tax collectors in Anatolia.

Apparently Spartacus made his point. His men showed no further signs of weakness, at least none that the Romans could see. If we believe one source, the Romans blinked next, but not on the Melia Ridge. If anything, the sight of a Roman prisoner on the cross might have stiffened their will. Rather, it was back in Rome, in the Forum, where the Roman people let their frustration spill over. Disappointed by the developing stalemate, they voted to recall Pompey from Spain where he was reestablishing order after the defeat of Sertorius.

Pompey had won the war against Sertorius in late 73 and early 72 B.C. He never managed to defeat Sertorius in the field, but Pompey inflicted enough damage to cause a mutiny. Rivals emerged among the rebels and made contacts with the Romans, who encouraged their plans to assassinate the leader. Betrayed by his allies, Sertorius was murdered at a banquet in his own tent. It was the summer or autumn of 73 B.C. The chief turncoat, Marcus Perperna, tried to continue the war against Rome, but sometime in winter or spring of 72 B.C., Pompey defeated him and had him executed. The rebellion in Spain was over.

The recall of Pompey was a popular act, voted in the Roman assembly. The Senate was no doubt less enthusiastic, because it meant that Pompey could march into Italy with his army intact, instead of dissolving it at the border, as commanders usually were required to do. Memories of Sulla gave a sinister tinge to Pompey's advance. Spartacus must have worried the senators more.

No one, however, could have hated the recall of Pompey more than Crassus. He had wanted the war against Spartacus to build his own career, not Pompey's. Now he would have to share the credit for victory. Thus Plutarch's claim that Crassus himself wrote to the Senate and asked that Pompey be recalled sounds preposterous, but it might just be true. Perhaps Crassus's agents in Rome had sniffed the change in the political winds. Perhaps they recognized the inevitability of the people's vote, and perhaps they advised Crassus to write to the Senate and thereby seem to be the master of events.

Crassus's letter is supposed to have asked for the recall of another general besides Pompey, Marcus Terentius Varro Lucullus. Marcus, governor of Macedonia in 72 B.C., had just led a successful campaign against the Bessi, a tough Thracian people once described as "worse than snow." Marcus Lucullus is not to be confused with his brother Lucius Licinius Lucullus, who was busy at the time commanding Roman troops against Mithridates in Anatolia but is better known today for his love of gastronomy—hence the adjective *Lucullan*. By asking for *two* generals to help him, Crassus downgraded Pompey's importance.

It was a Machiavellian plan, but Spartacus's next move was even more so. Apparently he got wind that Pompey was coming. It is not difficult to imagine Roman soldiers, lining the walls, hurling taunts at the enemy: Pompey was coming and they had better watch out. Pompey had a reputation: his nickname, earned in the Sullan era, was "the teenage butcher." His name might indeed have frightened some of the rebels, but Spartacus saw through it.

If Spartacus understood Pompey as a threat, he also recognized an opportunity. Pompey gave Crassus and Spartacus a common enemy. They both wanted to keep him out of the war, which would explain Spartacus's next move: he offered Crassus a peace treaty. In particular, he offered something very Roman, which was to ask Rome to accept him into its *fides*. *Fides* is an important Latin word with a rich set of meanings. It means "faith" or "trust" and, in this case, "protection." By accepting someone into its fides, Rome accepted a set of mutual obligations. We might call it an alliance but the Romans would not have done so, since there was no legal contract between the two parties. Instead moral ties bound them. The Romans considered the object of their fides to be a client, not an ally; they considered themselves to be his patron.

The ties of fides could prove binding indeed. The Second Punic War (218–201 B.C.), for instance, the worst war in Rome's history, began because Hannibal attacked the Spanish city of Saguntum, which had no alliance with Rome, merely a relationship of fides. However seriously Rome took a fides relationship, the man who negotiated it, usually a general, regarded it with even more importance. He became the personal patron of Rome's client, with whom he enjoyed especially intense ties. If Crassus had accepted Spartacus's offer, he would have become the Thracian's patron.

Doing so would have been repugnant. Rome regarded a request for fides as a formal act of surrender, but even so, it conferred a "most beautiful dignity" on the client. By accepting the Thracian into his fides, Crassus would have conceded not only Spartacus's dignity but also Spartacus's right to settle his men somewhere in safety. That would never do. To grant such honor to runaway slaves and gladiators was out of the question. Rome wanted Spartacus's head, not his handshake. Crassus disdainfully ignored the offer.

Yet, what magnificent gall on Spartacus's part the proposal was! Far from conceding defeat, he asserted his right to respect. If nothing else this tactic might have been a morale booster for his men. If he was stuck in Crassus's trap, Spartacus did not show it. In fact, he was about to demonstrate his ability to escape, because his cavalry had finally arrived. It was now about February.

Spartacus waited for a storm. He chose a night of snow and wind. An old hand like him would have guessed that in these conditions, the Roman garrison would be "below strength and at that time off its guard," as one ancient source says. The sources disagree as to just how he made the attack. One writer says that he used the cavalry to spearhead the charge through the ill-maintained defenses. Another says that he filled in a small part of the trenches with earth, wood, and branches for his army to cross. A third writer agrees that Spartacus filled in part of the trenches but with the corpses of prisoners whom he had executed and the carcasses of cattle. On another occasion, in A.D. 26, a Thracian army attacked a Roman camp by filling in its trenches with bushes, fences, and dead bodies, so we can imagine Spartacus using a variety of objects.

The sources disagree as well about the level of Spartacus's success. One writer says that he managed to extricate only one-third of his army before the Romans closed the gap again. Another insists that Spartacus got his entire army through. An ingenious scholar has tried to square the circle by saying that once Spartacus got part of his army through, Crassus had to abandon the fortifications or else he would have been caught between two threats. Hence the other two-thirds of the army was able to escape as well. In any case, the sources cite huge numbers of rebel slaves at large in the next phase of the war; they also mention Crassus's fear that Spartacus might now march on Rome. This suggests that, one way or another, Spartacus got most of his men out of Crassus's net.

Crassus had gambled and failed. Spartacus had paid a price in blood but he had broken free. It was a tremendous victory for the slaves and a bitter defeat for the Romans. There was nothing for the Romans now but to abandon the defenses they had worked so hard to build and to return to the pursuit. Once again, Spartacus had forced a campaign of maneuver and mobility, at which he excelled.

Spartacus displayed his mastery of the art of tactics. Breaking through fixed defenses is often difficult, particularly against defenders as good at fortifications as the Romans were. Spartacus, therefore, had reason for pride after his breakout but not for false hope. With Crassus behind him and Pompey expected to appear, the rebels continued to enjoy poor strategic prospects. Now, as always, Spartacus had only one reasonable goal: leaving Italy. But how? The Alps had overwhelmed them and the sea had betrayed them. Spartacus might think of finding new and trustworthy pirates somewhere. He might even contemplate persuading the army to march back north and give the Alpine passes another try. But not now; surely his battered people needed rest. That reasoning, at any rate, might explain the statement in the sources that his goal now was Samnium.

Samnium is a region of the south-central Apennines, lying north and northeast of Capua. It was famously rugged and anti-Roman. Sulla's army had destroyed Samnium's elite military manpower at the Battle of the Colline Gate in 82 B.C., so Samnium could offer Spartacus little support from its free population. With the help of local slaves, however, the rebels might have carved out a retreat in Samnium's remote hills. Perhaps they had already found assistance there in their march north in spring 72 B.C. Spartacus's knowledge of Samnium might even have dated back to his days in the House of Vatia in Capua. So Spartacus led his army northward through Bruttium and back into Lucania, heading for Samnium.

But it was not to be. The rebel army broke up again. As one source says, "they began to disagree among themselves." As before, the split had an ethnic component. A large contingent of Celts and Germans decided to go off on their own. Their leaders were named Castus and Cannicus (or Gannicus). The sources put the group at well over thirty thousand men but the figures are, at best, educated guesses. It is not clear if all the Celts and Germans in the rebellion joined them, nor do we know if any other nationalities chose the splinter group.

In any case, we needn't conclude that the split was just a matter of tribal politics. A reasonable person might have argued that Spartacus had failed and needed to be replaced; his Sicilian strategy, it could have been said, had wasted valuable time and lives. If he had saved the army on the Melia Ridge, he had also brought it there in the first place. According to the sources, before he learned about the breakup, Crassus was afraid that Spartacus was leading his men toward Rome again. This may be just what Castus and Cannicus wanted to do. Dreaming of storming the enemy's citadel, perhaps they scorned the idea of retreating to Samnium.

So, for the second time, the rebel army broke in two. Crassus surely took heart.

TO THE DEATH

9

THE CELTIC WOMEN

I T WAS JUST before dawn and the light was still dim. In approximately March, 71 B.C., in the hills of northern Lucania, the two women probably felt a chill in the air as they climbed the mountainside. Budding branches alternated with green-clad pines, and there might even have been some snow on the peak. The women were Celts, members of the breakaway army of rebel slaves led by Castus and Cannicus. Privacy is a rare luxury in an army on the move. This morning, though, they had needed to get away from the crowd in order to carry out monthly rituals. They might have been druids, and privacy, a sacred grove, and precision in timing were essential elements of Celtic religion.

The nature of their rite is unclear. Celtic rituals were legion; as Caesar wrote, "the whole of the Gallic people is passionately devoted to matters of religion." Celtic women commonly met in small groups to call on the gods. "The magic of women" galvanized many in Celtic society. As for the two women on the mountain, Sallust says that they were "fulfilling their monthly things." Some scholars take this as a reference to menstruation, while others consider it a reference to the phases of the moon, pointing out that the Celtic religion paid close attention to the calendar. (The moon is still visible in predawn light.) Plutarch says that the women were "sacrificing on behalf of the enemies" (that is, Rome's enemies: the women's own soldiers). These possibilities are not mutually exclusive. Many religions connect the menstrual and lunar cycles, and many communities link their success with women's fertility.

The two women stumbled upon the sight of Roman soldiers, six thousand men carrying out the mission of circling around the enemy and taking unobserved a ridge of the same mountain the women were climbing, Mount Camalatrum. Crassus had sent the men under the command of Caius Pomptinus and Quintus Marcius Rufus while he prepared to lead the main attack from another direction. The men under Pomptinus and Rufus had gone to the trouble of camouflaging their helmets, an effort that kept them invisible from any scouts that the rebels might have posted. The Romans were on the verge of achieving complete strategic surprise when the two women discovered them. If they managed to sound the alarm, the Romans' battle plan would unravel and yet another of Crassus's traps would snap shut empty.

Unfortunately for Crassus the two women rose to the occasion. They did not panic, which is no surprise, given the ancient evidence. A Roman writer says Celtic women were always ready to help beleaguered husbands by charging into battle, where they would bite and kick the enemy. Archaeological evidence shows elite Celtic women buried with chariots and weapons. So, on that day in 71 B.C., hurrying back to camp in order to sound the alarm was easy.

The incident symbolizes how much had gone wrong for the rebels and yet how formidable they remained. Their divided forces paid less attention to security than to religion. Yet religion encouraged a spirit of resistance, as the Celtic women show.

Earlier, the news that the rebels had divided their forces had probably proven a tonic to Crassus. Any gloom over the prospect of Spartacus's whole force careening toward Rome had given way to enthusiasm over the possibility of picking apart the new, smaller armies, one at a time. Having followed them from Bruttium, no doubt taking the Via Annia again, Crassus turned first to the easier target. The breakaway group had made camp beside a lake in Lucania.

The lake piqued the ancient sources' interest because of its unusual property of turning from drinkable to bitter and back again. That sounds like a seaside lake, and it would be reasonable to place it near the coastal Lucanian city of Paestum. The "lake" might in fact have been the marsh that stretched between Paestum and the mouth of the Silarus (modern Sele) river before land reclamation projects dried it up in the 1930s.

Many armies marched through Paestum. Lucanians conquered it around 400 B.C. when it was still a Greek colony called Poseidonia. The legions annexed Lucanian Paestum in 273 B.C., after the city made the mistake of supporting Rome's enemy, Pyrrhus. The ancient city's ruins lie practically within sight of the beaches where the Allies landed in 1943, en route to Salerno, about thirty-five miles away to the north. The Germans fought at Paestum for nine days before they withdrew. Archaeologists have found tens of thousands of so-called acorn missiles at Paestum, and some suggest that they date to Crassus's campaign in 71 B.C. Acorn missiles are named for the small nuts that they resemble in size and shape. They were made of stone, baked clay, or lead. Sling missiles were a weapon of choice against cavalry, and Spartacus deployed horsemen effectively, so it would have made sense for Crassus to have loaded up on them.

Five miles east of Paestum, on the edge of today's Cilento hills, above the modern town of Capaccio, there rises craggy Mount Soprano; some identify it with the ancient Mount Camalatrum. The plain at the foot of the mountain is a fertile area, not far from the

Via Annia; it would have been a good place to raid for supplies. The Lower Silarus river ran through the plain, about ten miles away to the northwest. At this time of year the river would have looked silvery, swollen with mountain runoff. A strong sea breeze blows here on the plain. The insurgents might have smelled the scent of freedom in it. *Riyos*, which many scholars believe was the Gauls' word for "free," might have echoed around the lake.

Admittedly, there is another candidate for the Lucanian lake: a mountain lake (now dry) near the inland Lucanian city of Volceii (modern Buccino), some forty miles northeast of Paestum. This lake's water was drinkable in spring, thanks to the runoff of melting snow, but turned brackish in summer. But soon afterward the rebels seem to have been in the vicinity of Capaccio, which tips the scales in favor of locating the Lucanian lake near it.

It was here, beside the lake, that the two Celtic women made their fateful trip up the mountain. The sources imply that they made it down again and they warned their men about the threat. The Romans "were in danger," say the sources. But Crassus saved the day. He arrived from another direction and caught the enemy by surprise. Faced with Crassus and his men, the Celts could not deal with the other Romans, under Pomptinus and Rufus, who were hiding on the mountainside. Those Romans now gave a loud cry, ran down from above, and took the Celts from the rear. Under attack from two directions, the terrified rebels ran for their lives. The Romans would have pursued and slaughtered them if not for the sudden appearance of help.

Spartacus had arrived. His presence in spite of the split with Castus and Cannicus is not surprising. Neither Paestum nor Volceii is far from the point where the turnoff for Samnium leaves the Via Annia; the breakaway group would have continued on the Via Annia toward Capua and then taken the Appian Way to Rome. Evidently, the Thracian had not given up on his wayward colleagues.

Indeed, perhaps he stayed close because he hoped to win them back. His timely appearance made Crassus give up the hunt and saved the breakaway army.

But Crassus attacked a second time. The second battle took place at a spot called Cantenna. Three miles south of Capaccio lies the town of Giungano (modern name), behind which rises Mount Cantenna. Perhaps this is the Cantenna of the ancient source; as is the case with Camalatrum, its location is unknown, but all indications put Cantenna in northern Lucania.

When Crassus attacked the second time, Spartacus and his men had not yet moved off. But Crassus managed to distract them, thereby leaving the men under Castus and Cannicus on their own. After barely surviving the first attack, they were physically weak and perhaps demoralized. The failure to stand and fight had violated every rule of Celtic and Germanic culture; now they paid a price for their safety in shame.

Before attacking, Crassus had laid the groundwork well. He had divided his forces in two marching camps, each with its own trench and earthworks. He placed both camps near the enemy in a gesture of self-confidence and intimidation. Crassus set up his headquarters tent in the larger of the two camps. Then, on a designated night, he pulled all his troops out and posted them in the foothills of the mountain. He left his headquarters tent in the camp, though, in order to fool the enemy.

Next, Crassus split his cavalry into two groups. He sent one unit out under Lucius Quinctius, his legate, with orders to tempt Spartacus with a feigned battle. It is a tribute to Quinctius's professionalism that he executed this delicate maneuver well. Then again, the example of the decimation of Mummius's troops after they had failed to carry out a similar maneuver against Spartacus no doubt focused the minds of Quinctius's men. In any case, they followed orders and neutralized Spartacus's forces while avoiding losses of their own.

The other group of cavalry had a job that also called for finesse. Arguably, they had the more difficult task. They had to approach the German and Celtic forces under Castus and Cannicus and lure them out to fight; then they had to simulate retreat. The goal was to lead the enemy into a trap. Crassus and his infantrymen were waiting, perhaps around a bend in the hills. The rebels followed Crassus's cavalrymen right into the ambush. At this point the Roman cavalry fell back onto the wings. Drawn up in battle formation, opposite the rebels, was hard Roman iron.

It was Crassus's dream and Spartacus's nightmare: a pitched battle against the Roman army. The rebels' best hope was to flee to safety. Whether that was still possible, now that the trap had been sprung, is doubtful. Besides, even if they could have fled, the men of Castus and Cannicus were unlikely to have done so. They had the stain of their flight at Camalatrum to wipe out. They stood and fought.

For Celts, battle was a religious act. Beforehand, they vowed to their war god the booty they hoped to take. Their thoughts went to the aftermath of a successful battle, when they could sacrifice captive animals, bury the enemy's weapons, and cut off the heads of his slaughtered chiefs. If they lost the battle—well, a man's ultimate offering to the gods was his own body, and a pious Celt would have given it gladly.

The odds did not favor them against Crassus. He probably outnumbered them and his men certainly far outstripped the enemy in weapons and discipline. Castus and Cannicus no doubt displayed good leadership skills but they are unlikely to have matched Spartacus's tactical gifts. Above all, the Celtic way of war stood in the way of success.

Unlike the Romans, who emphasized coordination and discipline, Celts thought of battle as a series of heroic duels. Celts—and Germans—grouped themselves in battle around their hero chiefs, fighting along with him to victory or death. This was no way to counteract the military science of the legions. As a Roman veteran, Spartacus knew this, and no doubt he labored mightily to cure his men of this notion. But Spartacus was gone.

Cantenna proved to be a crushing Roman victory. No figures of their losses survive. The sources disagree about the number of rebel casualties. One tradition cites 30,000 or 35,000 dead, while Plutarch records 12,300. The larger figures can be discarded as implausible; not even the lowest can be taken at face value. It is safest to say that the rebels suffered very large losses. Both traditions agree that Castus and Cannicus died on the battlefield. Plutarch states that this was "the most valiant battle of all" that Crassus fought. The author was referring to the stiff resistance that the Celts and Germans put up. On his account, only two dead men out of 12,300 were found with back wounds. All the rest kept their places in the battle and fought the Romans to the death.

If that is true, it was a very Celtic ending. The Celts idealized a hero's death on the battlefield and despised the thought of flight. For example, not a single Gaul turned in flight during the Battle of Bibracte (near the modern Autun, France) against the Romans in 58 B.C., as Caesar noticed. The Celts considered it better to take one's own life, in fact, than to surrender. The Celts long honored the principle of suicide in defeat, from the famous Hellenistic statue of the Dying Gaul and his wife to the suicide of the British queen Boudicca. Castus, Cannicus, and many thousands had kept their honor. But the glory of Gaul and Germany lay dead on a field in Lucania.

We hear nothing of prisoners but there probably were some. Others might have escaped and made it back to Spartacus's army. One wonders if the two Celtic women who went up Camalatrum were there at Cantenna, perhaps at the edge of the battlefield, praying for their men. If so, did they die with them, perhaps by suicide?

Crassus had the right to relish victory. Outside of textbooks, no army works like a machine, but even so, Crassus had trained his men to give him their best. Brutal discipline had finally paid off. Machiavelli, who would say that it is better for a prince to be feared than loved, would have approved of Crassus's methods. Crassus had avenged defeat on the Melia Ridge. He had achieved more through one night of cunning than he had in weeks spent moving masses of earth.

After the battle, the Romans took in a rich haul of loot from the defeated army, but the greatest treasures had propaganda value. According to Livy, they found five fasces with rods and axes, tokens of a Roman magistrate's power to beat and behead. The loss of the fasces had shamed the lictors, the magistrate's attendants who normally carried them; the recovery honored Crassus's men. More important, they recovered five Roman eagles and twenty-six battle standards. The standards symbolized the Roman army. Each standard was a long pole decorated with various symbols and insignia. Every century, cohort, and legion had its own standard. The legion's standard was a single silver eagle. Officers called standard-bearers carried the standards in battle, often taking them into the teeth of the enemy. At the Battle of Pydna in 168 B.C., a standard-bearer hurled his standard into the enemy, and many men died in order to win it back. Every Roman standard had, as it were, blood on it.

Roman standards embodied the unit. The men revered, even worshipped their standards. Losing a standard in battle was a disgrace, while recapturing a standard was a mark of distinction, especially if achieved by force of arms. Emperor Augustus (29 B.C.–A.D. 14) was so proud of getting back Rome's lost standards from the Parthians (that is, Iranians) that he had coins issued to commemorate the feat—and he acquired them through negotiation, not battle. By taking back such a collection of Roman honor, Crassus had practically won a second battle.

Spartacus no doubt had Roman battle standards of his own to brandish, taken in past victories, but on this day he probably did not win any new symbols for rallying his troops. He would have to find other ways to put his great communications skills to work. Surely he mourned Castus and Cannicus as he had mourned Crixus. This time, though, he did not have the leisure to hold funeral games or force Roman prisoners to fight as gladiators in their honor. Like the Celts and Germans, Thracians were men of honor, but Spartacus was enough of a Roman to think of survival. It was, he knew, no shame to live and fight again another day.

Spartacus convinced his men "to retreat towards the Peteline Mountains." Debate swirls over just where that was. Among the locations proposed are the Cilento hills southeast of Paestum, the hills around the city of Atena Petilia (the modern Atena Lucana) in the Campus Atinas, and the Picentini mountains (on the grounds that "Peteline" represents a manuscript error). The simplest explanation is to have "Peteline Mountains" mean the mountains around the city of Petelia, possibly the Sila mountains, a time-honored haunt of brigands and bandits. Petelia was a city in Bruttium, probably the modern Strongoli, near Croton and almost two hundred miles southeast of Paestum: in other words, to reach Petelia, Spartacus would have had to drag his tired troops nearly all the way back to the Melia Ridge. Yet all indications are that the final events of the war took place within a brief span of time, far too brief for Spartacus's army to have marched two hundred miles and back.

Another source provides the missing piece of the puzzle. It says that Spartacus set up camp near the headwaters of the Silarus river, not far from the modern town of Caposele. The valley of the Upper Silarus skirts the Picentini mountains, lying to the west. Caposele sits on what was a border region in ancient times between northwestern Lucania, southwestern Apulia, and northeastern Samnium. Caposele lies about forty-five miles north of Paestum, a few days' march away. The nearness of the two sites, the presence of the Picentini, and the vicinity of Samnium (Spartacus's goal after the Melia Ridge) all make the area of Caposele a strong candidate for the place "towards the Peteline Mountains" where the next events unfolded.

Wherever Spartacus and his men were heading, they probably did not get very far before the Romans caught them. Crassus had sent a contingent of troops after them, under the command of his lieutenants, Lucius Quinctius and Cnaeus Tremellius Scrofa. Scrofa served as quaestor, and Quinctius was the cavalry commander who had tricked Spartacus at Cantenna. Why Crassus himself did not undertake this important mission is unclear. Presumably he wanted his men to assess the enemy's intentions before he committed the bulk of his army.

Once again Crassus had misplaced his trust. Neither Quinctius nor Scrofa exercised the appropriate caution as they pursued Spartacus. Instead they clung to his heels, oblivious to the danger of his turning on them. Suddenly he did, and the Roman army fled in panic. In spite of the disappointment of recent defeat, the veteran fighter still had tricks in him. Things went so badly for the Romans that Scrofa was wounded and the men barely carried him away to safety. They might have wondered what awaited them at camp: a medal or decimation.

The sources contain two different stories about Spartacus's next move. This is not surprising, as ancient observers had to piece together the truth from the few surviving rebel eyewitnesses and from the claims of Roman commanders. Ultimately they might have had to guess at Spartacus's plans.

According to the first account, Spartacus now began to lead his army toward the city of Brundisium (modern Brindisi). Now more than ever, he had only one reasonable goal: leaving Italy, and the sooner the better. A southern Italian port city on the Adriatic coast, Brundisium was the maritime gateway to the East. Sulla, for instance, had landed there when he returned to Italy in 83 B.C. from the First Mithridatic War, ready to begin his bloody march of conquest up the

Appian Way, which stretched 364 miles from Brundisium to Rome. Perhaps Spartacus hoped to find ships at Brundisium to take him and his fellow Thracians home; perhaps this time he would meet pirates who kept their promises. Failing that, there was Apulia, the region in which Brundisium lay; it was rich in food and potential recruits. So, the rebels went back on the march.

From Paestum, the road to Brundisium led through Caposele (another reason to identify it with the place "towards the Peteline Mountains," if only military history were neat and logical). An ancient highway from Italy's Tyrrhenian coast to the Adriatic ran through the valley of the Upper Silarus. Not far from the headwaters of the river, near the city of Aquilonia, Spartacus would have reached the Appian Way. From there, Brundisium lay about 175 miles away to the southeast. This is presumably just the route that he started his army on after their victory over Quinctius and Scrofa.

But bad news stopped them in their tracks. The situation in Brundisium had changed. Spartacus learned that Marcus Lucullus had landed there with his troops, fresh from his success in Thrace. Better now to march into the Underworld than into Brundisium.

The second account takes off perhaps from that point. It begins with the men on the road. They were wearing their armor, perhaps to be ready for further Roman attacks. Fresh from their success over Crassus's deputies, they had grown overconfident. "Success destroyed Spartacus," writes Plutarch, "because it aroused insolence in a group of runaway slaves." They no longer considered it worthy of their dignity merely to engage in a fighting retreat. Instead of continuing to obey their commanders, they threatened them with their weapons. In short, the men mutinied.

Mutinies are usually the work of soldiers who want less, not more fighting and Plutarch inspires less trust the more he ascribes motives. These reasons make the tale of the mutiny suspect, but there are grounds for believing it. Victorious armies do not like to retreat, especially if they are people's armies, in which the ordinary soldier is used to voicing his opinion. Death before disgrace is a familiar motif of ancient warfare, not least in accounts of Thrace. Spartacus himself had encouraged this way of thinking. At the very outset of the revolt, back in the House of Vatia, he had said that freedom was better than the humiliation of being put on display for others. One of the rebels, perhaps Spartacus himself on Vesuvius, had said that it was better to die by iron than by starvation.

Besides, the mutineers' goal had some merit. Having just successfully tricked Crassus's lieutenants, it was reasonable for them to try tricking Crassus himself. With Pompey on his way, it was better to bring things to a head quickly than to let Rome build its military muscle. Spartacus might have objected that Crassus had learned too much by now to fall for a trick. But the men insisted.

Spartacus' army probably stood on the Appian Way. If they marched south on it they would soon cross a bridge over the river Aufidus (Ofanto). Roaring for a hundred miles to the Adriatic Sea, the Aufidus passed close to the the the town of Cannae. There, about 150 years earlier, in 216 B.C., Hannibal gave Rome its greatest battlefield defeat in history, killing perhaps fifty thousand men in one day.

History, strategy, honor, and mutiny all swirled around Spartacus. Rhetoric might change the mutineers' minds, but only careful reflection could illuminate the right path. Spartacus paused, then he moved his army.

10

SPARTACUS

THE THRACIAN WAS practically at the gates. His slaves and gladiators had already reached the Appian Way, and a march of fifty miles would bring them to Venusia (modern Venosa). An ancient city planted in the shadow of an extinct volcano, majestic Mount Vultur (modern Vulture), Venusia had been a Roman colony for two hundred years. Now, in the spring of 71 B.C., it would have been well advised to firm up its walls. Surely raiding parties had already looted outlying farms.

And raids were perhaps the least of it. People were saying this of the rebels: "they indiscriminately mix murder, arson, theft, and rape." They took Roman citizens prisoner. One Roman matron was supposed even to have killed herself in torment over the violation of her sexual honor. Venusians could imagine worse still, based on recent experience. After joining the rebels against Rome in the Social War, Venusia had been stormed and recaptured by a Roman army in 88 B.C.

One of the inhabitants of Venusia in 71 B.C. was a freedman named Horatius. Although an ex-slave, he was unlikely to have sympathized with Spartacus, because Horatius represented a success story. If the ancient biographical tradition can be trusted, he had started out selling salted fish: he was the kind of petty retailer who, in Cicero's opinion, could turn a profit only by making a habit of lying. Currently, however, he was an auction broker, a profession that made up in profitability what it lacked in prestige. The prosperous freedman might have feared Spartacus as much as any blueblood did.

But Horatius need not have worried. Spartacus's rabble in arms would not disrupt his road to success. If not then in 71 B.C., then soon afterward Horatius would own a farm as well as a town house. Six years later, in 65 B.C., his wife (her name is not recorded) would give birth to their son, Quintus. He would prove to be a talented child. Horatius sent the boy not only to the best school in Venusia and then to a better school in Rome but, finally, to university in Athens—where he shared classes with the son of Cicero, no less. Quintus would live to become Rome's most polished poet: Quintus Horatius Flaccus, better known as Horace.

In the end it would all work out for Horatius's family, but for one moment in 71 B.C. he held his breath. Or so we might imagine: Horatius, the poet Horace's father, is a real historical figure but his situation as Spartacus approached Venusia is an educated guess. For that matter, Spartacus's approach is itself a deduction from sources that are too sketchy and contradictory to permit certainty about the last phase of the war. In any case, it seems that Spartacus turned south and away from Venusia. He led his army down the valley of the Upper Silarus river toward the Romans' camp—again, a plausible itinerary but not certain. What is clear is that, as one source says, "he gave up on all [his other plans] and came to blows with Crassus." Why?

The ancient sources disagree about Spartacus's motivation. One says that his men forced him to fight the Romans, while the other says that he made the choice on his own. Was it the mutiny or the bad news from Brundisium? Historically, only one possibility can be right but the contradiction may reflect Spartacus's own mixed motives. The Roman in Spartacus surely knew that the odds of battle were against him. As a Thracian chieftain, though, he would have embraced a fight to the death for freedom.

Meanwhile, Crassus was a moving target. As soon as he got the news of Spartacus's approach, Crassus went on the march himself. He was eager to fight. Like many of the rebels, Crassus wanted to force a confrontation before Pompey arrived but he marched as much on political as on military grounds. Crassus wanted the credit for victory.

Naturally, Crassus wanted to win. He had grounds for optimism. Since taking command in the fall, Crassus had improved the odds considerably in Rome's favor. He had inflicted repeated and considerable battle losses on the enemy (dead, wounded, and prisoners) in northern Lucania, on the Melia Ridge, and at Cantenna. In addition, Spartacus had lost the men of the Celtic-German splinter group and perhaps other individual defectors as the going got rough. At its zenith, Spartacus's army had consisted of about 60,000 men. It was "still of great size," says one source, but it was surely much diminished. It would be surprising if he had more than 30,000–40,000 soldiers left, but that is just an educated guess.

The Romans seem to have done better. Crassus had suffered some losses among his 45,000 or so legionaries on the Melia Ridge and in the engagement "toward the Peteline Mountains." After the end of the rebellion, the Romans liberated three thousand Roman citizens held prisoner by the rebels; how many of them were soldiers is not known. At an educated guess, Crassus now had 40,000 legionaries. In other words, the Romans matched the rebel army in size and may have outnumbered it.

That did not bode well for Spartacus's men. The Romans were used to taking on larger armies and beating the odds through their superior training and leadership (especially at the centurion level). They had better arms and armor than the enemy and were surely better fed. They knew that reinforcements were on the way and from two directions but they were cocky enough to take on the enemy on their own.

The rebels could count. They cared little about expectations, however, because they didn't want an ordinary battle; they wanted a grudge fight. They wanted to avenge their fallen friends. They wanted to achieve the hero's death that Thracians, Celts, and Germans had all been raised to desire. They wanted to kill Romans because rebel slaves knew what awaited them if captured. A group of Sicilian slaves in the Second Sicilian Slave War (104–100 B.C.), for example, chose suicide over surrender; another group killed each other in captivity, according to some sources, rather than let the Romans send them to the lions. Spartacus's men might have reasoned that if the coming battle was to be a slaves' Thermopylae, then so be it.

It was 71 B.C., probably April. As the rebels marched southward through the Upper Silarus valley, the Romans marched northward. There was symmetry to the location. Spartacus's first clash with a Roman army had taken place on Vesuvius, the most fatal volcanic region in Italy. Now, on a plausible interpretation of the evidence, the last act would unfold in one of Italy's most dangerous earthquake zones, the valley of the Upper Silarus. In A.D. 79, Vesuvius erupted and destroyed Pompeii and Herculaneum. In 1980, an earthquake centered in Conza (ancient Compsa, a city near the Appian Way), killed 3,000 people, injured more than 10,000, and left 300,000 homeless.

The Silarus begins almost unnoticeably in the north, winding through a maze of hills. Then the river flows southward for twenty miles following a regular course, guarded on either side by mountain walls as high as five thousand feet. The Picentini mountains rise in rocky highlands to the west, while the massifs of Mounts Marzano and Ogna (modern names) wall off the eastern side of the valley. The space between the mountains is nowhere wider than about three miles. Much of the valley is hilly; the widest stretch of plain is about two miles wide. The valley ends dramatically in the south, where the curtain wall of mountains stops abruptly at the plain, leaving the Silarus to flow toward the sea over its middle and lower courses. As one looks back toward the Upper Silarus from the plain, the mountains seem to retreat gracefully from each other at the valley's entrance, only to throw up a rock wall again where the river turns.

Green and well watered, the valley's air is fresh but humid, and clouds are not uncommon. It might look as much like upstate New York or Quebec as the Mediterranean if not for the many groves of olive trees. No doubt slaves tended them in Roman times. If one enters the valley from the plain, past the hot springs of Contursi Terme (modern name), one smells the unmistakable odor of sulfur. About ten miles to the north sits the town of Oliveto Citra, on a hill overlooking the river.

Oliveto Citra claims the honor of being the site of Spartacus's last battle. So does the town of Giungano, fifty miles away in the hills near Paestum. Neither claim can be verified, but Giungano can be ruled out, since in fact it was probably the site of a different battle, the one in which Crassus defeated Castus and Cannicus. Oliveto Citra lies southwest of a plain that stretches for about two miles and which would indeed have made a good battlefield. Each side might have seen advantages in the relatively narrow space: the numerically superior Romans could not outflank the rebels, while Spartacus's cavalry had only limited space to maneuver. If ancient conditions were like today's, the valley contained olive trees and deep-plowed soil. But in the west, the pockmarked cliffs of the Picentini mountains mark deep gorges, while on the east, the long ridge of the Ogna massif stands guard. A Roman breastplate was once found in these fields. Still, one breastplate does not a battlefield make: it is safer to say that the battle probably took place somewhere in the valley of the Upper Silarus.

When his scouts located the rebels, wherever that was, Crassus marched up to them and pitched his camp close by. It was a provocative act, an expression of his eagerness to fight. It was also risky. When the sources criticize Crassus for moving too quickly in his zeal to beat Pompey, they may have been referring to this moment.

"He [Crassus] was digging a trench," say the sources, "when the slaves sallied forth and started fighting with the workers." This might mean a trench around the Romans' camp, but more likely it is a reference to a ditch or ditches dug to keep Spartacus's cavalry from outflanking the legions, constructed just as Sulla had done at the Battle of Orchomenus in Greece in 85 B.C. As the Roman general Corbulo would later say, "you defeat the enemy with a pickaxe." Crassus's men might also have been building strongholds at the end of the trench for the emplacement of light and mobile catapults known as scorpions. Caesar used this tactic fifteen years later in his invasion of Gaul. Scorpions fired short, heavy arrows that delivered a vicious sting, as the name of the machine suggests. We know of a case in which a scorpion arrow pierced a cavalry commander's body and pinned him to his horse.

The rebels attacked the trenches. The Romans whom Spartacus had faced in the first two years of the revolt might have turned and run toward safer ground. Crassus's men stayed and fought. More Romans arrived, and then more slaves, and now it was a melee.

Nothing suggests that either general joined the fray at the trench. Sulla's veterans might have thought back to their chief's behavior at Orchomenus when Mithridates' men attacked his ditch diggers. Seeing his soldiers flee, Sulla had jumped down from his horse, grabbed a standard, run through the crowd of deserters toward the enemy, and shouted words of abuse. He, for one, planned to die with honor; they could later declare, when asked where they betrayed their leader, "At

Orchomenus!" He turned the men around and, after furious fighting, saved the day.

The situation was different at the Silarus. Plutarch, who tells the tale, makes it sound as if Spartacus's men attacked the ditch diggers on their own initiative and so forced their leader's hand. "Seeing the necessity," Plutarch writes of what happened next, "Spartacus arranged his entire army in battle formation." But it is just as likely that Spartacus had sent his men out deliberately. A veteran like Spartacus should have foreseen Crassus's trenches and their threat to the rebel cavalry. A successful flank attack by the rebel cavalry could break up Rome's light infantry, whose job it was to send a steady stream of slings and arrows against the enemy. A cavalry ride surely played a role in Spartacus's battle plan—and he is likely to have had a battle plan. He may not have wanted to fight at first, but once he realized the inevitability of battle, Spartacus would have set his mind to work. A man like him did not let events hold him prisoner. He would probably have held a council of war and hammered out plans with his lieutenants.

Spartacus might have hoped to squeeze out a victory by first disrupting the Roman formations with his cavalry. A successful offensive by horsemen could deprive the Romans of their missile capability. Then his infantry would attack. Instead of a howling, hell-for-leather charge, Spartacus would try to decapitate the enemy by killing its leadership.

Crassus too surely had a battle plan. Apparently, he intended to neutralize the enemy cavalry and thereby ensure the freedom of his light infantry to rain missiles on the rebels. Light javelins, slingshot missiles, scorpion bolts and arrows—perhaps even fire arrows—were the likeliest projectiles. Meanwhile, his legions would beat back an anticipated charge by the enemy. Then they would counter with a much more disciplined and formidable charge of their own and thereby win the battle.

The two generals now prepared their armies for battle. This was a long process, more a matter of hours than of minutes. On the Roman side, the military tribunes carefully supervised the exit of the troops from camp and their deployment in the field. Absent other evidence, we might imagine that the legions were drawn up in the standard triple-line pattern. The rear line would serve as reinforcements, if needed. On the rebel side, preparations are likely to have been less regimented. Nonetheless, Spartacus's lieutenants probably kept things on a tighter rein than the Romans would have wished. It would not be surprising if the lines each extended for about a mile.

In the rebels' front there probably stood veteran troops who knew how to keep calm in battle. The Romans' weapons might have gleamed with spit and polish. After all, only at the eleventh hour did legionaries remove their shields from protective covers. The rebels' arms and armor were probably duller and far less uniform in quality. But many of the pieces recalled the Romans from whose corpses they had been stripped. Likewise, the rebels' standards, hoisted under the Italian sun, had traveled a path of victory from Vesuvius to Mutina to Bruttium.

Before the fight began, each commander addressed his troops or at least the portion of them within earshot. Crassus's words do not survive. Spartacus engaged in a bold gesture. After calling for his horse to be brought to him, he drew out his sword and addressed his soldiers. According to Plutarch, he said "that if he won he would have many horses, and good ones, from the enemy, but if he lost, he would not need any." Then he slaughtered the animal.

Now and then an ancient general sent away his horse and fought on foot, in order to encourage the men. But Spartacus took a further step and engaged in a religious ritual, the solemn gesture of a man facing death, a gesture that stood out for its drama but not for its pursuit of the sacred: Every ancient people considered war a religious act and consulted the gods before battle. The Romans, for instance, brought chickens along with them on military campaigns; they considered these birds sacred. They fed the birds before battle and took it as a favorable sign if the chickens ate with gusto and let food drop from their beaks. Celtic armies consulted priests and bards before battle. We can assume that Spartacus's army always carried out pre-battle rituals but no details survive except in one case, the battle of the Silarus.

Thracians, like many ancient peoples, including Celts and Germans, regarded the horse as sacred. An incident from one of Rome's various wars in Thrace echoes Spartacus's act. Around 29 B.C. a Roman army of invasion stood poised to fight a battle with a Thracian tribe, the Moesians. At the last moment, the Moesian commander stood before his battle line and sacrificed a horse. Then he vowed to slaughter the Roman leaders as human sacrifices—and to eat their intestines. Spartacus apparently left Crassus's viscera out of it.

By killing the horse—his own mount, no less—Spartacus made a vow in the hope of victory. He also made policy decisions about tactics and morale. Generals normally fought on horseback. By killing his horse, Spartacus might have improved the men's morale but at the price of limiting the general's vision and mobility. Without his horse, Spartacus could not change plans once the fighting began nor flee if things went badly. But the men may have seen only his courage and generosity. Perhaps they responded, as Thracians usually did before battle, by singing and dancing in sight of the enemy; perhaps the Celts among them redoubled the taunts they customarily leveled at the enemy. On either side, commanders signaled; banners waved; trumpets blared. Then they fought.

Two armies collided at the Silarus and so did two worlds. It was a clash of military science and heroic ideals, precisely the sort of battle to give birth to legends. What few details have survived are in large part melodramatic; the skeptical reader might choose to dismiss them altogether. Yet the story is more unusual than implausible. Besides, several authentic details of Roman combat can be culled from the sources.

When the signal for battle was given, we might expect that each side's infantry attacked. The rebels are likely to have cheered and charged. The Romans had been trained to advance slowly. They would have come to within about fifty feet of the enemy and thrown their javelins. Then they would have drawn their swords and charged. The legionaries would have raised a shout, one meant as much to encourage themselves as to terrify the enemy.

All of this is speculation, and it leaves out key points. Roman battles were complex affairs; commanders sent in cavalry, called for reserves, wheeled their men around, retreated and reformed their lines, looked for gaps in the enemy's position—all at the proper times. Too little is known about this engagement even to guess about these details. The Silarus was an epic fight, involving sixty thousand men or more, but the ancient world cared mainly about what Spartacus did that day. How not, when he turned the battle into a duel? Spartacus's strategy was to target Crassus. "He pushed toward Crassus," writes one source, "through many weapons and wounds."

Crassus probably sat on horseback close to his army's front line, the usual position of a Roman general in battle. From here he observed, exhorted, and commanded. He was close enough to the fighting to inspire his men, call for reserves, or make mental notes for future reference. Not for Crassus the safety of the rear: he "exposed his body to danger," says one source. But Spartacus ran even a greater risk because he stood in the front line itself and he fought on foot.

For a general to stand in the front line was rare but not unheard of. Hannibal, for instance, stood in the front rank at Cannae in 216 B.C. and both Caesar and Catiline would each do so at times in the decades following Spartacus's revolt. But what was indeed rare in ancient warfare was to turn a clash among tens of thousands of men into a contest between two generals. Spartacus embodied a throw-back to the old Thracian ideal of one man with a sword.

But not just Thracians. By singling out the enemy general, Sparta-cus acted like a *Roman* seeking Rome's highest military honor. Called the *spolia opima* ("splendid spoils"), this distinction went only to one historically attested Roman in the entire history of the republic. Mar-cus Claudius Marcellus won this prize from a Gallic chieftain in 222 B.C. More recently, at some point between 79 and 76 B.C. in Spain, the renegade Roman commander Sertorius had challenged the procon-sul Metellus to a battlefield duel; Metellus declined. Sertorius, how-ever, did not then charge Metellus's army with his loyal retainers, as Spartacus did with Crassus.

Attacking Crassus was brave and foolhardy. Penetrating the enemy line was always dangerous, and more so since the Romans would fight tooth and nail to protect their commander. No doubt Spartacus had a retinue around him, perhaps a bodyguard of picked men, but to protect Crassus the legionaries would swarm them and eventually break through. Spartacus had to gamble on speed: to kill Crassus quickly before the Romans killed him, and then to hope that the legion crumbled at the news of its general's death. It was a desperate move but arguably a good one under the circumstances. Attacking Crassus risked death; charging an entire legion assured it.

Spartacus's charge is one of the unforgettable events of ancient warfare. It was a real-life *aristeia*, to use a Greek word, borrowed by the Romans. Aristeia is an epic story of a warrior's heroic deeds. The Romans marveled at his courage. Spartacus "fought *fortissime*," writes one author, that is, "with the height of personal bravery." As he bat-tled toward Crassus, "he killed two centurions who fought hand to hand with him." Centurions always led from the front and held their ground: "They shall not pass" might have been their motto. As much as any legionary, they knew how to fight at close quarters. While protecting himself with his large, rectangular shield, a centurion's practiced eye could find a target for his sword in the enemy's head or torso. But centurions were not trained to face a gladiator.

Spartacus never reached Crassus. Two different versions of Spartacus's fate survive. "In the end," according to one account, "when those around him had fled, he stood his ground, surrounded by many, and although he defended himself, he was cut down." The second report says "Spartacus was wounded in the thigh by a short javelin. He got down on one knee, thrust his shield before him and continued to fight off those who were attacking him, until he himself and the large number of men around him were surrounded and fell."

The differences are clear. One story says that Spartacus's friends abandoned him, while the other has them fight and die with him. One report mentions a javelin wound in the thigh, which forces Spartacus to his knee, while the other report says nothing of wounds or kneeling. The little javelin (*doration* in the Greek text, so *iaculum* or *telum* in Latin) is just the sort of weapon to have been thrown by Rome's light infantry. Spartacus's men had tried to stop the Romans from digging an anticavalry trench. Apparently the Roman pickaxe had prevailed, which held back the enemy horse and allowed a Roman light infantryman to do what Roman centurions could not: to bring down Spartacus. How demeaning for a gladiator not to fall in hand-to-hand combat.

It is impossible to choose between the two versions, so we have to settle for the common details: Spartacus was surrounded, he defended himself, and he died fighting.

For all their fear and loathing of gladiators and rebel slaves, Roman writers stood in awe of Spartacus's courage that day. The historian Sallust (86–35 B.C.) first sounded this note by commenting that "he did not die quickly or unavenged." Florus (circa A.D. 100–150) paid Spartacus the compliment of saying that "he died almost an *imperator.*" In Latin, *imperator* means "commander" but it was a special title of honor, symbolizing the bond between a winning general and his men. After a victory, his soldiers saluted the winner as imperator. Sulla, Pompey, Caesar, and Augustus all made great use of the term. By Florus's day, *imperator* was the generic title for "emperor." In short, nothing became Spartacus's life so well as his manner of losing it.

Compared to Spartacus, the tens of thousands of other soldiers on the field receive scant attention from the sources. It is clear that they fought hard and long. "The battle was long and strongly contested because of the desperation of so many myriads of men," says one source. A hard-fought Roman battle could last as long as five hours.

Battle inspired, terrified, and disoriented its participants. Always loud, the sound of battle echoed between the hills, leaving men uncertain about the location of a given action. Commanders might have had to guess the course of action by watching dust clouds raised by charging troops.

One source uses a metaphor from the arena to characterize the rebels' fighting spirit: "As befit an army led by a gladiator, the battle was fought *sine missione*—to the death." *Sine missione* is a technical term for a bout in which the producer denies a defeated gladiator the chance to live. The Romans knew that no opponent was more dangerous than one who cannot live but can still kill.

By killing Spartacus the Romans had turned the tables on his strategy. They apparently inflicted the psychological shock on his men that Spartacus had hoped to inflict on the Romans. After he was killed, the rest of his army fell into disorder. The loss of cohesion in pitched battle is fatal. The legionaries, we can imagine, now pushed and chopped their way into the rebels' lines, opening up pockets here, there, and everywhere. The bravest of the rebels would have stayed and fought but many would have run—if they still could. "They were cut down *en masse*," says one source. Another puts it more admiringly: "They met with a death worthy of real men."

They may have owed their courage in part to their women, who likely stood in the rear ranks. The Triballi, a tough Thracian people, are said to have stationed women there during one battle. They rallied any wavering men with cries and taunts. It was deserved humiliation, but at least the women did not kill them, as Cimbri women are said to have done under similar circumstances.

By the battle's end, the Romans had crushed Spartacus's army. The Romans paid a price for victory: the rebels, it is estimated, had killed about a thousand Roman soldiers. At about 2.5 percent of Crassus's troops, that amounted to what was probably a lower-than-average death rate for the winning side in a Roman infantry battle (based on the limited surviving evidence). The Romans caused massive carnage in turn.

One source claims sixty thousand rebel dead, but that is preposterous. A more honest assessment of rebel casualties concludes that "a slaughter of them came about that cannot be counted." Still, thinking out loud is permissible. Lopsided casualty ratios were not unusual in ancient battles; soldiers who broke and ran were at the mercy of those in pursuit. We know of cases in Roman history in which the defeated army is said to have seen more than half of its men killed or taken prisoner. If there is an element of exaggeration in those figures, there is also the fact that victorious cavalry could ride down an enemy in flight, and infantrymen could encircle their foes and cut them to pieces. If the victorious Romans suffered a death toll of 2.5 percent, it is possible that the defeated rebels suffered several times as many deaths: it is not difficult to imagine 5,000 to 10,000 deaths out of 30,000–40,000 rebel soldiers.

Indeed, the sheer number of slippery corpses and scattered weapons might have slowed down the Romans' pursuit of their broken foe. Bodies might have been piled up two or three high, and even the air might have seemed to be thick with blood. A large number of rebels managed to flee into the nearby mountains. We might assume that any man who could do so took women and children with him rather than leave them to the Romans. Crassus had to engage in extensive mopping-up operations after winning the battle. The shock waves spread even further, as survivors took the fight both north and south.

Contrary to myth, Spartacus was not crucified. Crassus could never have asked the question that led to the chorus shouting, "I am Spartacus!" That response is a brilliant Hollywood touch—but it is entirely fictional.

Spartacus died in battle and his corpse was never found. This may seem hard to imagine in the case of so famous a man: surely, someone recognized him. But the slave commander might have worn ordinary armor: finery would not have suited a man who outlawed gold and silver, divided loot equally, and killed his own horse. Spartacus's final struggle might have left only the badly disfigured body of a soldier dressed in ordinary armor. Then the tide of battle flowed over it, no doubt rendering it unrecognizable in the end. Crassus was denied the chance to decorate a trophy with the arms and armor of his rival.

Spartacus had failed. He had freed tens of thousands of slaves and built them into an army that even some free people joined. He had upended much of the southern Italian countryside. Conquering legion after legion, he had taxed Rome's resources for more than two years. But in the end, Spartacus went down the same path of catastrophe as Hannibal and, in later years, Cleopatra. Spartacus's defeat was both a failure of the intellect and of the imagination. Any thoughtful analyst would have reached the conclusion that sooner or later, the Roman army would crush the insurgency in Italy. Most of the insurgents, however, could not imagine a safe and happy life over the Alps in a strange country. Spartacus built an army that was bold enough to win if it would only quit while it was ahead, but not wise enough to see this.

Whether Spartacus's leadership failed is a difficult question. He did not fail on the battlefield, where he excelled as a commander, as long as he maintained limited goals. Nor did he fail in training or inspiring the troops. Spartacus did not attempt to abolish slavery

altogether nor did he make a serious effort to conquer the city of
Rome, but he offered grand ideals nonetheless. He gave his followers realistic but noble goals: freedom, equality, honor, prowess, vengeance, loot, and even the favor of the gods. But not even Dionysus's
favorite could convince them of his ultimate strategic goal: Spartacus
failed to persuade his men to cross the Alps. It is doubtful that anyone could have persuaded them. Desperate men are easy to inspire
but difficult to reassure. After proving to his army that the gods had
turned against Rome and its legions, he could not persuade them that
disaster lay around the corner unless they fled Italy.

Spartacus suffered the common fate of prudent revolutionaries:
he lit a fire that he could not put out. He discovered as well that the
very vigor that makes insurgent armies successful also makes them
fragile. Rebel forces, built from scratch, are notoriously volatile and
willful. Spartacus's army suffered from massive internal divisions
between Italian-born and emigrants and, especially, from divisions
among different ethnic and national groups. The mix of Thracians,
Celts, Germans, and Italians was unstable, yet it was all there was.
Spartacus had no choice but to fight with the men he had.

Given those limitations, Spartacus acted well when Crassus
brought on the inevitable crisis. It was prudent and proper for him
to cross into Sicily. Spartacus cannot be blamed for being double-
crossed by the pirates, especially if they were bribed and bullied by
Verres, the Roman governor of Sicily. Did Spartacus botch the crossing by raft or was it beyond the technical capabilities of all but the
best-supplied forces?

Spartacus was a failure against Rome but a success as a mythmaker.
No doubt he would have preferred the opposite, but history has its
way with us all. Who, today, remembers Crassus? Pompey? Even Cicero is not so well remembered. Everyone has heard of Spartacus.

Strangely enough, though, they often remember the wrong man.
Neither firebrand nor idealist, the real Spartacus wanted to mix hope

and prudence. Ultimately, one suspects, he would have been happy to carve out a small space free of Rome and retire as a king or lord in a corner of Thrace. But history taught him a hard lesson: unlike games in the arena, revolutions spill out of control.

Meanwhile, thousands of corpses lay back near the Silarus River. We can make educated guesses as to their fate. The bodies of officers might be transported back to Rome. For ordinary Roman soldiers, it was standard practice to be cremated on the battlefield, where their ashes would be buried in a mass grave. The corpses generated a thick cloud of smoke as the flames consumed them and filled the valley with a sickly sweet smell. Before the pyre was lit, the legions would give their fallen comrades a final salute. They marched around the pyre in full armor to the blare of trumpets. It is possible that arms and armor were tossed into the flames. Numerous animal sacrifices ended the ceremony.

The rebels probably did not receive similar treatment. Wood was too expensive to waste on them, so their corpses were likely to have been dumped into a mass grave. The body that had been Spartacus probably ended up in an anonymous mound of flesh in a trench covered with dirt.

Somewhere between the headwaters of the Silarus and the spot where the river breaks out of the mountains into the plain, somewhere along the ancient highway between Italy's two seas, somewhere between the road to Cannae and the beaches where the Allies would land one day, Spartacus was laid to rest.

11

THE VICTORS

Spring belongs to Venus, goddess of gardens and love. In Capua, the famous roses bloom. Crowds thicken in the city's perfume market, where exotic scents fill the air. Meanwhile, in 71 B.C., six hundred eighty-one years since the legendary founding of Rome, in the consulship of Publius Cornelius Lentulus Sura and Cnaeus Aufidius Orestes, the machinery of the Roman state grinds on. On April 1—the kalends of April, to the Romans—a Capuan slave named Flaccus inspects a sack of coins. He is the property of the house of Novius, a prominent business family in Capua. The slave confirms the authenticity of the coins, seals the sack, inscribes his name on an ivory rod attached to it, and completes a tiny step in the vast process of sending the Roman people its taxes. Taxes are as timeless as the blooming roses.

Meanwhile, on the outskirts of Capua, the Roman people exact another payment. Down the road to Rome, as far as the eye can see, there stretches a line of slaves dying on crosses. It is the end of Spartacus's revolt.

The crucified were Crassus's last victims. They had done everything they could to avoid this fate. After surviving defeat in battle in Lucania, a still considerable number of rebels had fled rather than surrender. They had lost Spartacus and their other leaders but apparently they chose new ones. If pitched battle no longer lay within their means, they could still carry out guerrilla operations. The sources say that they went into the mountains—perhaps the Picentini they knew so well. Crassus and his army followed them. The rebels divided into four groups, no doubt hoping that by scattering, they would increase the odds of survival. Apparently, they failed; Crassus claimed to have captured them all.

Crassus took six thousand rebels alive. He then marched them to Capua, a distance of about seventy-five miles, assuming that they were captured in the Picentini mountains. Were any of the original seventy-four gladiators who raised the rebellion among them? If so, they would not have had long to contemplate the irony of their return to the city where they had first broken out of the House of Vatia. Crassus had in mind a punishment that the Roman world considered "terrible," "infamous," "utterly vile," and "servile." He planned to crucify them.

In the Western world, crucifixion has a profound religious meaning because of the crucifixion of Jesus. In ancient times, crucifixion signified capital punishment; the cross was the equivalent of the gallows but far crueler. The Romans considered crucifixion the supreme penalty, reserved for rebellious foreigners, violent criminals, brigands, and slaves. Verres had crucified an alleged agent of Spartacus, thereby unwittingly subjecting a Roman citizen to a punishment from which he was exempt. Spartacus, as we know, had purposely crucified a Roman prisoner in the battle of the Melia Ridge. He wanted to warn his men what they could expect from the Romans, and he was right.

This crucifixion of six thousand people may be the largest recorded mass crucifixion of the ancient world. Only Octavian Caesar, the future emperor Augustus, matched it, in 36 B.C. when he captured and crucified six thousand slave rowers from the fleet of his rival, Sextus Pompey. In both cases, the figure 6,000 is an approximation and, like most ancient statistics, it must be taken with a grain of salt. But ancient sources mention other mass crucifixions, among them: 800 men crucified in 86 B.C., with their wives and children killed before their eyes, under Alexander Jannaeus, king of independent Judaea; 2,000 rebels from Tyre crucified along the Mediterranean shore by Alexander the Great in 332 B.C.; 2,000 rebels crucified in Judaea by the Roman official Quintilius Varus in 4 B.C.; and 3,000 rebels crucified in Babylon by the Persian king Darius in 519 B.C. Supposedly 500 people a day were crucified during the six-month Roman siege of Jerusalem in A.D. 70, a shockingly high total of 90,000 crucifixions— if true.

If crucifying 6,000 slaves was extreme, the action bears Crassus's signature. The man built his career on the willingness to go the extra mile, from buying a legion to decimating a cohort to walling off the "toe" of the Italian "boot." Why not cap his victory with a spectacular, cruel, and extravagant gesture of Roman justice?

We find crucifixions disgusting, but Romans probably tolerated them as a grim necessity. Nowadays many people reject the death penalty as cruel and unusual or criticize a tough interrogation technique like waterboarding as torture, while other people accept them. The purpose of crucifixion, in Roman eyes, was less revenge than deterrence. Most Romans considered the slave revolt a crime inflicted on the people of Italy. They disregarded the injustice of slavery and noted only the devastation of the countryside. The sight of slaves in arms had aroused the Romans' fear, anger, and indignation. Now they wanted peace of mind promised by a sight burned forever into the mind's eye, a warning to Italy's slaves never to repeat their rebellion.

In Capua, the freedman Publius Confuleius Sabbio might have walked outside the city walls to take in the sight. Sabbio had done so well in the cloak-weaving business that, in the early to middle first century B.C., he was able to build a large town house decorated with elegant and ornate mosaics. He welcomed guests with his favorite greeting, *Recte omnia velim sint nobis*, "I would like all things to go well for us!" The ex-slave would probably have faced the prisoners on the crosses with less kind words. He was a city dweller; they were country folk; he had achieved success in the Roman order; they had threatened to destroy it. Although Sabbio had also once faced the threat of the cross, he may well have thought that Crassus had made things go well indeed.

He had not done so on the cheap: crucifying six thousand people was surely expensive. Perhaps Crassus advertised himself afterward as the man who paid for all the lumber, nails, rope, and leather for whips. He was the man who arranged for six thousand posts to be transported to intervals along the road and affixed to the ground, and who had guards stand watch over the dying rebels for days, including nighttime. He might have presented himself once again as a man whose huge wealth paid outsized dividends to the Roman people. Some of the owners of the six thousand slaves might have seen matters differently, since every cross represented a lost investment. Slave owners might have been willing to accept the rebels back, as owners had done after the First Sicilian Slave War, in a time of labor shortage. They might have argued that a good whipping would make any rebel docile again before Crassus slammed that door shut.

Crassus had the rebels crucified along "the whole road to Rome from Capua," as the ancient sources say. By doing so, he followed the protocols of Roman justice and advanced his political career. Roman jurists recommended crucifying notorious brigands at the scene of their crimes, which made Capua, the birthplace of Spartacus's revolt, the logical place to erect the crosses. Roman authorities also favored the most crowded roads for crucifixions, in order to impress the maximum number of people, so the road between Capua and

Rome made sense. In politics, as in transportation, all roads led to Rome, so naturally Crassus erected his crosses on the way to the capital city.

It is usually assumed that the "road to Rome from Capua" was the Appian Way. In fact, two roads connected Capua and Rome; the other road was the Via Latina. The Appian Way was more famous but the Via Latina was an important road too. The Appian Way (132 miles) was fourteen miles shorter than the Via Latina (146 miles) and took a day's less travel: it took five or six days to reach Rome from Capua on the Appian Way compared to six or seven days on the Via Latina. Whichever road Crassus chose would have been crowded with crosses.

Roman crucifixion normally consisted of three elements: scourging, carrying of the cross by the condemned, and lifting. We might imagine a lamentable parade of the condemned, marching slowly north toward Rome through a landscape of spring flowers, their flesh torn and beaten from the whip, their throats parched. They might have included women as well as men, since Roman justice did provide for the crucifixion of women. The Romans even crucified dogs, in an annual ritual, so perhaps children too ended up on Crassus's crosses. The victims carried only the crossbar; the upright stake had already been fixed in the ground. When the condemned person reached the assigned stake, the executioners hoisted him into place via a ladder and poles.

All of the condemned suffered cruelly, yet experiences on the cross varied. Depending on how the victim was hanged, he might have suffocated within minutes or survived in agony for days. The sources make clear that the hanged could linger: they record cases of men talking from the cross, making legal contracts from the cross, and being cut down and spared after a bribe to the officer on guard. Some victims were displayed with special grotesqueness, to mock them, and some were crucified upside down.

Some of the condemned were tied to the cross by rope while others were nailed to it. Archaeologists have found the bones of one crucifixion victim in Israel, dated to the first century A.D. Possibly named Yehohanan, his feet were nailed to the cross but his arms seem to have been tied to the crossbar by rope. The victim was twenty-four years old and stood five feet five inches tall, probably shorter than the average height of the northern European males who predominated among Spartacus's rebels. Yehohanan's right anklebone still has a nail and piece of wood attached to it.

Perhaps some of Spartacus's followers remained defiant on the cross. The ancient sources record cases of crucified men who laughed, spit on spectators, or even sang victory songs when nailed to the cross.

We can only hope that the slaves on the road to Rome died quickly instead of suffering prolonged pain. After they died, the authorities would probably not have hurried to cut them down. The longer their corpses remained hanging, rotting, and stinking, the more they would deter future rebels. As lowly criminals, the slaves were probably hanged close to the ground; high-status prisoners were raised three feet above ground level. All corpses were food for vultures, but dogs too could pick at the lower ones. Eventually, somebody had the job of taking down the remnants and hauling them to the nearest garbage dump. It is unlikely that the slaves received a proper burial; perhaps someone eventually burned the heaps of rotting flesh to spare the citizens the lingering smell.

It had taken Crassus six months to defeat the rebels. Since he entered office no later than November, 72 B.C., the revolt was over by the end of April, 71 B.C. The crosses should have been in place by May. Perhaps celebrants of the Floralia, the Roman equivalent of May Day, wearing traditional flower wreaths in their hair, went out to stare at the condemned. Through fields of red poppies and opposite hillsides of yellow broom, in valleys and over passes, along waterways and beside aqueducts, past junctions and way stations, milestones and mausoleums, villas and vineyards, gateways and gardens, the line of crosses marched on and on. Chariots and chain gangs, flocks of sheep and herds of cows, schoolchildren skipping along and senators carried in litters, bandits sneaking through the night and bakers up before dawn, they all passed by and saw. If any gladiators happened to view the crosses on the way between Capua and Rome, they might have taken the lesson especially to heart.

Perhaps we should imagine Crassus at the head of a column of soldiers, riding between the crosses, heralded by trumpeters, headed for Rome on a macabre victory lap. It was his moment; surely he made the most of it. As long as the slaves hung on their crosses, they would bring Crassus the publicity he craved. His hunger might have gone deep.

In spite of his success, Crassus feared oblivion in the public eye. In half a year he had defeated Spartacus, a man who had held Rome at bay for one and a half years before that. Crassus had tried Rome's patience, however, by walling off Spartacus rather than finding and destroying him in battle. He had, furthermore, required help from other generals, so Crassus could not claim sole credit for victory.

His rival Pompey had turned injury to insult. It had happened this way: in addition to the rebels whom Crassus followed into the mountains, a second group of survivors remained at large. They fled Lucania and went north, perhaps after concluding belatedly that Spartacus had been right, after all, about crossing the Alps. Considerations of timing as well as a hint in ancient sources suggest that these were Celtic and German refugees from the battle of Cantenna. Five thousand people, they made it as far as Etruria (Tuscany) in central Italy when their luck ran out. They landed right into the path of Pompey and his victorious army, marching back from Spain. Showing no mercy to runaway slaves, Pompey wiped them out.

Pompey wrote a letter to the Senate announcing his success. According to one source, the letter said "Crassus had defeated the runaway slaves in open battle but he, Pompey, had torn up the very roots of the war." A clever putdown, it touched a sore truth. Crassus had killed Spartacus but left insurgents at large. They could still make life miserable for free Italians, as would become painfully clear about a year later.

In his prosecution of Verres, Cicero refers to an incident in early 70 B.C. that he calls "the troubles at Tempsa." Tempsa was a town in Bruttium known for its copper mines. Where there were mines there were slaves. The "troubles at Tempsa," Cicero says, involved "the remnants of the Italian war of the fugitive slaves."

Just what were those troubles? Cicero doesn't say. They were bad enough to be reported to a meeting of the Roman Senate but not so bad that the senators sent an army to deal with them. According to Cicero, Gaius Verres should have handled the problem. He happened to be in the vicinity, on his way back to Rome after finally completing his extended term as governor of Sicily. A delegation from the town of Vibo Valentia, near Tempsa, led by an important local inhabitant named Manius Marius, went to Verres and asked for his help. A "small band" of rebels was at large, Marius told him. Surely the insurgents looked with eager eyes at the villas that dotted Vibo's fertile territory. As a governor, Verres would have had a modest military escort, and Marius wanted them to restore order.

Cicero claims that Marius's pleas fell on deaf ears; Verres preferred the company of his mistress on the seashore to helping the citizens of Vibo. Cicero may be telling the truth, but it may also be that things were more complicated: perhaps the rebels scattered before Verres could intervene. Or perhaps the "small band" was really too large for Verres's men. In any case, once the rebels had sacked the territories of Tempsa and Vibo, they melted into the hills. In Rome, the Senate shrugged.

The senators had other business at hand. War still raged against Mithridates while pirates continued to terrorize the Mediterranean.

At home, Cicero was prosecuting Verres—his term as governor of Sicily had ended on December 31, 71 B.C.—on charges of corruption. Cicero was brilliant and a former quaestor but he was young; Verres was defended by the greatest advocate of the day, Hortensius.

But the most diverting spectacle of domestic politics was the rivalry between Crassus and Pompey. By summer, both men had reached Rome with their armies. Normally, Roman generals were required to disband their armies once they entered the boundaries of Italy, but these two generals were exceptions because they each had fought rebel slaves. Crassus commanded 35,000–40,000 troops; Pompey about 25,000–30,000. Neither man disbanded his army. They sat outside the city, waiting and wheeling and dealing.

Each man wanted to be elected consul for 70 B.C., preferably at the expense of the other. Rome had two consuls each year; surely Pompey and Crassus would have preferred to share their year of office with a lesser figure. Neither could get his wish without the consent of Rome's power brokers. Roman elections mobilized a mass electorate but they were heavily weighted in favor of the rich and powerful. No one could be elected without the support of a few, well-connected people. In the end, the generals agreed to a deal: when elections were held in July, Crassus and Pompey were each chosen as consul for the following year.

They would take office on January 1, 70 B.C. With political success assured, the two generals might have each disbanded his army, save for one remaining item of business: the victory parade. Every Roman general aspired to the supreme honor of celebrating a triumph. A triumph was a spectacular victory march through the city of Rome with his army, culminating in a sacrifice to Jupiter on the Capitoline Hill and a feast. The general who celebrated a triumph was called *triumphator.*

Two other victorious generals had returned to Italy in 71 B.C. and they too wanted triumphs. They were Marcus Lucullus, who had been summoned home to fight Spartacus after winning victories in Thrace, and Quintus Caecilius Metellus Pius, proconsul and Pompey's colleague in Spain.

Every triumph was different. Few details of the triumphs of 71 B.C. survive, but on a plausible (but by no means certain) reconstruction, a triumph proceeded as follows.

All Rome turned out on the day of a triumph. The triumphator began the morning outside the city with an assembly of his troops. He addressed them and distributed honors to a few and cash gifts to everyone. Then the triumphal parade began, entering Rome through the special *porta triumphalis,* "triumphal gate," which was otherwise closed. The parade headed toward the Capitol via a long and very visible route. The Senate and the magistrates led the way, followed by trumpeters. Then came floats, displaying paintings of sieges and battles and heaps of spoils, with gold and silver prominent. Next came the white bulls or oxen headed for the slaughter, accompanied by priests. Freed Roman prisoners of war came next, dressed as the triumphator's freedmen. Prominent captives marched in chains, usually headed for execution.

Then, preceded by his lictors, came the victorious general. Dressed in a special toga decorated with designs in gold thread, the triumphator rode in a four-horse chariot. He carried a scepter and wore a wreath of Delphic laurel. A slave stood beside him and reminded him that he was mortal. His grown sons rode on horseback behind his chariot, followed by his officers and the cavalry, all on horseback. Finally came the infantry, marching proudly, singing a combination of hymns and bawdy songs about their commander. Caesar's men, for instance, mocked their chief as "the bald adulterer."

The climax of the day came on the Capitoline Hill. There, after the execution of the enemy leaders, the triumphator attended the sacrifice to Jupiter. He gave the god a portion of the spoils as well as his laurel wreath. Afterward he appeared as the guest of honor at a banquet on the Capitoline. Throughout the city the people feasted at public expense. Finally, the pipes and flutes accompanied the triumphator home at night.

To celebrate a triumph, a commander had to receive permission of the Senate and a vote of the People of Rome. He also had to fulfill certain requirements. He had to have won a victory in a foreign war over a declared enemy. He had to have killed at least five thousand of the enemy and brought the war to a conclusion—one of many reasons for inflated body counts in ancient texts. He had to have held public office and fought in the theater officially assigned him. As a final matter of dotting the *i*'s and crossing the *t*'s, he had to have carried out the proper religious ceremonies before fighting.

His victory over Spanish rebels allowed Pompey to request—and receive—a triumph. So did Pompey's co-commander in Spain, Metellus Pius, and likewise Marcus Lucullus. Crassus, however, did not qualify for a triumph, in spite of his official commission and his victories, because his enemies were slaves. It was beneath the dignity of the Roman people to celebrate a triumph over a servile foe. Crassus had to settle for an *ovatio* instead.

An ovatio was a stripped-down version of a triumph. Like a triumph, it featured a victory parade through the city, leading up to the Capitol and culminating in a sacrifice to Jupiter. There was money for the soldiers and feasts for the people. But the general did not ride on a chariot as the triumphator did; he either walked or, in Crassus's day, rode a horse. He did not wear the triumphator's gold threads but instead the standard purple-bordered toga of a magistrate. He had no scepter. Trumpets were banned; the victor had to settle for flutes. Finally, he wore a myrtle wreath instead of laurel.

As minor as this last detail seems to us, apparently it meant a great deal to the Romans. Crassus swallowed his pride when it came to accepting an ovatio instead of a triumph, but a myrtle wreath was too much. He asked the Senate for a special decree, a private bill as it were. The Senate complied, allowing Crassus to wear a laurel wreath at his ovatio.

Marcus Lucullus's triumph probably took place first, well before the end of the year. Metellus Pius, Crassus, and Pompey followed in late December, apparently within the space of a few days. Scholars reconstruct the order of events thus: Metellus Pius came first because of his rank as a former consul, then Crassus the ex-praetor, and finally Pompey, who, in spite of his military prowess, was a mere Roman knight.

Within the space of about a week, about a hundred thousand men marched through the city and accepted the cheers of a public grateful that peace had been restored in the heart of the empire and in one province, if not everywhere. These were very lavish affairs to judge from a surviving detail of Metellus Pius's triumph, that he served five thousand thrushes for the public feasting. The cost for these birds alone was sixty thousand sesterces, which was roughly equivalent to the annual pay of about a hundred legionaries.

By the time of Pompey's triumph, Rome had crowned four brows with laurel wreaths in one year. It was the last day of December, 71 B.C. The Spartacus War was officially history. The legend had already begun.

CONCLUSION

IN THE CONSULSHIP of Quintus Caecilius Metellus Celer and Lucius Afranius, the year we call 60 B.C., a small army marches southward from Rome under the command of Gaius Octavius. Down the great highways of Italy the men tramp, past Capua and Vesuvius, across the hills of Lucania and under the peaks of Mount Pollino, where they finally turn eastward into Bruttium and Italy's far south. Their goal is in sight. A dirty mission, and one postponed by the Senate for a decade, it is nonetheless essential to Roman honor. They have come to exorcise the ghost of Spartacus.

For Octavius, it is a detour from his destiny. He has been named governor of Macedonia, a province across the Adriatic Sea and gateway to the Thracian front, with its rebellious tribes. Victory in arms there might lead to a triumph, which is an ambitious Roman's dream. Octavius is the very model of the young man on the make. The product of the local aristocracy of a central Italian town, he has married into a prominent Roman family and is climbing the ladder of political and military office. Greatness beckons, but before Octavius can board ship at Brundisium, he has a job to do in Italy.

Eleven years after the end of the great uprising, the last of the rebel's men still controlled the hills around the plain of Thurii in Bruttium. A rich agricultural region, the plain housed many villas. Spartacus had once scored a great coup here; Thurii is the only city that he and his men ever captured. No wonder the remnants of Spartacus's army chose to make their way back to these hills after Crassus's victory in 71 B.C.

As far as we can tell, they survived as raiders, not revolutionaries, content to huddle in the hills and sally forth for supplies. They no longer dared to face the legionaries' iron on the open plains. Perhaps the dreamers among them hoped that Spartacus was still alive somewhere and that he would return—after all, his body had never been found. But Spartacus was dead, and a long row of crosses signaled the fate that awaited those who came out in the open to fight Rome.

They continued on local raids for eight years, until the tide of another failed uprising washed up on them. In 63 B.C., the renegade Roman aristocrat Catiline tried to raise a revolt of debtors and slaves, but the Senate crushed it. Survivors of that lost cause fled to Thurii and reinforced the Spartacans. The Senate now decided to wipe out the maroon communities around Thurii. Enter Octavius.

"He put an end to them on his journey": so say the sources, without wasting too many words on the fate of rebel slaves. But we can imagine the details: from the Roman cavalrymen suddenly riding in to the crash of swords, some of them perhaps even wielded in defense by men trained in the House of Vatia long ago. We can hear the screams and the crackle of the flames and finally, the hammering of nails into the inevitable crosses on the roadside.

Whether Octavius knew it or not, his mopping-up operation marked the end of an era. It had lasted about three generations, from the outbreak of the First Sicilian Slave Revolt, circa 135 B.C., until

60 B.C. Each of the two Sicilian slave wars had continued for several years, while Spartacus's uprising lasted more than two years. No further slave uprisings of that magnitude would follow. For example, Catiline's "conspiracy," as Cicero famously called it, took Rome three months to suppress, and it was largely an operation of free men rather than of slaves.

All was not peaceful with Rome's slaves or gladiators, however. Having learned its lesson with Spartacus, the Senate now recognized the revolutionary potential of gladiators and moved to stop it. During the Catiline crisis of 63 B.C., for example, the Senate decreed that gladiators be sent out of Rome and moved to Capua and other Italian cities. Both sides recruited gladiators to the political gangs whose violence plagued Roman politics in the decade of the 50s, as civil war loomed between Caesar and Pompey. When Caesar finally crossed the Rubicon in 49 B.C. and marched on Rome, his rival Pompey seized Caesar's gladiators at Capua and distributed them among Roman colonists to be guarded: the gladiators were a thousand or more men. The senators were right to worry about gladiators.

No new Spartacus arose to rally Italy's slaves. Leaders of his caliber do not come often, and any who did would have had a hard time convincing men to risk the fate of Spartacus's followers. Slaves took up arms again but in the service of one or another of Rome's revolutionary politicians rather than under the banner of a rebel slave. The best-known case is that of Sextus Pompey, son of Pompey the Great, who ran a successful pirate fleet from Sicily between 43 and 36 B.C. His men included thirty thousand runaway slaves.

Spartacus was dead, but his legend was alive and well. Twenty years after Spartacus's death, Caesar cited the lessons of Spartacus's revolt when he fought Celts and Germans in Gaul. Thirty years after Spartacus's death, the Roman general Mark Antony threatened the republic with his armies. There were no rebel slaves among them but Cicero branded the man "a new Spartacus" nonetheless. Spartacus echoed in Horace's poetry fifty years after his death. A hundred years after his death, Spartacus's name came up at the specter of a gladiators' revolt in central Italy.

From Caesar to Tacitus to Augustine, the Roman elite never forgot Spartacus. Two of the first historians to write about him were Sallust (86–35 B.C.) and Livy (59 B.C.–A.D. 17). To Sallust, Spartacus was a great man, a hero and patriot who tried to keep his soldiers from committing atrocities and who wanted to lead them out of Italy homeward. But Sallust despised the Senate and much of Rome's political elite, so his sympathy for a rebel slave makes sense. Livy, a more establishment figure, saw a darker Spartacus, to judge by what little remains of his chapters on the revolt of the gladiators. To Livy, Spartacus was the man who had terrorized Italy.

The voices of ordinary people and slaves are nearly impossible to recover, but they may have left the trace of a whisper. To them, Spartacus might have been a figure of resistance and hope, a reminder of Rome's Achilles' heel. The evidence is especially speculative, but we should consider it. Let us begin with Crassus's chosen instruments of punishment. Pieces of the six thousand crosses on which Spartacus's men hanged might have ended up as relics in the hands of ordinary Italians. The Romans believed in the magical value of a nail or piece of cord used in a crucifixion. Wrapped in wool and placed around the neck, these amulets were thought to cure malarial fevers. The Romans also believed that the hair of a crucified person could ease the disease. Malaria was endemic to Roman Italy, and people sought whatever relief they could find. We can imagine soldiers grabbing nails and cord from the slaves' crosses and cutting hair from victims' corpses and then perhaps even selling such items. If only in amulets kept in Italians' cupboards, the memory of the slaves' final agony lingered.

In Rome there was precedent for treating great men like demigods. For example, the Gracchi brothers had been assassinated (in

133 and 122 B.C.) after trying to put through land reform for the common people of Rome. They enjoyed a virtual martyr cult, including statues and daily offerings, while the places where they died were considered sacred. In 86 B.C., to take another case, Romans erected statues to a now-obscure praetor, Marius Gratidanus, and offered wine and incense to thank him for currency reforms. Slaves could not erect statues to Spartacus, but they could bless his memory and keep it alive.

Worshipping great men might have come naturally to Roman slaves. Slaves took part in the rituals of the little religious community that every Roman household represented. It was standard practice for slaves to worship the *genius*—that is, the "life force"—of their master. Many would have preferred worshipping the memory of the man who had tried to free them.

A painting in Pompeii, though fragmentary and puzzling, may tell us something about popular memory. A cartoon-like fresco, it labels one of its characters as Spartacus: literally, SPARTAKS, which is the Oscan version of the Latin name Spartacus. Oscan was the language of Pompeii. After Sulla planted a colony of his veterans there in 80 B.C., Latin quickly dominated the city's public life, but the Oscan language lingered. Did it record the great rebel gladiator? In truth, Pompeii could not have forgotten Spartacus easily.

A reminder of Spartacus dominated Pompeii's skyline: Vesuvius, visible throughout the city, and once the scene of Spartacus's triumph. Some Pompeians might have suffered personally from his raids, which ravaged the local countryside. As a gladiator, moreover, Spartacus had an added claim to Pompeii's attention, because Pompeians were ardent fans. Archaeological evidence shows this, at least for the first century A.D.

The Spartacus fresco decorated a building on a busy street. In A.D. 79 its location was the entrance hall of a private house. But the fresco was painted much earlier, well before the volcanic eruption of A.D.

79; in fact the fresco had been covered over by two layers of plaster by then and was no longer visible. It is possible that the room where it was found was part of a tavern next door; the evidence suggests that the architecture had been changed before A.D. 79. The painting is monochromatic, with reddish chestnut-colored figures drawn on a white background, a common style in pre-Roman Campania. It looks a little bit like a modern comic strip.

The Spartaks fresco depicts a series of combats. On the far right there is a trumpeter. To his left ride two horsemen armed with lances, helmets, and round shields. The first rider looks like he is trying to escape the second, but without success: the second horseman spears him in the thigh. To the left of the horsemen two men are fighting on foot. They are armed with swords, large body shields, and helmets. Finally, on their left, comes a rectangular shape, possibly an altar.

Some say the fresco depicts an actual battle, but it is clearly a gladiatorial combat. The two pairs of fighters and their arms and armor point to this conclusion. So does the altar, which recalls the tombs around which the earliest gladiatorial games took place. And then there is the trumpeter. Musicians accompanied gladiatorial games, and they sometimes dressed like animals. This trumpeter is wearing a mask, possibly representing a bear. He may be draped in a bearskin cloak as well. We know of another example of a trumpeter in the games who wore a mask and bearskin. That man's stage name was Ursus Tubicen, "the Bear Trumpeter," presumably in reference to the instrument's deep roar.

Each of the four gladiators is labeled. The names of the men on foot are illegible while the name of the conquering horseman is FEL . . . POMP . . . , plausibly restored as Felix the Pompeian, which also means "the lucky Pompeian." The wounded horseman is clearly labeled SPARTAKS.

But was he *the* Spartacus? The experts disagree. Some say yes and argue, moreover, that the fresco depicts Spartacus's last battle. Some even suggest that the man who commissioned the painting—Felix of Pompeii?—had claimed to have wounded Spartacus. The fresco depicts gladiators, not soldiers, but it depicts Spartacus in combat, and so it might have been meant as a symbol of his revolt.

Much debate revolves around the fresco's use of the Oscan language. In the conventional view, Oscan disappeared in Pompeii after 80 B.C., so the fresco can't refer to Spartacus's revolt. But Oscan inscriptions from the first century A.D. are found elsewhere in southern Italy, so the fresco might indeed refer to Spartacus's revolt.

In fact, after 80 B.C. native Pompeians might even have wanted to flaunt the Oscan language as a sign of lcoal pride. The sources refer to bitter and protracted tension at Pompeii between Oscan-speaking natives and Latin-speaking colonists. Perhaps the Spartaks fresco was thumbing its nose at the colonists by reminding them of an enemy who had humiliated Rome.

The evidence does not permit certainty, but the reader might accept this hypothesis: The fresco offers a snapshot of myth turning into history. Spartaks is Spartacus as one segment of the public remembered him. Outside of books and schoolrooms, historical truth usually becomes myth. Spartacus was larger than life; he was whatever people made of him. They might even have made him into a religious figure—the Spartaks fresco suggests that, too. The possible presence of a tomb in the fresco points to funeral games, a common subject of Italian wall painting, documented in other wall painting at Pompeii. A funeral was a religious occasion; it was also, from time to time, an occasion for gladiators. It was a time-honored Italian custom to celebrate the death of a great man with a gladiatorial combat beside his tomb: a death for a death, as it were.

In the fields of southern Italy, Spartacus might have entered the Orphic-Dionysiac pantheon as a symbol of hope. If the Roman elite shivered at the thought of Spartacus returning, the slave masses might have thrilled at it.

It remained a bloody time for many of those who survived Spartacus. His followers were slowly annihilated. Many of the other important figures in this drama also met with disaster. Oddly, the minor characters seem to have done better than the great men, but perhaps that is a misreading of the sources, which revel in lurid details about the elite while passing over secondary players.

To take the lesser figures first, it seems that defeat by Spartacus was not a career killer. For example, as praetor in 73 B.C., Varinius had barely escaped Spartacus. Yet there is evidence that eight years later, in 65 B.C., he held office as governor of the province of Asia (western Turkey).

The consuls Gellius and Lentulus recovered from the dishonor of their defeats by Spartacus in 72 B.C. They were elected censors for the year 70. From 67 to 65 they served as commanders under Pompey in the war against the pirates; they were entrusted with guarding the Italian coast and patrolling the Tyrrhenian Sea. How ironic if any of the pirates who had betrayed Spartacus ended up in their hands! Both men remained active in politics, where they supported Pompey over Caesar. Rumor stained Gellius with domestic scandal: Gellius's adopted son is said to have committed adultery with Gellius's second wife.

In 72 B.C., Quintus Arrius had served as propraetor and helped Gellius defeat Crixus. He worked his way through the maze of Roman politics over the next two decades, appearing now as a friend of Crassus, now of Caesar, but never of Cicero, who repaid the compliment by denigrating Arrius in his writings. Arrius retired from public life in 52 B.C., in a violent era when peaceful retirement was rare for senators.

Turn to the principal players in the defeat of Spartacus and the record gets bloody. Verres, for example, may have saved Sicily from Spartacus, but that did not help him in 70 B.C. when Cicero exposed the former governor for having looted the island. Facing a likely conviction after Cicero's devastating prosecution, Verres did not wait for the verdict. He fled Rome for Massilia (modern Marseilles), where he would spend the next quarter century in self-imposed exile. Finally, in 43, Roman politics caught up with him. In that year Mark Antony had him murdered, allegedly because Verres refused to turn over to him art treasures that Verres had stolen long ago in Sicily. That last detail, however, is probably too good to be true. Ironically, Cicero himself was murdered at Antony's command in the same year. Antony took revenge on the orator for having skewered him in public speeches, just as Cicero had once denounced Verres.

It was Pompey who had advised Verres to go into exile. Similar advice might have saved Pompey's neck, but Pompey was too ambitious and, for a time, too successful, to do such a thing. During the decade of the 60s, Pompey was the first man in Rome. He won top military commands: Pompey cleared the seas of pirates, finally defeated Mithridates, and added the Levant to the Roman Empire. Still, Pompey was no dictator, and in 60 B.C. he entered into a deal with Crassus and Caesar to run Rome as a triumvirate. But the First Triumvirate, as historians call this arrangement, eventually fell apart. In the end, things came down to civil war (49–45 B.C.) between supporters of Pompey and those of Caesar. Defeated at the battle of Pharsalus in northern Greece in 48, Pompey sailed to Egypt. He was murdered as he stepped ashore. Caesar, of course, was assassinated four years later, on the Ides of March, 44 B.C.

Crassus avoided this civil war because he was dead. In 53 B.C. he too had met a violent end. Building on his success against Spartacus, Crassus served as consul twice and as censor, championed the tax collectors of the province of Asia (western Turkey), dabbled in social and political reform, and built up formidable connections and influence. Finally he won a great command in the East and left Italy in 55 B.C. to conquer Parthia, as the Persian kingdom of the day was known. But the Parthians were no army of ill-equipped slaves.

The Parthians excelled at cavalry, both heavy- and light-armed, and were famous archers. Crassus had only infantrymen, apart from a small cavalry corps led by his son Publius and manned by Gauls. He failed to understand the challenge that faced him. After staging in Syria, Crassus crossed into western Mesopotamia. The enemy met him near the city of Carrhae. After crushing the Gallic cavalry and killing Publius, the Parthians faced a demoralized enemy. Crassus agreed to negotiate but was killed in a scuffle with the enemy. They cut off his head and his right hand. His men either surrendered or fled, but most were caught and either killed or taken captive.

The story goes that Crassus's decapitated head suffered a final indignity. It reached the court of the Parthian king at the city of Seleucia, near modern Baghdad. There Crassus's head supposedly showed up as a prop in a performance of Euripides' tragedy *The Bacchae*.

Of the three Roman generals who closed in on Spartacus in 71 B.C., only Marcus Lucullus died of natural causes. Lucullus celebrated a triumph for his success in Thrace, but the rest of his public life was not easy. His older brother, Lucius Lucullus, won great military success against Mithridates but made important enemies in Roman politics who forced him out of power. They made trouble at Rome for both brothers over the next decade. Lucius went insane and died around 56 B.C. His grieving brother Marcus buried him on the family estate in the countryside near Rome and then died shortly afterward.

After the frustration of serving under Gellius in 72 B.C., Cato the Younger went on to greatness and tragedy. He became the Late Republic's leading member of the old guard; no one defended the Senate's privileges more stubbornly. Although Cato distrusted Pompey, he detested Caesar, so Cato fought for Pompey in the civil war that broke out in 49 B.C. After serving in Sicily, Epirus, and Asia Minor, in 46 B.C. Cato ended up in North Africa, where Caesar defeated Cato and pardoned him. Cato preferred suicide. Like Spartacus, his name became legendary. Cato lives on as an icon of republican virtue.

Thracian rebels would continue to rise in arms against Rome for a century after Spartacus's death. Big revolts broke out in 11 B.C., A.D. 11, and A.D. 26, which forced Rome to send in the legions. Finally, in A.D. 46, Rome formally annexed Thrace, which had been a client state, as a province. Six years later a Thracian from the tribe of the Bessi received Roman citizenship as a reward for loyal service in the Roman navy, where he had been a marine for twenty-six years. His name was Spartacus—or, rather, to use the variant spelling of his citizenship record, Sparticus. Sparticus assimilated, unlike the gladiator. Yet the great rebel, too, had once served Rome; if fate had taken a different turn, Spartacus might have headed toward Roman citizenship in 73 B.C. instead of rising in revolt. But Rome was a much more open society in A.D. 52 than it had been 125 years earlier.

It is in the shadow of Vesuvius that our story ends. In A.D. 14, an old man lay dying just west of Vesuvius, at the foot of the mountain or perhaps on its slopes: in either case, within the territory of the Italian city of Nola. He called for a mirror, had his hair combed and his sagging jaws set. Surrounded by his friends, he asked wittily whether he had played his part well in the comedy of life. He displayed a coolness in the face of death that a gladiator would have envied. But he was no gladiator: he was the first man in Rome, the "father of his country," as the Senate called him. Gaius Julius Caesar Octavianus, better known as Augustus, Rome's first emperor. As Augustus made his exit, Spartacus took a bow with him.

Nola lies at the foot of Mount Vesuvius. When Spartacus and his men poured down from the summit in 73 B.C., they victimized the territory of Nola. As he lay dying, Augustus is unlikely to have turned his attention to local history. But in truth, Augustus had reason to look up toward the summit and think of the slaves who had once ruled the mountain. Without them, he might never have become emperor.

As a young man, Augustus held the honorary title of Thurinus, "the man from Thurii." The sources disagree as to the origin of that title, but the likeliest explanation is a souvenir from his father. Augustus's father was Gaius Octavius, the man who had cleaned out the nests of Spartacus's remaining followers around Thurii in 60 B.C. If Octavius senior had lived, he might well have gone on to other titles. As governor of Macedonia, he won a smashing victory over Thracian rebels; he was on his way back home to Rome in 58 B.C. to claim a triumph when he suffered an untimely death. His son was cheated of the bragging rights of having a *pater triumphator*, but he was entitled to call himself "Thurinus." Not exactly military glory on the grand scale, but the label recalled the senior Octavius's finest hour.

The son would begin his career with an honor attached to his name. Ironically, his father's marriage turned out to be even more helpful to his son than his military success, for Octavius had married Julius Caesar's niece. Caesar would adopt the boy, and young Thurinus grew up to become Octavian Caesar and then Augustus.

The shrewd Augustus might have considered, nonetheless, how much he owed Spartacus, at least indirectly. Spartacus's rebellion had helped to make it possible for Augustus to end the republic and become emperor. As scholars have pointed out, Spartacus had more symbolic than actual importance in the history of the later Roman Republic. Yet symbols matter. If Romans clamored for order and if they willingly submitted to dictatorship, it was in small part the result of Spartacus's *symbolic* power.

GLOSSARY OF KEY NAMES

ARRIUS, QUINTUS. As propraetor in 72 B.C., Arrius served on the staff of the consul Gellius.

BATIATUS—SEE Vatia.

CAESAR, JULIUS (100–44 B.C.) The famous Roman statesman made a veiled reference to Spartacus's revolt in his *Gallic War.*

CANNICUS (also known as **Gannicus**) Celtic co-commander of a breakaway rebel army that was defeated by Crassus in Lucania in 71 B.C.

CASTUS Celtic co-commander of a breakaway rebel army that was defeated by Crassus in Lucania in 71 B.C.

CATO, MARCUS PORCIUS, or **CATO THE YOUNGER** (95–46 B.C.) Fought against Spartacus under the consul Gellius in 72 B.C.

CICERO, MARCUS TULLIUS (106–43 B.C.) Makes several references to Spartacus, especially in his orations against the former governor of Sicily, Verres.

CRASSUS, MARCUS LICINIUS (d. 53 B.C.) The Roman general who, holding a special command, defeated Spartacus.

CRIXUS (d. 72 B.C.) Celtic gladiator and Spartacus's colleague as leader of the revolt against Rome.

GELLIUS, LUCIUS (ca. 136–50s B.C.) Consul in 72 B.C. who suffered the humiliating defeat in battle by Spartacus.

GLABER, CAIUS CLAUDIUS Praetor, defeated in 72 B.C. by Spartacus at Mount Vesuvius.

HERACLEO Active in Sicily, this pirate humiliated Verres by sailing into Syracuse's Great Harbor under his nose.

LENTULUS, GNAEUS CORNELIUS CLAUDIANUS Consul in 72 B.C., was defeated in battle by Spartacus.

LUCULLUS, LUCIUS (118–56 B.C.) Prominent Roman statesman and victorious commander against Mithridates, 73–66 B.C.

LUCULLUS, MARCUS Consul in 73 B.C., governor of Macedonia, victor over the Thracian Bessi, he was recalled to Italy to help defeat Spartacus. Brother of Lucius.

MITHRIDATES (120–63 B.C.) King of Pontus, he led a serious and long-lasting revolt against Rome with which Spartacus or at least some of his followers sympathized.

MUMMIUS Officer under Crassus, he was defeated by Spartacus in 72 B.C.

OENOMAUS Celtic gladiator and one of the original leaders of the revolt, he was killed early in the rebellion.

OCTAVIUS, GAIUS Father of the emperor Augustus, he defeated the last of Spartacus's followers in 60 B.C.

POMPEY, OR GNAEUS POMPEIUS MAGNUS (106–48 B.C.) One of the two leading Roman statesmen of his generation. Pompey defeated Sertorius in Spain and was recalled to Italy to help defeat Spartacus.

PUBLIPOR "Publius's boy," he joined Spartacus's rebellion and guided the slaves through Lucania.

SERTORIUS, QUINTUS (ca. 126–73 B.C.) Renegade Roman general and brilliant guerrilla soldier, he led a ten-year rebellion in Spain.

SPARTACUS (d. 71 B.C.) Thracian, Roman auxiliary soldier, bandit, and gladiator, Spartacus led the most famous slave revolt of antiquity for two years in Italy, 73–71 B.C.

THRACIAN LADY Spartacus's female companion, whose name has not survived, was a prophetess of Dionysus who preached Spartacus's mission.

VARINIUS, PUBLIUS Praetor in 73 B.C., Varinius suffered several defeats against Spartacus, including one in which he lost his horse and nearly his life.

VATIA, CNAEUS CORNELIUS LENTULUS The likely name for the man who is also called Batiatus, the gladiatorial entrepreneur who owned Spartacus at the time of his revolt.

VERRES, GAIUS (d. 43 B.C.) Rendered infamous by Cicero for his corruption as governor of Sicily, Verres probably protected the island from Spartacus.

NOTE ON SOURCES

What follows is a description of the main works used to write this study and a guide to further reading. It is not a complete list of references but a representative sample, with the emphasis on English-language scholarship. I include a few works in foreign languages that I have found essential, but many fine studies in French, German, and Italian have been omitted.

The indispensable reference book for classics and ancient history is *The Oxford Classical Dictionary*, 3rd ed. (Oxford: Oxford University Press, 1999). Excellent maps of the ancient world can be found in Richard J. A. Talbert, ed., *The Barrington Atlas of the Ancient Greco-Roman World* (Princeton: Princeton University Press, 2000).

SPARTACUS

The best place to begin is with Brent Shaw's excellent edited collection and translation of the main documents of the revolt, *Spartacus and the Slave Wars* (Boston: Bedford/St. Martins, 2001). The book also includes the main documents on the two Sicilian slave revolts as well as other Roman slave uprisings; it also has a fine introductory essay. Theresa Urbainczyk's *Spartacus* (London: Bristol Classical Press, 2004) offers a concise and prudent overview. M. J. Trow's *Spartacus: The Myth and the Man* (Stroud, England: Sutton, 2006) is a highly readable work by a nonscholar. Keith Bradley's *Slavery and Rebellion in the Roman World, 140 B.C.–70 B.C.* (Bloomington: Indiana University Press, 1989) has an outstanding chapter on Spartacus. F. A. Ridley, *Spartacus: The Leader of the Roman Slaves* (Ashford, England: F. Maitland, 1963), is a concise and often accurate little book by a socialist activist and writer. Several important books on Spartacus have appeared in

European languages; two of the best are Jean-Paul Brisson, *Spartacus* (Paris: Le club français du livre, 1959) and Antonio Guarino, *Spartaco* (Napoli: Liguori 1979). Guarino sees Spartacus as more bandit than hero; the argument does not convince but it is highly stimulating. The standard scholarly encyclopedia article is (in German) F. Muenzer, "Spartacus," in August Pauly, Georg Wissowa et al., *Paulys Real-encyclopädie der classischen Altertumwissenschaft*, 83 vols. (Stuttgart: 1893–1978), vol. 3 A: columns 1527–36 and Supplementary volume 5: column 993. There is a great deal of value, especially on topography, in the works of Luigi Pareti, particularly his *Storia di Roma e del Mondo Romano III: Dai prodromi della III Guerra Macedonica al "primo triumvirato" (170–59 av. Cr.)* (Turin: Unione Tipografico-Editrice Torinese, 1953), 687–708 and Luigi Pareti with Angelo Russi, *Storia della regione lucano-bruzzia nell' antichità* (Rome: Edizioni di storia e letteratura, 1997), 459–69.

A 1977 scholarly symposium held in Bulgaria contains many important essays, most in English: Khristo Miloshev Danov and Aleksandur Fol, eds., *SPARTACUS Symposium Rebus Spartaci Gestis Dedicatum 2050 A.: Blagoevgrad, 20–24.IX.1977* (Sofia: Editions De L'Académie Bulgare Des Sciences, 1981). Also in 1977 the Japanese Spartacus scholar Masaoki Doi published in English a valuable bibliography of scholarship on Spartacus, but copies are not easy to find: *Bibliography of Spartacus' Uprising, 1726–1976* (Tokyo: n.p., 1977).

The ancient evidence for Spartacus is notoriously inadequate. All of the Greek and Latin sources are collected in one place, in the original languages, in Giulia Stampacchia, *La Tradizione della Guerra di Spartaco di Sallusto a Orosio* [*The Tradition of the Spartacus War from Sallust to Orosius*] (Pisa: Giardini, 1976), which also offers (in Italian) a careful and measured study of the narrative of the revolt as seen through the various sources. The most important ancient work about Spartacus was probably the *Histories* of Gaius Sallustius Crispus, better known as Sallust (86–35 B.C.). A failed politician who commanded a legion for Julius Caesar, Sallust was a teenager at the time of the Spartacus War. He wrote extensively about Spartacus in his *Histories*, and, to judge from what remains of this work, he wrote trenchantly, but only pieces have survived. The basic Latin edition is B. Maurenbrecher, *C. Sallusti Crispi Historiarum Reliquae.*, vol. 2, *Fragmenta* (Leipzig: Teubner, 1893). For an excellent translation and historical commentary of the surviving fragments of Sallust's *Histories*, see Patrick McGushin, *Sallust: The Histories: Translated with Introduction and Commentary*, 2 vols. (Oxford: Clarendon, 1992–94).

The great Roman historian Titus Livius, or Livy (59 B.C.–A.D. 17) also wrote about Spartacus, but that section of his work survives only in a sketchy summary probably written centuries later.

The two most complete histories of Spartacus's revolt to survive from antiquity are by Plutarch (ca. A.D. 40s–120s) and Appian (ca. A.D. 90s–160s). They are useful but problematic. Both writers were Greek, and both moved in government circles in the heyday of the Roman Peace. Both wrote about Rome's past, drawing their information from earlier writings that no longer survive, and each preserved important details. But Appian condensed his sources imperfectly, and Plutarch cared less about history than biography. His account of Spartacus, for example, is just a section of his biography of Spartacus's conqueror, Marcus Licinius Crassus. Plutarch has a maddening habit of sacrificing narrative for a good moral. And Plutarch is our best single source about Spartacus! Still, Plutarch was careful and worldly, and a cautious reader can get a lot from him. There is an important historical commentary in Italian in M. G. Bertinelli Angeli et al., *Le Vite di Nicia e di Crasso* (Verona: Fondazione Lorenzo Vallo: A. Mondadori, 1993). An excellent historical commentary on Appian can be found in Emilio Gabba, *Appiani: Bellorum Civilium Liber Primus* (Firenze: La Nuova Italia Editrice, 1958).

Other Roman and Greek writers provide important details about Spartacus, all drawn, more or less accurately, from earlier histories. The most important of them are Velleius Paterculus (ca. 20 B.C.–A.D. 30s?), Frontinus (ca. A.D. 30–104), Florus (ca. A.D. 100–50), and Orosius (ca. A.D. 380s–420s). An important study of Florus on Spartacus is H. T. Wallinga, "Bellum Spartacium: Florus' Text and Spartacus's Objective," *Athenaeum* 80 (1992): 25–43. Cicero lived through Spartacus's revolt as a grown man and referred to it in several of his speeches, most notably in his orations against Verres, especially Oration 6 (also known as II, 5). An English translation of the speech by Michael Grant is conveniently found in Cicero, *On Government* (Hardmondsworth, England: Penguin, 1994), 13–105. For an overview, see M. Doi, "Spartacus' uprising in Cicero's works," *Index* 17 (1989): 191–203.

Two brilliant but speculative and ultimately unconvincing studies argue that Spartacus's revolt was primarily nationalist and anti-Roman rather than a slave revolt: W. Z. Rubinsohn, "Was the Bellum Spartacium a Servile Insurrection?" *Rivista di Filologia* 99 (1971): 290–99, and Pierre Piccinin, "Les Italiens dans le 'Bellum Spartacium,'" *Historia* 53, no. 2 (2004): 173–99. See also Piccinin, "À propos de deux passages des œuvres de Salluste et Plutarque," *Historia* 51, no. 3 (2002): 383–84 and Piccinin, "Le dionysisme dans le Bellum Spartacium," *Parola del Passato* 56, no. 319 (2001): 272–96.

The following are important studies of specific topics in the history of Spartacus's revolt: R. Kamienik, "Die Zahlenangaben ueber des Spartakus-Aufstand und ihre Glaubwuerdigkeit," *Altertum* 16 (1970): 96–105, on the number of rebels at various points in the revolt; K. Ziegler, "Die Herkunft des Spartacus," *Hermes* 83 (1955): 248–50, on the possibility that Spartacus was a Maedus; M. Doi, "Spartacus' uprising and ancient Thracia, II," *Dritter Internationaler Thrakologischer Kongress*, vol. 2 (Sofia: Staatlicher Verlag Swjat, 1984), pp. 203–7, and M. Doi, "The origins of Spartacus and the anti-Roman struggle in Thracia," *Index* 20 (1992): 31–40, on the influence of Spartacus's Thracian background; G. Stampacchia, "La rivolta di Spartaco come rivolta contadina," *Index* 9 (1980): 99–111, on the rural character of Spartacus's supporters; C. Pellegrino, *Ghosts of Vesuvius: A New Look at the Last Days of Pompeii, How Towers Fall, and Other Strange Connections* (New York: Morrow, 2004), 147–66, on Spartacus's sojourn on Mount Vesuvius; E. Maróti, "De suppliciis: Zur Frage der sizilianischen Zusammenhänge des Spartacus-Aufstandes,"*Acta Antiquae Hungariae* 9 (1961): 41–70, on Spartacus's planned crossing to Sicily; Maria Capozza, "Spartaco e il sacrificio del cavallo (Plut. *Crass.* 11, 8–9)," *Critica Storica* 2 (1963): 251–93, on Spartacus's sacrifice of a horse during his last battle. Allen Mason Ward, *Marcus Crassus and the Late Roman Republic* (Columbia: University of Missouri Press, 1977), esp. pp. 83–98, ch. 4, "The War With Spartacus," offers a fundamental study of the crucial last six months of the war.

The titles of the following all make the subjects clear: R. Kamienik "Gladiatorial games during the funeral of Crixus: Contribution to the revolt of Spartacus," *Eos* 64 (1976): 83–90; M. Doi, "Why did Spartacus stay in Italy?" *Antiquitas: Acta Universitatis Wratislaviensis* 598 (1983): 15–18; M. Doi, "On the Negotiations between the Roman State and the Spartacus Army," *KLIO* 66 (1984): 170–74; M. Doi, "Female Slaves in the Spartacus Army," in Marie-Madeleine Mactoux and Évelyne Geny, eds., *Mélanges*

Pierre Lévêque, II: Anthropologie et Société, Annales litter. de l'Univ. de Besançon, 377; Centre de rech. d'histoire anc., 82 (Paris: Les Belles Lettres, 1989): 161–72; R. M. Sheldon, "The Spartacus Rebellion: A Roman Intelligence Failure?" *International Journal of Intelligence and Counterintelligence* 6, no. 1 (1993): 69–84. Also valuable are B. Baldwin, "Two Aspects of Spartacus's Slave Revolt," *Classical Journal* 62 (1966–67): 288–94 and J. Scarborough, "Reflections on Spartacus," *Ancient World* 1, no. 2 (1978): 75–81.

Study of the "Spartaks" fresco begins with the publication by Italian archaeologist Amadeo Maiuri, *Monumenti della pittura antica scoperti in Italia.; Sezione terza; La pittura ellenistica romana; fasc. 2. Le pitture delle case di "M. Fabius Amandio," del "Sacerdos amandus" e di "P. Cornelius Teges" (reg. I, ins. 7)* (Rome: La Libreria dello Stato, 1938). Jerzy Kolendo makes the case for skepticism in "Uno spartaco sconosciuto nella Pompei osca: Le pitture della casa di Amando," *Index* 9 (1980): 33–40 and "Spartacus sur une peinture osque de Pompei: Chef de la grande insurrection servile ou un gladiateur inconnu originaire de la Thrace?" *Antiquitas: Acta Universitatis Wratislaviensis* 10 (1983): 49–53. Fabrizio Pesando weighs possible changes in the architecture of the building where the fresco was found in "Gladiatori a Pompei," in Adriano La Regina, ed., *Sangue e Arena* (Milan: Electa, 2001), 175–98. A sensible overview of the debate in English can be found in A. van Hoof, "Reading the Spartaks fresco without red eyes," in Stephan T. A. M. Mols and Eric Moormann, eds., *Omni pede stare: Saggi architectonici e circumvesuviani in memoriam Jos de Waele* (Naples: Electa Napoli and Ministeri per i Beni e le Attività Culturali, 2005), 251–56.

SPARTACUS IN FICTION, FILM, AND IDEOLOGY

Brent D. Shaw offers an excellent overview of Spartacus in Western culture before Marx in the eighteenth and nineteenth centuries, with a look forward to the present, in "Spartacus Before Marx: Liberty and Servitude," *Princeton/Stanford Working Papers in Classics* Version 2.2, November 2005, http://www.princeton.edu/~pswpc/pdfs/shaw/110516.pdf. On Marxist scholarship on Spartacus in the Soviet Union, see Wolfgang Zeev Rubinsohn, *Spartacus' Uprising and Soviet Historical Writing* (Oxford: Oxbow, 1987).

Three twentieth-century novels about Spartacus are available in English:

Lewis Grassic Gibbon, *Spartacus* (New York: Pegasus, 2006), originally published in 1933; Arthur Koestler, *The Gladiators*, trans. Edith Simon (New York: Macmillan, 1939), a work by a disillusioned ex-communist who sees in Spartacus's revolt the excesses of revolution; and Howard Fast's famous 1951 *Spartacus*, republished in 1996 by North Castle Books (Armonk, N.Y.) with a brief introductory essay by Fast about his experiences as an American communist in the McCarthy era.

Stanley Kubrick's 1960 film is available in DVD in several versions; the Criterion Collection version is the best. A 2004 remake, "Spartacus—The Complete TV Miniseries," is also available on DVD. A fascinating and enjoyable collection of essays about Kubrick's film is Martin M. Winkler, *Spartacus: Film and History* (Malden, Mass., and Oxford: Blackwell, 2007).

Khachaturian's ballet *Spartacus*, with choreography by Yuri Grigorovich and performed by the Bolshoi Ballet, is also available on DVD. The 1990 Arthaus DVD version, one of two starring Irek Mukhamedov as Spartacus, is probably the best. Recordings of the music alone are available.

Among documentaries on Spartacus, there is *The Real Spartacus*, a 2001 production of Britain's Channel 4; *Decisive Battles—Spartacus*, from the History Channel in 1994, available in DVD; *Spartacus, Gladiator War*, from National Geographic in 2006.

ROME AND ROMANS

A good introductory textbook to Roman history is Mary T. Boatwright, Daniel J. Gargola, and Richard Talbert, *The Romans* (New York: Oxford University Press, 2004). Michael Crawford, *The Roman Republic*, 2nd ed. (Cambridge, Mass.: Harvard University Press, 1993), offers a brief and incisive scholarly analysis. A lively and accessible overview is Philip Matyszak, *Chronicle of the Roman Republic* (London: Thames & Hudson, 2003). A classic and more detailed alternative is Thomas Rice Holmes, *The Roman Republic and the Founder of the Empire*, 3 vols. (Oxford: Clarendon, 1923). There are excellent introductory essays in Nathan Rosenstein and Robert Morstein-Marx, *A Companion to the Roman Republic* (Malden, Mass., and Oxford: Blackwell, 2006).

Tom Holland offers a vivid account of the final decades of the Roman

Republic in *Rubicon: The Last Years of the Roman Republic* (New York: Anchor, 2005). A scholarly introduction is Mary Beard and Michael Crawford, *Rome in the Late Republic: Problems and Interpretations,* 2nd ed. (London: Duckworth, 1999). The indispensable scholarly analysis of Roman politics in those years is Erich S. Gruen, *The Last Generation of the Roman Republic* (Berkeley: University of California Press, 1974).

An essential reference book for Roman officials is T. Robert S. Broughton, with the collaboration of Marcia Patterson, *The Magistrates of the Roman Republic,* 2 vols. (New York: American Philological Association, 1951–52). See also T. Corey Brennan, *The Praetorship in the Roman Republic* (Oxford: Oxford University Press, 2000).

On the economy of late Republican Italy, see Neville Morley, *Metropolis and Hinterland: The City of Rome and the Italian Economy, 200 B.C.–A.D. 200* (Cambridge, England: Cambridge University Press, 1996), and Nathan Rosenstein, *Rome at War: Farms, Families, and Death in the Middle Republic* (Chapel Hill: University of North Carolina Press, 2004).

On the demography of late Republican Italy, see P. A. Brunt, *Italian Manpower 225 B.C.–A.D. 14* (Oxford: Clarendon Press, 1971); Tim G. Parkin, *Roman Demography and Society* (Baltimore: Johns Hopkins University Press, 1992); W. W. Scheidel, "Human Mobility in Roman Italy, I: The Free Population." *Journal of Roman Studies* 94 (2005): 1–26, and "Human Mobility in Roman Italy, II: The Slave Population," *Journal of Roman Studies* 95 (2005): 65–79.

On individual Roman politicians of the Spartacus War, see Arthur Keaveney, *Sulla: The Last Republican* (London: Routledge, 2005); Arthur Keaveney, "Sulla and Italy," *Critica Storia* 19 (1982): 499–544; Allen Mason Ward, *Marcus Crassus and the Late Roman Republic;* Frank E. Adcock, *Marcus Crassus, Millionaire* (Cambridge: England: W. Heffer & Sons, 1966); B. A. Marshall, *Crassus: A Political Biography* (Amsterdam: Adolf M. Hakkert, 1976); B. A. Marshall, "Crassus's Ovation in 71," *Historia* 21 (1972): 669–73; B. A. Marshall, "Crassus and the Command Against Spartacus," *Athenaeum* 51 (1973): 109–21; P. Greenhalgh, *Pompey: The Roman Alexander* (London: Weidenfeld & Nicolson, 1980); Robin Seager, *Pompey the Great: A Political Biography* (Oxford: Blackwell, 2002); Anthony Everitt, *Cicero: The Life and Times of Rome's Greatest Politician* (New York: Random House, 2003); B. A. Marshall and R. J. Baker, "The Aspirations of Q. Arrius," *Historia* 24, no. 2 (1975): 220–31; I. Shatzman, "Four Notes on Roman Magistrates," *Athenaeum* 46 (1968): 345–54.

On Sertorius, see Philip O. Spann, *Quintus Sertorius: Citizen, Soldier, Exile* (Fayetteville: University of Arkansas Press, 1976); Christoph F. Konrad, *Plutarch's Sertorius: A Historical Commentary* (Chapel Hill: University of North Carolina Press, 1994). On Mithridates, see Adrienne Mayor, *Mithridates* (Princeton: Princeton University Press, forthcoming).

Other valuable studies include Mary Beard, *The Roman Triumph* (Cambridge, Mass.: Harvard University Press, 2007); John Percival, *The Roman Villa: An Historical Introduction* (London: B. T. Batsford, 1976); James S. Ackerman, *The Villa: Form and Ideology of Country Houses* (London: Thames & Hudson, 1990); Carol Humphrey Vivian Sutherland, *The Romans in Spain, 217 B.C.–A.D. 117* (London: Methuen, 1939); John S. Richardson, *The Romans in Spain* (Oxford: Blackwell, 1996); John S. Richardson, *Hispaniae: Spain and the Development of Roman Imperialism, 218–82 BC* (Cambridge, England: Cambridge University Press, 1986); Wilfried Nippel, *Public Order in Ancient Rome* (Cambridge, England: Cambridge University Press, 1995).

GLADIATORS

Two accessible and readable recent introductions to the subject are Alison Futrell, *The Roman Games* (Oxford: Blackwell, 2006) and Fik Meijer, *The Gladiators: History's Most Dangerous Sport* (New York: St. Martin's, 2003). Susanna Shadrake, *The World of the Gladiator* (Stroud, England: Tempus, 2005), offers reconstructions of gladiatorial combat, as does Marcus Junkelmann, *Das Spiel mit dem Tod: So kampften Roms Gladiatoren* (Mainz am Rhein: von Zabern, 2000); the latter is in German but the excellent photos speak for themselves. An English-language summary of some of Junkelmann's ideas is found in Marcus Junkelmann, "Familia Gladiatoria: The Heroes of the Amphitheatre," in *Gladiators and Caesars: The Power of Spectacle in Ancient Rome*, Eckart Koehne and Cornelia Ewigleben, eds., English version edited by R. Jackson (Berkeley: University of California Press, 2000), pp. 31–74; see also M. Junkelmann, "Gladiatorial and Military Equipment and Fighting Technique: A Comparison," *Journal of Roman Military Equipment Studies* 11 (2000): 113–17.

Karl Grossschmidt and Fabian Kanz, *Gladiatoren in Ephesos: Tod am*

Nachmittag (Vienna: Osterreichisches Archaeologisches Institut, 2002), summarizes important discoveries from a gladiators' cemetery in Ephesus. Luciana Jacobelli, *Gladiators at Pompeii* (Los Angeles: John Paul Getty Museum, 2004), focuses on the important evidence of the first century A.D. but contains much of interest.

Other valuable books on gladiators and their place in Roman society and culture include Donald G. Kyle, *Spectacles of Death in Ancient Rome* (London and New York: Routledge, 1998); and Thomas Wiedemann, *Emperors & Gladiators* (London and New York: Routledge, 1992). Katherine E. Welch theorizes a Roman initiative behind Campania's first stone amphitheaters: Katherine E. Welch, *The Roman Amphitheatre: From Its Origins to the Colosseum* (New York: Cambridge University Press, 2007), along with an article by the same author, "The Roman arena in late-Republican Italy: A new interpretation," *Journal of Roman Archaeology* 7 (1994): 59–80. Carlin A. Barton, *The Sorrows of the Ancient Romans: The Gladiator and the Monster* (Princeton: Princeton University Press, 1993), is speculative but often insightful. On gladiators in the armed gangs and bodyguards of the Late Republic, see Andrew Lintott, *Violence in Republican Rome* (Oxford: Oxford University Press, 1999), 83–85.

SLAVES

The best introduction to Roman slavery is Keith Bradley, *Slavery and Society at Rome* (Cambridge, England: Cambridge University Press, 1994). See also his very thoughtful earlier study, *Slaves and Masters in the Roman Empire: A Study in Social Control* (Brussels: Latomus, 1984). The little book by Michael Massey and Paul Moreland, *Slavery in Ancient Rome* (London: Bristol Classical Press, 2001), is also a good start. Thomas Wiedemann, *Greek and Roman Slavery* (London: Routledge, 1981), is an excellent collection of documents. J. C. Dumont, *Servus: Rome et l'Esclavage sous la République: Collection de l'École Française de Rome* 103 (Rome: École Française de Rome, 1987), is fundamental on slavery in the Republic. Two important introductory studies are John Bodel, "Slave Labour and Roman Society," in Keith Bradley and Paul Cartledge, eds., *The Cambridge World History of Slavery*, vol. 1 (Cambridge, England: Cambridge University Press, 2008), and Willem Jongman, "Slavery and the growth of Rome: The transformation of Italy in the second and first centuries BCE," in Catherine Edwards and Greg Woolf, eds., *Rome the Cosmopolis* (Cambridge, England: Cambridge University Press, 2003), pp. 100–22.

Moses I. Finley, *Ancient Slavery and Modern Ideology* (Princeton: Markus Wiener, 1998), is an essential discussion of the problem of slavery in the classical world. See also Joseph Vogt, *Ancient Slavery and the Ideal of Man*, trans. Thomas Wiedemann (Cambridge, Mass.: Harvard University Press, 1975); Keith Hopkins, *Conquerors and Slaves* (Cambridge, England: Cambridge University Press, 1978); Niall McKeown, *The Invention of Ancient Slavery*, Duckworth Classical Essays (London: Duckworth, 2007).

F. Hugh Thompson, *The Archaeology of Greek & Roman Slavery* (London: Duckworth, 2003), is valuable, but there remains much work to do on this subject. See Jane Webster, "Archaeologies of Slavery and Servitude: Bringing 'New World' Perspectives to Roman Britain," *Journal of Roman Archaeology* 18, no. 1 (2005): 161–79.

On the Roman slave trade, see John Bodel, "*Caveat emptor*: Towards a Study of Roman Slave Traders," *Journal of Roman Archaeology* 18 (2005): 181–95 and the debate represented by such works as W. V. Harris, "Demography, Geography and the Sources of Roman Slaves," *Journal of Roman Studies* 89 (1999): 62–75, and W. Scheidel, "Quantifying the Sources of Slaves in the Early Roman Empire," *Journal of Roman Studies* 87 (1997): 156–69.

REVOLTS AND RESISTANCE

There is an excellent introduction to the subject in Bradley, *Slavery and Rebellion in the Roman World, 140 B.C.–70 B.C.* See also Theresa Urbainczyk, *Slave Revolts in Antiquity* (Stocksfield, England: Acumen, 2008). Although the emphasis is on Greece, not Rome, a seminal discussion is found in Paul Cartledge, "Rebels and *Sambos* in Classical Greece: A Comparative View," in his *Spartan Reflections* (London: Duckworth, 2001), 127–52. Brent Shaw's *Spartacus and the Slave Wars*, cited above, offers translations of the major sources and a valuable introductory essay. Also useful is Zvi Yavetz, *Slaves and Slavery in Ancient Rome* (New Brunswick, N.J.: Transaction, 1988). Wolfgang Hoben, *Terminologische Studien zu den Sklavenerhebungen der roemischen Republik* (Wiesbaden: Steiner, 1978), represents an important study of the terminology of revolt used in the ancient sources. On the First Sicilian Slave War, see P. Green, "The First Sicilian Slave War," *Past and Present* 20 (1961): 10–29, with objections by W. G. G. Forrest and T. C. W. Stinton, "The First Sicilian Slave War," *Past and Present* 22 (1962): 87–93. On the Sicilian revolts, see also G. P. Verbrugghe, "Sicily 210–70 B.C.: Livy, Cicero and Diodorus," *Transactions and Proceedings of the American Philological Association* 103 (1972): 535–59 and G. P. Verbrugghe, "Slave rebellion or Sicily in revolt?" *Kokalos* 20 (1974): 46–60.

Thomas Grünewald has written a fascinating study in *Bandits in the Roman Empire: Myth and Reality*, trans. John Drinkwater (London and New York: Routledge, 2004).

WARFARE

Adrian Goldsworthy offers a concise introduction to the Roman way of war in *Roman Warfare* (New York: Smithsonian, 1999). His *The Complete Roman Army* (London and New York: Thames & Hudson, 2003), is a detailed overview of the legions and auxilia. For futher study, see his *The Roman Army at War, 100 BC–AD 200* (Oxford: Clarendon, 1996). Peter Connolly, *Greece and Rome at War* (London: Greenhill, 2006), offers superb illustrations and sound history. Catherine Gilliver, *The Roman Art of War* (Charleston, S.C.: Tempus, 1999), offers thoughtful analysis. Philip Sabin, *Lost Battles: Reconstructing the Great Clashes of the Ancient World* (London: Hambledon Continuum, 2008), combines wargaming and scholarship to reconstruct the ancient battlefield. See also Sabin's important article, "The Face of Roman Battle," *Journal of Roman Studies* 90 (2000): 1–17.

Some valuable studies of Roman logistics, equipment, marching order, and discipline are M. C. Bishop and J. C. N. Coulston, *Roman Military Equipment from the Punic Wars to the Fall of Rome* (London: B. T. Batsford, 1993); Jonathan Roth, *The Logistics of the Roman Army at War (264 B.C.–A.D. 235)* (Leiden: Brill, 1999).

On piracy in the Roman Mediterranean, see Philip De Souza, *Piracy in the Graeco-Roman World* (Cambridge, England: Cambridge University Press, 1999), and the still valuable Henry Arderne Ormerod, *Piracy in the Ancient World: An Essay in Mediterranean History* (Liverpool: University Press of Liverpool, 1924).

On the Roman ideal of single combat, see S. P. Oakley, "Single Combat in the Roman Republic," *Classical Quarterly* 35, no. 2 (1985): 392–410. See also the stimulating remarks of J. E. Lendon in *Soldiers and Ghosts: A History of Battle in Classical Antiquity* (New Haven: Yale University Press, 2006), especially pp. 172–232.

On "barbarian" warfare, see Christopher Webber, *The Thracians 700 BC–AD 46* (Oxford: Osprey, 2001); Stephen Allen, *Celtic Warrior, 300 BC–AD 100: Weapons, Armour, Tactics* (Oxford: Osprey Military, 2001); J.-L. Brunaux, *Guerre et Religion en Gaule: Essai D'Anthropologie Celtique* (Paris: Editions Errance, 2004); Daithi O Hogain, *Celtic Warriors: The Armies of One of the First Great Peoples in Europe* (New York: St. Martin's, 1999).

On guerrilla warfare and counterinsurgency, see Robert B. Asprey, *War in the Shadows: The Guerrilla in History*, vol. 1 (Garden City, N.Y.: Doubleday, 1975); Robert Taber, *War of the Flea: The Classic Study of Guerrilla Warfare* (Washington, D.C.: Brassey's, 2002); and C. E. Calwell, *Small Wars: Their Principles and Practices*, 3rd ed., with an introduction by Douglas Porch (Lincoln: University of Nebraska Press, 1996).

THRACIANS, CELTS, AND GERMANS

Introductions to the ancient Thracians include Ralph F. Hoddinott, *The Thracians* (London: Thames & Hudson, 1981); Alexander Fol and Ivan Mazarov, *Thrace & the Thracians* (New York: St. Martin's, 1997); L. Casson, "The Thracians," *Metropolitan Museum of Art Bulletin* 35, no. 1 (1977): 2–6. N. M. V. de Vries, "Die Stellung der Frau in der Thrakischen Gesellschaft," *Dritter Internationaler Thrakologischer Kongress* 2 (1984): 315–21, is fundamental on Thracian women.

There is a large bibliography on the Celts. Two good introductions are Barry Cunliffe, *The Ancient Celts* (Oxford: Oxford University Press, 1997), and John Haywood, *Atlas of the Celtic World* (London: Thames & Hudson, 2001). For the documents, see Philip Freeman, *War, Women and Druids: Eyewitness Reports and Early Accounts of the Ancient Celts* (Austin: University of Texas Press, 2002). On Celtic women, see Miranda Green, *Celtic Goddesses: Warriors, Virgins and Mothers* (London: British Museum, 1995); Peter Berresford Ellis, *Celtic Women: Women in Celtic Society and Literature* (London: St. Edmundsbury, 1995).

For an introduction to the ancient Germans, see Anthony King, *Roman Gaul and Germany* (Berkeley: University of California Press, 1990).

For general considerations on Romans and barbarians, see Barry W. Cunliffe, *Greeks, Romans, and Barbarians: Spheres of Interaction* (New York: Methuen, 1988); Peter S. Wells, *Beyond Celts, Germans, and Scythians: Archaeology and Identity in Iron Age Europe* (London: Duckworth, 2001).

RELIGION

Mary Beard, John North, and Simon Price, *Religions of Rome*, 2 vols. (Cambridge, England: Cambridge University Press, 1998), is an essential history and sourcebook. Valerie Warrior offers a concise introduction in *Roman Religion* (Cambridge, England: Cambridge University Press, 2006).

On the messianic aspects of the Roman slave revolts, see N. A. Mashkin, "Eschatology and Messianism in the Final Period of the Roman Republic," *Philosophy and Phenomenological Research* 10, no. 2 (1949): 206–228, and P. Masiello, "L'Ideologica Messianica e le Rivolte Servili," *Annali della Facoltà di lettere e filosofia* 11 (1966): 179–96.

A concise analysis of the Bacchanalia affair of 186 B.C. can be found in J. A. North, "Religious Toleration in Republican Rome," *Proceedings of the Cambridge Philological Society* 25 (1979): 85–103. See also P. G. Walsh, "Making a Drama out of a Crisis: Livy on the Bacchanalia," *Greece & Rome* 43 (1996): 188–203. A detailed and sophisticated analysis bringing in an archaeological perspective is J.-M. Pailler, *Bacchanalia: La repression de 186 av. J.-C. à Rome et en Italie (BEFAR 270)* (Rome: École Française de Rome, 1988).

On Thracian religion, see Ivan Marazov, "Thracian Religion," in Alexander Fol and Ivan Marazov, *Thrace and the Thracians* (New York: St. Martin's, 1977), pp. 17–36; S. E. Johnson, "The Present State of Sabazios Research," in H. Temporini and W. Haase, eds., *Aufstieg und Niedergang der roemischen Welt*, vol. 2, no. 17.3 (1984): 1583–1613; Alexander Fol, *The Thracian Dionysos: Book One: Zagreus* (Sofia: St. Kliment Ohridski University Press, 1991); Alexander Fol, *The Thracian Dionysos: Book Two: Sabazios* (Sofia: St. Kliment Ohridski University Press, 1994); N. Dimitrova, "Inscriptions and Iconography in the Monuments of the Thracian Rider," *Hesperia* 71, no. 2 (2002): 209–29.

On Celtic religion, see Jean Louis Brunaux, *The Celtic Gauls: Gods, Rites and Sanctuaries* (London: Seaby, 1988); Miranda J. Green, *The World of the Druids* (London: Thames & Hudson, 1997); Nora K. Chadwick, *The Druids* (Cardiff: University of Wales Press, 1997).

On the use of Dionysus as a political symbol in the Hellenistic world, see Walter Burkert, "Bacchic *Teletai* in the Hellenistic Age," in Thomas H. Carpenter and Christopher A. Faraone, eds., *Masks of Dionysus* (Ithaca: Cornell University Press, 1993), pp. 259–75, esp. pp. 259–70.

On heroization and divine honors for great men in the late Roman Republic, see Stefan Weinstock, *Divius Julius* (Oxford: Clarendon, 1971), pp. 287–97; Itta Gradel, *Emperor Worship and Roman Religion* (Oxford: Clarendon, 2002), pp. 27–53. On the widespread belief that successful Roman Republican generals were supernaturally inspired, see J. P. V. D. Balsdon, "Sulla Felix," *Journal of Roman Studies* 41, nos. 1–2 (1951): 1–10.

ITALIAN TOPOGRAPHY AND ARCHAEOLOGY

Basic introductions to the Italian geographical context of Spartacus's revolt include Timothy W. Potter, *Roman Italy* (Berkeley: University of California Press, 1990); R. Ross Holloway, *The Archaeology of Ancient Sicily* (London and New York: Routledge, 2000), and guidebooks in the Blue Guide series such as Paul Blanchard, *Southern Italy* (London: A&C Black, 2004). H. V. Morton, *A Traveller in Southern Italy* (London: Methuen, 1969) is impressionistic but stimulating.

R. J. Buck published a series of studies on the ancient roads of Lucania between 1971 and 1981: R. J. Buck, "The Via Herculia," *Papers of the British School at Rome* 39 (1971): 66–87; R. J. Buck, "The Ancient roads of eastern Lucania," *Papers of the British School at Rome* 42 (1974): 46–67; R. J. Buck, "The Ancient roads of southeastern Lucania," *Papers of the British School at Rome* 43 (1975): 98–117; R. J. Buck, "The Ancient roads of northwestern Lucania and the battle of Numistro," *Parola del Passato* 36 (1981): 317–47.

The following regional and local studies are helpful: On the archaeology and history of Campania, see Martin Frederiksen, *Campania* (Hertford, England: Stephen Austin & Sons, 1984). On Capua, see Stefano De Caro and Valeria Sampaolo, *Guide of Ancient Capua* (Santa Maria Capua Vetere: Soprintendenza Archeologica delle province di Napoli e Caserta, 2000). On ancient Lucania, see Elena Isayev, *Inside Ancient Lucania: Dialogues in History and Archaeology* (London: Institute of Classical Studies, University of London, 2007). There is a brief but illuminating discussion of the Roman Republican era at Metapontum in Joseph Coleman Carter, *Discovering the Greek Countryside at Metaponto* (Ann Arbor: University of Michigan Press, 2006); Antonio De Siena, *Metaponto: Archeologia di una Colonia Greca* (Taranto: Soprintendenza Archeologica della Basilicata, Scorpione Editrice, 2001); Franco Liguori, *Sybaris Tra Storia e Leggenda* (Castrovillari: Bakos, 2004).

Laura Battastini argues that Spartacus's battle with Lentulus took place in the northern Tuscan Apennines near the village of Lentula: *Lentula, La dinastia dei Lentuli Corneli, la guerra di Spartaco e la storia di antichi villaggi dell'Appennino Tosco Emiliano*, 2nd ed. (Rastignano: Editografica, 2000). R. Luongo opens a window into the journey of Spartacus's army in the region of the Picentini mountains: R. Luongo, "L'esercito di Spartaco nella regione dei Monti Picentini," *Rassegna Storica Salernita* 42, n.s. 21.2 (2004): 21–32. Enzo Greco's study of Spartacus on the Strait of Messina is illuminating if unconvincing: Enzo Greco, *Spartaco sullo stretto ovvero Le origini di Villa San Giovanni e Fiumara di muro* (Rome: Gangemi Editore, 1999).

Domenico Raso offers a plausible theory of Crassus's military works in the Aspromonte Mountains in Domenico Raso, "TINNARIA: Antiche opere militari sullo Zomaro," *Calabria sonosciuta* 37 (January–March 1987): 79–102, and Domenico Raso, *Zomaro: La montagna dei sette popoli, tra i misteri della montagna calabrese* (Reggio di Calabria: Laruffa, 2001).

On Roman roads, see Raymond Chevallier, *Roman Roads*, trans. N. H. Field (Berkeley: University of California Press, 1976); Ray Laurence, *The Roads of Roman Italy: Mobility and Cultural Change* (London and New York: Routledge, 1999); Romolo Agosto Staccioli, *The Roads of the Romans* (Rome: "L'Erma" di Bretschneider, 2003); Ivana della Portella, Giuseppina Pisani Sartorio, Francesca Ventre, *The Appian Way from Its Foundation to the Middle Ages*, trans. from the Italian (Los Angeles: J. Paul Getty Museum, 2004) and A. R. Amarotta, "La Capua-Reggio (e il locus Popilli) nei pressi di Salerno," *Atti della Accademia Pontaniana* 33 (1984): 289–308.

A brief but valuable introduction to the archaeological evidence for Spartacus's revolt is found in A. Russi, "La romanizzazione: il quadro storico," in Dinu Adamesteanu, ed., *Storia della Basilicata, vol. 1: L'Antichità*

(Rome: Editori Laterza, 1999), 531–37, and in the same volume, A. Small, "L'occupazione del territorio in età romana," p. 577. For the coin horde buried at Siris, see A. Siciliano, "Ripostiglio di monete repubblicane da Policoro," *Annali dell' Istituto Italiano di Numismatica* 21–22 (1974–75): 103–54. For the treasure buried at Palmi, in an olive grove twenty-five miles north of Cape Caenys, see P. G. Guzzo, "Argenteria di Palmi in ripostiglio," *Atti e memorie della Società Magna Grecia* 18–20 (1977–79): 193–209.

MISCELLANEOUS

On tattooing in Greece and Rome, see C. P. Jones, "Stigma: Tatooing and Branding in Graeco-Roman Antiquity," *Journal of Roman Studies* 77 (1987): 139–55. On tattooing in Thrace, see A. Mayor, "People Illustrated," *Archaeology* 52, no. 2 (March–April 1999): 54–57.

The best introduction to crucifixion and the Romans is Martin Hengel, *Crucifixion in the Ancient World and the Folly of the Message of the Cross* (Philadelphia: Fortress, 1977). For a concise overview, see Haim Cohn and Shimon Gibson, "Crucifixion," *Encyclopaedia Judaica*, 2nd ed., vol. 5, Michael Berenbaum and Fred Skolnik, eds. (Detroit: Macmillan, 2007), pp. 309–10, or J. J. Rousseau and Rami Arav, "Crucifixion," in *Jesus and his World: An Archaeological and Cultural Dictionary* (Philadelphia: Fortress, 1995), pp. 74–78. On the evidence of material culture, see J. Zias, "Crucifixion in Antiquity: The Anthropological Evidence," www.joezias.com/CrucifixionAntiquity.html, and J. Zias and E. Sekeles, "The Crucified Man from Giv'at ha-Mivtar: A Reappraisal," *Israel Exploration Journal* 35 (1985): 22–27. On medical questions regarding crucifxion, see M. W. Maslen and Piers D. Mitchell, "Medical Theories on the cause of death in crucifixion," *Journal of the Royal Society of Medicine* 99 (2006): 185–88.

For a stimulating if speculative theory about the enduring, Celtic way of war, see Grady McWhiney, *Attack and Die: Civil War Military Tactics and the Southern Heritage* (Tuscaloosa: University of Alabama Press, 1981).

NOTES

In citing ancient authors, I follow the abbreviations of the standard reference work, *The Oxford Classical Dictionary* 3rd ed. (Oxford: Oxford University Press, 1999). I cite the titles of ancient works, however, in English translation. References to the fragments of Sallust's *Histories* come from the following edition unless otherwise stated: B. Maurenbrecher, C. *Sallusti Crispi Historiarum Reliquae*, vol. 2, *Fragmenta* (Leipzig: Teubner, 1893).

INTRODUCTION

5 Ronald Reagan: in the so-called "Westminster Speech" before the British Parliament in London, June 8, 1982, http://www.heritage.org/Research/Europe/WM106.cfm.

CHAPTER ONE: THE GLADIATOR

13 *murmillo:* Florus, *Epitome* 2.8.12.

13 "of enormous strength and spirit": Sallust, *Histories* frg. 3.90.

14 "sharp iron": In Latin, *ferra acuta*. See Marcus Junkelmann, "Familia Gladiatoria: The Heroes of the Amphitheatre," in *Gladiators and Caesars: The Power of Spectacle in Ancient Rome*, Eckart Koehne and Cornelia Ewigleben, eds., English version edited by Ralph Jackson (Berkeley: University of California Press, 2000), 66.

16 the city of Capua: The ruins of ancient Capua are located in today's city of Santa Maria Capua Vetere. The modern city called "Capua" was, in fact, ancient Casilinum.

16 slave sale carved on a Capuan tombstone: The stele of Publilius Satyr,

published by Theodor Mommsen et al., *Corpus Inscriptionum Latinarum*, 17 vols. (Berlin: 1863–1986), vol 10, 8222.

17 served in an allied unit: Florus, *Epitome* 2.8.7.

18 Second Book of Maccabees: 2 Maccabees 12:35.

18 became what the Romans called a *latro:* Florus, *Epitome* 2.8.8.

18 no less a source than Varro: Sosipater Charisius 1.133 (ed. Keil).

21 "like wild beasts": Livy, *History of Rome* 42.59.

21 "are absolutely mad about war": Strabo, *Geography* 4.4.2, translated by Philip Freeman as *War, Women, and Druids: Eyewitness Reports and Early Accounts of the Ancient Celts* (Austin: University of Texas Press, 2002), pp. 12–13.

21 the going rate for a Gallic slave: Diodorus Siculus 5.25.3–4.

21 40 million amphoras of wine: André Tchernia, "Italian Wine in Gaul at the End of the Republic," in Peter Garnsey, Keith Hopkins, and C. R. Whitaker, eds., *Trade in the Ancient Economy* (Berkeley: University of California Press, 1983), pp. 92, 97–98.

21 many Thracians supported Mithridates: Cassius Dio, frg. 101.

22 "Peace is displeasing to [their] nation": Tacitus, *Germania* 14.

23 "Tell your masters to feed their slaves!" Dio Cassius 77.10.2.

23 The best evidence comes from Pompeii: All of these examples come from the earlier ludus in Pompeii and appear in Luciana Jacobelli, *Gladiators at Pompeii* (Los Angeles: John Paul Getty Museum, 2004), pp. 48–49, 65–66.

24 "erect and invincible": Seneca, *Letters* 37.2.

25 "to run a risk for freedom": Appian, *Civil Wars* 1.116.539.

25 "more thoughtful and more dignified": Plutarch, *Crassus* 8.3. For the translation of the Greek word *prâotês* as "dignified," see Hubert Martin, Jr., "The Concept of Prâotês in Plutarch's *Lives*," *Greek, Roman and Byzantine Studies* 3 (1960): 65–73.

25 an elite few free-souled, prudent men: Sallust, *Histories* frg. 98A.

25 a few "nobles" among the insurgents: Sallust, *Histories* frg. 98A.

CHAPTER TWO: THE THRACIAN LADY

30 our sole source: Plutarch, *Crassus* 8.4.

30 scene on a tombstone of a slave dealer: The Kapreilios Relief shows

two women and two children accompanying a file of eight slaves marching in a chain gang, chained by the neck and preceded by a guard. See J. Kolendo, "Comment Spartacus devint-il esclave?" in Chr. M. Danov and Al. Fol, eds., *SPARTACUS Symposium Rebus Spartaci Gestis Dedicatum 2050 A.: Blagoevgrad, 20–24.IX.1977* (Sofia, Bulgaria: Editions De L'Académie Bulgare Des Sciences, 1981), p. 75, and M. I. Finley, "Marcus Aulus Timotheus, Slave Trader," in *Aspects of Antiquity: Discoveries and Controversies*, 2nd ed. (New York: Penguin, 1977), 154–66.

31 nomadic people: Plutarch, *Crassus* 8.3.

31 modern experts: Personal communications, Professor Harry Greene, Cornell University, and Professor Luca Luiselli, University of Rome.

32 "great and fearful power": Plutarch, *Crassus* 8.4.

32 "lucky end": Plutarch, *Crassus* 8.4, mss. a, b, c.

32 "unlucky end": Plutarch, *Crassus* 8.4, mss. d, e, f.

32 "something sacred and prophetic": Tacitus, *Germania* 8.

32 "a woman to make your heart tremble": Phyllis Mack, *Visionary Women: Ecstatic Prophecy in Seventeenth-Century England* (Berkeley: University of California Press, 1992), p. 17.

32 Columella: Columella, *On Agriculture* 1.8.6.

33 Syrian prophetess named Martha: Plutarch, *Life of Marius* 17.1–3.

33 snake made Spartacus a Thracian hero: Demosthenes 18.259–260; Alexander Fol and Ivan Mazarov, *Thrace and the Thracians* (New York: St. Martin's, 1997), pp. 28–29.

35 two slave revolts in Sicily: Diodorus Siculus 34.2.46, 36.4.4, with commentary of Jean Christian Dumont, *Servus: Rome et l'Esclavage sous la République*, Collection de l'École Française de Rome 103 (Rome: École Française de Rome, 1987), pp. 263–64.

35 "new Dionysus": E. Candiloro, "Politica e cultura in Atene da Pidna alla guerra mitridatica," *Studi classici et orientali* 14 (1965): 153–54 and n.71.

35 "raged through every part of Italy": Claudian, *Gothica* 155–56.

35 One historian: Emilio Gabba, *Appiani: Bellorum Civilium Liber Primus* (Firenze: La Nuova Italia Editrice, 1958), pp. 317, cf. 211–12.

38 kill a man through his chest: Frank Driever and Burkhard Medea, "Thoracic Stab Wound Caused by a Grilling Scewer [*sic*]," *Archir für*

Kriminologie 211, nos. 5–6 (May–June 2003): 174–80, http://www .ncbi.nlm.nih.gov/sites/entrez?db=pubmed&cmd=Retrieve&dopt= AbstractPlus&list_uids=12872687.

39 found a sica: In one of his poems (*Carmina* 9.253), the Late Roman man of letters, Sidonius Apollinaris (ca. A.D. 430–489) describes Spartacus as wielding a sica in battle against Rome's consuls.

39 "Not satisfied with having made their escape": Florus, *Epitome* 2.8.3.

42 "dishonorable and barbaric": Plutarch, *Crassus* 9.1.

42 "many runaway slaves and certain free men": Appian, *Civil Wars* 1.116.540.

42 ten thousand fugitives joined: Florus, *Epitome* 2.8.3.

44 harvesting grapes and cutting hay: Varro, *Agriculture* 1.17.2.

44 steal your firewood: Cato, *On Agriculture* 144.3.

45 money has no smell: Suetonius, *Vespasian* 23.

45 Most of Rome's so-called allies: Appian, *Mithridatic Wars* 109.519–20.

46 "If roving Spartacus": Horace, *Odes* 3.14.14–20. Translation available at http://www.perseus.tufts.edu/cgi-bin/ptext?lookup=Hor.+Carm.+3.14.

47 *terror servilis:* Livy, *History of Rome* 3.16.3.

47 "If they come against us in force": Sallust, *Histories* frg. 3.93.

CHAPTER THREE: THE PRAETORS

52 "a *tumultus* of slaves": Caesar, *The Gallic War* 1.40.6.

53 strictly for the Saturnalia: Plutarch, *Sulla* 18.5.

54 "had a humble and unworthy name": Aulus Gellius, *Attic Nights* 5.6.20, translated by Brent D. Shaw, *Spartacus and the Slave Wars: A Brief History With Documents* (Boston: Bedford/St. Martin's, 2001), 164.

56 nation of horsemen: Homer, *Iliad* 14.227.

56 Thucydides respected: *Peloponnesian War* 2.96.2.

57 "were used to weaving branches": Sallust, *Histories* frg. 3.102.

58 "did not yet consider this a war": Appian, *Civil Wars* 1.116.541.

59 "confused roar": Tacitus, *Germania* 3.2.

59 immense mass grave: The site is at Ribemont-sur-Ancre. See Jean-Louis Brunaux and Bernard Lambot, *Guerre et Armament chez les gaulois 450–52 av. J.-C.* (Paris: Editions Errance, 1987), p. 84.

61 "fast-moving brawlers": Plutarch, *Crassus* 9.4.

62 "because of the unhealthiness": Sallust, *Histories* frg. 3.96A.

63 "the height of their disgrace": Sallust, *Histories* frg. 3.96.

64 "They roved throughout all of Campania": Florus, *Epitome* 2.5.

65 no longer willing to obey him: Plutarch, *Crassus* 9.8.

66 "a few farseeing people": Sallust, *Histories* frg. 3.98A.

67 "Some of them stupidly": Sallust, *Histories* frg. 3.98A.

CHAPTER FOUR: THE PATHFINDERS

72 "happened upon the farmers": Sallust, *Histories* frg. 3.97.

73 populated by slave shepherds: Juvenal, *Satires* 8.180; Horace, *Epistles* 2.2.177 sqq., *Epodes* 1.27 sqq.

73 "and having hastily found a suitable guide": Sallust, *Histories* frg. 3.98B.

74 reputation for sacrificing prisoners: Diodorus Siculus 5.32.5.

74 Reports of gruesome practices: Strabo, *Geography* 7.2.3.

74 "unbeknownst to the farmers": Sallust, *Histories* frg. 3.98B.

75 In a hill town north of the valley even today: For the town of Ricigliano, see http://ricigliano.asmenet.it/, and Piera Carlomagno, ed., *La Provincia di Salerno: Guida Turistica* (Sarno, Italy: Edizioni dell'Ippogrifo, 2004), pp. 362–63.

75 Some Late Republican tombstones: Vittorio Bracco, "I materiali epigrafici," in Bruno d'Agostino, ed., *Storia del Vallo di Diano*, vol. 1, *Età Antica* (Salerno: Pietro Laveglia Editore, 1981), p. 256.

75 "Nothing was too holy": Sallust, *Histories* frg. 3.98C.

76 "very wide field": Sallust, *Histories* frg. 3.98D.

78 "winding, narrow, and cramped": R. J. Buck, "The Ancient Roads of Southeastern Lucania." *Papers of the British School at Rome* 43 (1975): 113.

78 Oliveto Citra, Rocca da spide, and Genzano di Lucania: All the places mentioned lie within the borders of ancient Lucania; today some are in Basilicata and others in Campania.

79 "They were very knowledgeable": Sallust, *Histories* frg. 3.102.

79 "Of all the men in the region of Lucania": Sallust, *Histories* frg. 3.99.

79 "they were used to weaving rustic baskets": Sallust, *Histories* frg. 3.102.

80 They stretched hides: Sallust, *Histories* frg. 3.103.

80 "great and frightening": Plutarch, *Crassus* 9.7.

80 "After this": Appian, *Civil Wars* 1.116.542.

80 "In a short time they collected": Orosius, *Histories* 5.24.2.

82 "terrible slaughter": Florus, *Epitome* 2.8.5.

82 In Metapontum's countryside: By studying pollen and seeds, archaeologists can describe Metapontum's agricultural history in unusual
detail. See Joseph Coleman Carter, *Discovering the Greek Countryside
at Metaponto* (Ann Arbor: University of Michigan Press, 2006), pp.
242–43, 246–47.

83 one scholar takes this as a sign of haste: Aldo Siciliano, "Herakleia,
Acropoli—Tesoretti," in Lucilla De Lachenal, *Da Leukania a Lucania:
la Lucania centro-orientale fra Pirro e i Giulio-Claudii: Venosa, Castello
Pirro del Balzo, 8 novembre 1992–31 marzo 1993* ([Rome]: Istituto poligrafico e Zecca dello Stato, Libreria dello Stato, 1993), p. 143.

85 "their natural disposition": Livy, *History of Rome* 29.6, cf. 28.12.

85 "slaves, deserters, and the rabble": Appian, *Civil Wars* 1.117.547.

87 "They attained a certain level of skill": Caesar, *Gallic War* 1.40.5.

87 "from a small and contemptible start": Augustine, *City of God* 4.5.

88 even a slave is a human being: Florus, *Epitome* 2.8.1–2.

CHAPTER FIVE: THE STOIC

92 no longer merely ashamed but afraid: Plutarch, *Crassus* 9.8.

92 a police action but rather a war: Plutarch, *Crassus* 9.8; Florus, *Epitome*
1.34.3, 2.8.1–2, 12.

93 one if not several pitched battles: see, for example, "acie victi sunt,"
"they were defeated in a formal battle," Livy, *Periochae* 96.

94 "arrogance and presumption": Plutarch, *Crassus* 9.9. I assume that the
"German force" mentioned here is Crixus's army; see M. G. Bertinelli
Angeli et al., *Le Vite di Nicia e di Crasso* (Verona: Fondazione Lorenzo
Vallo, A. Mondadori, 1993), with commentary ad loc.

94 he began the campaign season with thirty thousand: Orosius, *Histories*
5.24.2.

96 "a vigorous man": Cicero, *Verres* 2.4.42.

96 compared Arrius to a boxer: Cicero, *Brutus* 242–43.

99 banging javelins on shields and shouting war cries: Ross H. Cowan,
"The Clashing of Weapons and Silent Advances in Roman Battles," *Historia* 56, no. 1 (2007): 114–17.

99 "threatening rumble": Horace, cited without reference by John Peddie, *The Roman War Machine* (Stroud, England: Sutton, 1996), p. 23.

99 "fought extremely fiercely": Orosius, *Histories* 5.24.4.

100 two-thirds of Crixus's men died: Appian, *Civil Wars* 1.117.544.

102 with a sudden rush: Plutarch, *Crassus* 9.9.

103 defeated Lentulus's legates and captured: Plutarch, *Crassus* 9.9.

103 abandoned the field in great confusion: Appian, *Civil Wars* 1.116.544.

103 "thoroughly destroyed": Florus, *Epitome* 2.8.10.

103 "more polluted, deformed": Cicero, *On the Response of Soothsayers* 25.

104 made the slaves spectators: Cicero, *On the Response of Soothsayers* 26.

104 purged himself of all his prior infamy: Florus, *Epitome* 2.8.9; cf. Orosius, *Histories* 5.24.3.

105 "As Spartacus was pressing forward": Appian, *Civil Wars*, 1.117.544.

106 "victory disease": Timothy M. Karcher, "The Victory Disease," *Military Review* (July/August 2003): 9–17, http://www.army.mil/prof_writing/volumes/volume1/september_2003/9_03_5.html.

106 "elated by his victories": Florus, *Epitome* 2.8.11.

106 "Terror," says one ancient writer: Orosius, *Histories* 5.24.5.

107 "many deserters": Appian, *Civil Wars* 1.117.545.

108 60,000 soldiers: Eutropius 6.7.2.

108 other figures: 90,000, Velleius Paterculus 2.30.6; over 100,000, Orosius, *Histories* 19; 120,000, Appian, *Civil Wars* 1.117.545.

108 "And at the same time Lentulus": Sallust, *Histories* 3.106, as translated, with my emendations, by Patrick McGushin, *Sallust: The Histories Translated with Introduction and Commentary*, vol. 2 (Oxford: Clarendon Press, 1994), 39.

109 "he changed his mind about going to Rome": Appian, *Civil Wars* 1.117.547.

110 crowns for just digging ditches: Aulus Gellius, *Attic Nights* 6.24–26.

110 malicious remark: Aurelius Victor, *On Illustrious Men.* 66.3.

111 sewer of Romulus: Cicero, *Letters to Atticus* 2.1.8.

CHAPTER SIX: THE DECIMATOR

115 A marble bust: For photos and bibliography, see http://viamus.uni-goettingen.de/fr/mmdb/d/singleItemView?pos=0&Inventarnummer=A%201452.

120 "Everyone who had a soldier's heart": Sallust, *Histories* frg. 4.21, with commentary ad loc.

122 location, isolation, and eradication: Mao Tse-Tung, *On Guerrilla Warfare*, translated from the Chinese and with an introduction by Samuel B. Griffith II (Urbana: University of Illinois Press, 1961), p. 30.

122 By November or thereabouts: Rome followed the lunar calendar until 46 B.C., and it regularly often fell out of synchronization with the solar calendar. "November," therefore, is a rough estimate.

122 According to Plutarch, an angry Senate: Plutarch, *Crassus* 10.1

124 According to one source, these were the legions: Appian, *Civil Wars* 1.118.549.

125 "Many of his men fell": Plutarch, *Crassus* 10.3.

125 "tremblers": Plutarch, *Crassus* 10.4.

126 he had made himself more fearful: Appian, *Civil Wars* 1.118.551.

126 One of our sources implies: Plutarch, *Crassus* 10.5–6.

126 In this version, Crassus's army: Appian, *Civil Wars*, 1.118.551.

127 "with contempt": Appian, *Civil Wars*, 1.118.551.

127 "defeated him and pursued him": Appian, *Civil Wars*, 1.118.551.

127 "Finally . . . Licinius Crassus": Florus, *Epitome* 2.8.12.

CHAPTER SEVEN: THE PIRATE

131 Heracleo: This was his name according to Cicero (*Verrines* 6.97); Orosius (6.3) calls him Pyrganio.

134 "great Italian war": Cicero, *Verrines* 6.2.5.

134 "war of the Italian fugitives": Cicero, *Verrines* 6.6.14.

134 the Senate extended Verres's governorship: Thomas Stangl, ed., *Cicero Orationum Scholiastae* (Vienna: Tempsky, [1912]), Scho. Cic. Gron. II 324.

134 "Gaius Verres strengthened the shores": Sallust, *Histories*, frg. 4.32.

137 "Once the Cilicians had made an agreement": Plutarch, *Crassus* 10.7.

137 "The narrowness of the passage": Thucydides, *Peloponnesian War* 4.24.5, in Robert Strassler, ed., *The Landmark Thucydides: A Comprehensive Guide to the Peloponnesian War* (New York: Simon & Schuster, 1998), p. 236.

139 the Sicels: Thucydides, *Peloponnesian War* 6.2.4.

139 "A number of huge jars": Cassius Dio, *Roman History* 11.14.29, Loeb Classical Library edition, pp. 439–40, http://penelope.uchicago.edu/Thayer/E/Roman/Texts/Cassius_Dio/11*.html; cf. H. H. Scullard, *The Elephant in the Greek and Roman World* (Ithaca: Cornell University Press, 1974), pp. 16, 149, 152.

139 "When they placed large, wide-mouthed jars": Sallust, *Histories* frg. 4.26.

140 Cape Caenys offered a narrower crossing: Some scholars place the crossing farther north, at Scilla, but that town lies outside the strait, where Plutarch, *Crassus* 10.3–4, insists on putting Spartacus.

140 "They tried to launch rafts": Florus, *Epitome* 2.8.13.

140 "The entangled rafts were hindering": Sallust, *Histories* frg. 4.27, in Patrick McGushin, trans. and ed., *Sallust: The Histories*, vol. 2 (Oxford: Clarendon, 1994), p. 43.

141 "that bravest of men": Cicero, *Verrines* 6.5.

CHAPTER EIGHT: THE FISHERMAN

144 the Romans claimed an immense body count: Appian, *Civil Wars* 1.119.552.

145 the Romans had got their courage back: Appian, *Civil Wars* 1.119.552.

146 the nature of the terrain: Plutarch, *Crassus* 10.7.

147 three hundred stades: Plutarch, *Crassus* 10.8.

149 a system of trenches: Appian, *Civil Wars* 1.118.551.

149 the Romans cut a trench from sea to sea: Plutarch, *Crassus* 10.8.

150 "annoyed the men": Appian, *Civil Wars* 1.119.553.

150 "He crucified a Roman prisoner": Appian, *Civil Wars* 1.119.553.

151 the Roman people let their frustration spill over: Appian, *Civil Wars* 1.119.554.

152 Crassus himself wrote to the Senate: Plutarch, *Crassus* 11.3.

152 "worse than snow": Paulinus of Nola, *Poems* 17.206.

152 Marcus Lucullus: Technically Marcus Varro is correct, since Marcus had been adopted as an adult by one Terentius Varro, but for simplicity's sake I use his birth name.

152 "the teenage butcher": Valerius Maximus 6.2.8.

152 accept him into its *fides*: Tacitus, *Annals* 3.73; cf. Appian, *Civil Wars* 1.120.556.

153 "most beautiful dignity": Tacitus, *Annals* 3.73.

153 "below strength": Sallust, *Histories* frg. 4.36.

154 A.D. 26: Tacitus, *Annals* 4.51.

155 "his goal now was Samnium": Appian, *Civil Wars* 1.119.552.

155 "they began to disagree": Sallust, *Histories,* frg. 4.37, in McGushin, trans., *Sallust: The Histories,* vol. 2, p. 44.

CHAPTER NINE: THE CELTIC WOMEN

159 "the whole of the Gallic people": Caesar, *Gallic War,* cited without reference in Jean-Louis Brunaux, *The Celtic Gauls: Gods, Rites, and Sanctuaries,* translated by Daphne Nash (London: Seaby, 1988), p. 102.

159 "The magic of women": Gallic inscription, cited by Philip Freeman, *The Philosopher and the Druids: A Journey Among the Ancient Celts* (New York: Simon & Schuster, 2006), p. 125.

159 "fulfilling their monthly things": Sallust, *Histories,* frg. 4.40.

160 "sacrificing on behalf of the enemies": Plutarch, *Crassus,* 11.5.

160 bite and kick the enemy: Ammianus Marcellinus, *Histories* 15.12.

162 *riyos:* personal communication, Professor Michael Weiss, Department of Linguistics, Cornell University.

162 "were in danger": Plutarch, *Crassus,* 11.5.

163 the town of Giungano: http://www.comune.giungano.sa.it/.

165 30,000: Orosius, *Histories* 5.24.6.

165 35,000: Livy, *Periochae* 97; Frontinus, *Stratagems* 2.5.34.

165 12,300: Plutarch, *Crassus* 11.5.

165 "the most valiant battle of all": Plutarch, *Crassus* 11.5.

165 Battle of Bibracte: Caesar, *Gallic War* 1.26.

167 "to retreat towards the Peteline Mountains": Plutarch, *Crassus* 11.6.

167 near the headwaters of the Silarus: Orosius, *Histories* 5.24.6.

168 Spartacus now began to lead his army: Appian, *Civil Wars* 1.120.557.

169 The second account takes off: Plutarch, *Crassus* 11.6.

169 "Success destroyed Spartacus": Plutarch, *Crassus* 11.6.

CHAPTER TEN: SPARTACUS

171 "they indiscriminately mix": Orosius, *Histories* 5.24.3.

171 One Roman matron: Orosius, *Histories* 5.24.3.

172 ancient biographical tradition: Suetonius, *Life of Horace.*

172 in Cicero's opinion: Cicero, *On Duties* 1.42.

172 "he gave up on all [his other plans]": Appian, *Civil Wars* 1.120.557.

172 his men forced him to fight the Romans: Plutarch, *Crassus* 11.8.

172 he made the choice on his own: Appian, *Civil Wars* 1.120.557.

173 "still of great size": Appian, *Civil Wars* 1.120.557.

173 three thousand Roman citizens: Orosius, *Histories* 5.24.7.

174 A group of Sicilian slaves: Florus, *Epitome* 2.7.9–12; Diod. Sic. 36.10.3.

174 an earthquake centered in Conza: http://en.wikipedia.org/wiki/Italy_
    Earthquake_of_1980.

176 moving too quickly: Sallust, *Histories* frg. 4.39; Plutarch, *Comparison of
    Nicas and Crassus* (*Crassus* 36 [3].2); cf. McGushin, ed., *Sallust: The
    Histories*, vol. 2, pp. 155–56.

176 "He was digging a trench": Plutarch, *Crassus* 11.8.

176 "you defeat the enemy with a pickaxe": Frontinus, *Stratagems* 4.7.2.

176 scorpion arrow pierced: Caesar, *African War* 29.

176 "At Orchomenus!": Plutarch, *Sulla* 21.2.

177 "Seeing the necessity": Plutarch, *Crassus* 11.8.

178 "that if he won he would have many horses": Plutarch, *Crassus* 11.9.

179 the Moesian commander stood: Florus, *Epitome* 2.26.13–16.

179 singing and dancing: There was a revolt in the southern Thracian moun-
    tains in A.D. 26. When besieged, the braver spirits "after the manner of
    their country were disporting themselves with songs and dances in
    front of the rampart" (Tacitus, *Annals* 4.47, http://www.perseus.tufts.
    edu/cgi-bin/ptext?lookup=Tac.+Ann.+4.47). See also Ralph F. Hoddi-
    nott, *The Thracians* (London: Thames & Hudson, 1981), p. 130.

180 "He pushed toward Crassus": Plutarch, *Crassus* 11.9.

180 "exposed his body to danger": Plutarch, *Crassus* 11.10.

181 "fought *fortissime*": Florus, *Epitome* 2.8.14.

181 "he killed two centurions": Plutarch, *Crassus* 11.9.

182 "In the end": Plutarch, *Crassus* 11.10.

182 "Spartacus was wounded in the thigh": Apian, *Civil Wars*, 1.120.557.

182 "he did not die quickly": Sallust, *Histories*, frg. 4.41 .

182 "he died almost an *imperator*": Florus, *Epitome* 2.8.14.

183 "The battle was long and strongly contested": Appian, *Civil Wars* 1.120.557.

183 "As befit an army led by a gladiator": Florus, *Epitome* 2.8.14.

183 no opponent was more dangerous: Seneca, *Controversies* 9.6, cited by Alison Futrell, *The Roman Games* (Oxford: Blackwell, 2006), p. 144.

183 "They were cut down *en masse*": Appian, *Civil Wars* 1.120.558.

183 "They met with a death": Florus, *Epitome* 2.8.14, in Brent D. Shaw, trans., *Spartacus and the Slave Wars: A Brief History with Documents.* (Boston: Bedford/St. Martin's, 2001), p. 155.

184 sixty thousand rebel dead: Livy, *Periochae* 97; Orosius, *Histories* 5.24.7. The casualty figure of 12,300 in Plutarch, *Pompey* 21.2, probably refers to the battle of Cantenna.

184 "a slaughter of them came about": Appian, *Civil Wars* 1.120.558.

CHAPTER ELEVEN: THE VICTORS

189 Capuan slave named Flaccus: Theodor Mommsen et al., *Corpus Inscriptionum Latinarum*, vol. 10 (Berlin, 1883), part 2, 8070.3.

190 they went into the mountains: Appian, *Civil Wars* 1.120.559.

190 "terrible": See the oft-cited "terrible cross" of the slaves in Plautus; Martin Hengel, *Crucifixion in the Ancient World and the Folly of the Message of the Cross* (Philadelphia: Fortress Press, 1977), p. 7, n. 13.

190 "infamous": "the infamous stake," *Latin Anthology* 415.23–24.

190 "utterly vile": Origen, *Commentary on Matthew*, 27.22ff. For the translation, see Hengel, *Crucifixion*, p. x.

190 "servile": Cicero, *For Cluentius* 66; *First Philippic* 2.

191 less revenge than deterrence: Pseudo-Quintilian, *Minor Declamations* 274.13, cited by Hengel, *Crucifixion*, p. 50.

191 the devastation of the countryside: See, e.g., Velleius Paterculus 2.30.5; Plutarch, *Crassus* 8.1; Ampelius 45.3; Otto Keller, *Pseudacronis scholia in Horatium vetustiora*, vol. 1 (Leipzig: Teubner, 1902), p. 274, 3.14.19.

191 fear, anger, and indignation: Livy, *History of Rome* 3.16.3, 21.41.10.

192 *Recte omnia velim sint nobis*: M. Pagano and J. Rougetet, "La casa del

liberto P. Confuleius Sabbio a Capua e i suoi mosaici," *Mélanges de L'École Française de Rome* 98 (1987): 753–65.

192 "the whole road to Rome from Capua": Appian, *Civil Wars* 1.20.559.

192 Roman jurists recommended: *Digest* 48.19.28.15, cited in Hengel, *Crucifixion*, p. 48.

192 Roman authorities also favored: Pseudo-Quintilian, *Minor Declamations* 274.13, cited in Hengel, *Crucifixion*, p. 50.

193 the crucifixion of women: Apuleius, *Golden Ass* 4.31; Josephus, *Antiquities* 18.3.4.

193 the Romans even crucified dogs: Pliny, *Natural History* 29.14.57.

193 the hanged could linger: Haim Cohn and Shimon Gibson, "Crucifixion," in Michael Berenbaum and Fred Skolnik, eds., *Encyclopedia Judaica*, 2nd ed., vol. 5 (Detroit: Macmillan, 2007), pp. 309–10.

194 cases of crucified men who laughed: Hengel, *Crucifixion*, p. 48.

195 "Crassus had defeated": Plutarch, *Crassus* 11.11.

196 "the troubles at Tempsa": Cicero, *Verrines* 6.39, 41.

196 "the remnants of the Italian war": Cicero, *Verrines* 6.39.

196 "small band": Cicero, *Verrines* 6.40.

198 "the bald adulterer": Suetonius, *Deified Julius* 51.

200 Marcus Lucullus's triumph: On the dates and other details of the four triumphs, see A. Degrassi, *Inscriptiones Italiae* XIII.1 (Rome: La Libreria dello Stato, 1947), p. 565.

200 five thousand thrushes: Varro, *Agricultural Topics* 3.2.15–16, repeated by Columella, *On Agriculture* 8.10.6. See discussion by Mary Beard, *The Roman Triumph* (Cambridge, Mass.: Harvard University Press, 2007), p. 49 and p. 346, n. 12.

200 roughly equivalent to the annual pay: see R. Alston, "Roman Military Pay from Caesar to Diocletian," *Journal of Roman Studies* 84 (1994): pp. 113–23.

CONCLUSION

202 "He put an end to them": Suetonius, *Deified Augustus* 3.1.

204 thought to cure malarial fevers: Pliny, *Natural History* 28.41, 28.46. See also Laura D. Lane, "Malaria and Magic in the Roman World," in David Soren and Noelle Soren, eds., *A Roman Villa and a Late Roman*

Infant Cemetery: Excavation at Poggio Gramignano, Lugnano in Teverina (Rome: L'Erma di Bretschneider, 1999), p. 640.

205 "life force": Itta Gradel, *Emperor Worship and Roman Religion* (Oxford: Clarendon, 2002), p. 37.

206 Ursus Tubicen: Hans-Günther Simon, "Zwei ausseregewöhnliche reliefverzierte Gefässe aus Langenhain, Wetteraukreis," *Germania* 53 (1975): 126–37, esp. 134.

207 bitter and protracted tension: Cicero, *For Sulla* 60–62.

211 He called for a mirror: The details come from Suetonius, *Deified Augustus*, 98.5–100.1.

ACKNOWLEDGMENTS

CHAPTERS OF THIS manuscript were read by and greatly improved through the comments of Kimberly Bowes, Judith Dupré, Mark Levine, Adrienne Mayor, Marcia Mogelonsky, Jan Parker, Matthew Sears, and Chaya Rivka Zwolinski. Many Cornell colleagues and students, past and present, offered advice and answered specific questions. I would like to thank in particular Annetta Alexandridis, Edward Baptist, Flaminia Cervesi, Nora Dimitrova, Michael Fontaine, Kathryn Gleason, Harry Greene, Martin Loicano, Elizabeth Macaulay-Lewis, Kathryn McDonnell, Michelle Moyd, Jon Parmenter, Eric Rebillard, Sidney Tarrow, Robert Travers, Rachel Weil, and Michael Weiss. I would also like to thank Josh Bernstein, Donald Kagan, Victor Davis Hanson, Anna Kirkwood, Kim McKnight, Josiah Ober, Priya Ramasabban, Philip Sabin, Nikola Theodossiev, and Rob Tempio.

I am deeply grateful to my two academic homes at Cornell University, the Department of History and the Department of Classics. The superb collection and the supportive staff of Cornell's John M. Olin Library helped make this book possible. I benefited from the comments received when I read portions of my manuscript at Cornell's Ancient Mediterranean Colloquium, Cornell's Peace Studies Seminar, and at the Duke–University of North Carolina Graduate Colloquium.

I was lucky enough to make several research trips to Italy. Among those who helped me there are Carmine Cozzolino, Marcella DeFeo, Umberto Del Vecchio, Maria Laura Frullini, Donato Punello, and Marcello Tagliente. Jim Zurer provided expert travel advice.

As in the past, Suzanne Lang provided invaluable secretarial and logistical assistance. Barbara Donnell, Michael Strauss, and Sylvie Strauss helped with typing.

I am greatly indebted to my editor at Simon & Schuster, Bob Bender, whose sage advice improved the manuscript thoroughly. I would also like to thank his assistant, Johanna Li. I am greatly indebted as well to my editors at Weidenfeld & Nicolson, Alan Samson and Keith Lowe, for their perceptive and productive reading of the manuscript. My literary agent and friend, Howard Morhaim, first suggested that I write about Spartacus.

My family is the true *sine qua non* of this book. I thank Sylvie and Michael for their support and patience and Marcia for more than I can say.

George Wood, my former student and friend, fell in Iraq in 2003. George was planning a career as a Roman historian. It is impossible for me to write about Rome without remembering him.

Josiah Ober and Adrienne Mayor have always been there, as friends and colleagues, for thirty years. Dedicating this book to them is but small recompense.

INDEX

Also by Barry Strauss

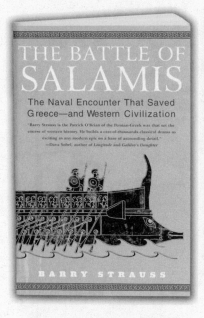

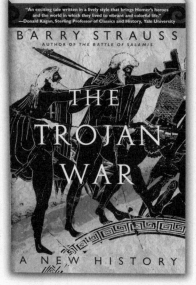

"Strauss is the Patrick O'Brian of the Persian-Greek war that set the course of western history. He builds a cast-of-thousands classical drama as exciting as any modern epic on a base of astounding detail."

—Dava Sobel, author of *Longitude* and *Galileo's Daughter*

"Strauss boldly treats the Trojan War not as mythology or poetry but as history. . . . An exciting tale written in a lively style that brings Homer's heroes and the world in which they lived to vibrant and colorful life."

—Donald Kagan, Sterling Professor of Classics and History, Yale University

Available wherever books are sold or at www.simonandschuster.com